THE VEGETARIAN HANDBOOK

OTHER BOOKS BY GARY NULL

The Complete Guide to Health and Nutrition
The New Vegetarian
Nutrition Sourcebook for the Eighties
The New Vegetarian Cookbook
The Complete Handbook of Nutrition

THE VEGETARIAN HANDBOOK

GARY NULL

ST. MARTIN'S GRIFFIN
New York

Design by Jaya Dayal

Library of Congress Cataloging-in-Publication Data

Null, Gary.
The vegetarian handbook, revised edition.

1. Vegetarianism.   2. Nutrition.   3. Cookery
(Vegetables)   I. Title.
TX392.N845   1987   641.5′636   87-16331
ISBN 0-312-14441-5 (pbk.)

First St. Martin's Griffin Edition: May 1996

10   9   8   7   6   5   4

CONTENTS

I

INTRODUCTION TO VEGETARIANISM

II

PROTEIN: THE LARGER PICTURE

III
REASONS FOR BECOMING A VEGETARIAN

ACKNOWLEDGMENTS

N early five years of research and hundreds of hours of interviews
have been necessary to create this book, and many people
assisted in the project. Drs. Doris Rapp, Marshall Mandell, Theron
Randolph, and William Philpott were of particular help. As clinical
ecologists, their findings are of special significance to this book. As
a result, I have quoted these experts throughout the text. One common criticism of any alternative health program has been its lack
of credibility. The question asked is, "What is your source?" At the
risk of overstatement, I put forth these people as my primary sources.

I wish to thank also Drs. Michael Schachter, Alan Levin, Richard
Podell, William Rhea, Richard Kunin, Claude Frazier, William Crook,
Ray Wunderlich, and Janice Phelps.

I want to give special acknowledgment to Trudy Golobic, who
worked tirelessly and creatively, editing and summarizing dozens
of hours of taped interviews and who, better than anyone, knows
the meaning of a long work week; David Merrill, a selfless, highly
skilled journalist whose contributions were invaluable to the final
manuscript; Philip Jay Hodes, Ed. D., whose criticism and editorial
input helped reduce the initial thousand-page manuscript to its current form; and Hillard Fitzky, for his years of research and effort and
special genius in helping to formulate and develop The Protein Combination Project.

I also wish to thank Mary Ann Reidy, M.S., for assisting in summarizing some of the tapes for the initial stages of this manuscript,
and for her commitment to the health movement.

PREFACE

The product of five years of research, this book presents what I consider to be a revolutionary advance in vegetarianism: the calculating power of the computer has been applied to the task of finding many new high-protein food combinations from vegetable sources, and dozens of brand-new recipes have been created based on these discoveries.

This book was written with several audiences in mind. Dieters, vegetarians, people with food allergies or who are suspected of having them, health professionals, researchers, and reporters have been asking me for years how to find the ideal diet. Each of these groups will, I hope, find special value for themselves in this book.

DIETERS

As any successful dieter can tell you—and they represent only a tiny percentage of perennial dieters—the way to lose weight and keep it off is to eat for good health and high energy, rather than for quick weight loss. Starve yourself and you'll eventually binge and regain the weight. Eat to feel well and you'll be rewarded with long-term positive changes.

This is the only diet that will work over a lifetime for everyone. In addition, this diet uses the insights of behavioral psychology and nutrition science to lead binge eaters, sweets addicts, and compulsive but previously unsuccessful dieters step by step to a new perspective on food and new, healthy eating habits they can adopt at their own pace.

VEGETARIANS

There are now fourteen million vegetarians in the United States—up from nine million only five years ago. And there are millions of other people who are concerned by the statistics on heart disease and hypertension and want to find out how to lower the amount of cholesterol and saturated fat in their diets. This book will help both of these groups lower their fat and sugar intake while enjoying a more varied, interesting diet than ever before.

PEOPLE WITH FOOD ALLERGIES

Clinical ecologists, medical doctors specializing in environmental allergies, have found that many of today's diseases can be traced to the foods we eat most frequently. Major offenders are beef, dairy products, eggs, wheat, corn, and cane and beet sugars. In fact, the clinical ecologists have found that almost any food that is eaten more frequently than once every four days can cause food allergies, and that, in seven out of ten cases, chronic health problems such as arthritis, depression, chronic fatigue, constipation, asthma, ulcers, eczema, colds and sore throats, and even severe mental illness— as well as water retention, bloating, and compulsive eating, all of special concern to dieters—can be alleviated by avoiding specific foods. As a result, they developed the concept of the four-day rotational (or rotary) diet in order to mitigate current allergies and prevent new ones from developing. Up until now, the benefits of a rotational diet have been largely unavailable to vegetarians, as all of the published diets have been created for meat eaters. This is the first book that has been designed to make a rotation diet easy and accessible to the vegetarian. We have compiled almost one hundred recipes, drawing on a wide variety of ingredients for each meal, to allow you maximum ease in designing your own rotational diet.

HEALTH PROFESSIONALS

Doctors, chiropractors, dentists, nurses, nutritionists, dieticians, athletic coaches, teachers, and other professionals concerned about the diets of patients, clients, students, or institutions will find this book helpful, both in conveying the importance of adopting a healthier life-style and in providing nuts-and-bolts instructions on how to do it.

RESEARCHERS AND JOURNALISTS

Researchers, students, science and health reporters, writers, journalists, and anyone seriously interested in learning more about vegetarianism will find in this book a history of vegetarianism and expositions of the main arguments both in favor of and against it.

THE PROTEIN COMBINATION PROJECT

For years, vegetarians have been told that "it's very hard to get enough protein on a vegetarian diet." They were urged to supplement their diet with foods from animal sources—milk, eggs, and other dairy products—and preferably to go back to eating at least fish. These warnings have not deterred the fourteen million people who are vegetarians today. Armed with many fine whole-foods and vegetarian cookbooks written over the last few years, more and more people have been enjoying the vegetarian food combinations that have been the mainstay of peasant diets for hundreds of years.

Only grudgingly have mainstream nutritionists conceded that it is possible to combine incomplete proteins from vegetable sources to make proteins as good as those found in meat. And now, with the Protein Combination Project described in part II, vegetarianism has arrived in the computer age. Like other modern vegetarians, I long ago learned the rules for combining two or more "incomplete" proteins to form, together, enough "complete" protein to sustain life. It was thought (1) that the egg was the most "perfect" protein because it contained all eight essential amino acids in the correct proportions for human use; (2) that animal proteins were the next best source, and that adding eggs, milk, yogurt, and other dairy products to vegetarian meals was the easiest way to be sure to get enough protein; and (3) that certain combinations of foods—grains and legumes, grains and milk products, seeds and legumes, and some nuts and seeds—approximated the completeness of egg protein by combining a food in which one or more essential amino acid was in short supply (the "limiting" amino acid) with another which had an excess of that amino acid.

This was all very useful until I learned that I was allergic to many of the high-protein staples of my vegetarian regimen—including eggs, milk, wheat germ, and brewer's yeast. These were foods I was eating every day! No wonder I often felt weak and tired as a runner, and couldn't improve my pace no matter how hard I trained.

I was advised by the clinical ecologists I consulted not only to eliminate these foods; but, in order to prevent new sensitivities from developing, to *rotate* my foods: never to eat any single food more frequently than once every four days. How could I do that, adhere to my principles as a vegetarian, and still get enough protein? I knew

I was not alone with this dilemma. One estimate is that as much as 70 percent of the U.S. population probably suffers from chronic food sensitivities. Clearly, I—and the millions of other food-sensitive people in the country—needed some new foods. I resolved to fill in the blank spaces in the vegetarian repertoire of food combinations.

To do so, I needed to find out the total protein and specific amino acid content of *all* the available foods. Then, with the aid of a computer, I could list hundreds of new food combinations that approach the protein-completeness of the perfect egg.

Now, finally, the results of this formidable research project are in—and there are a few surprising discoveries:

- Animal foods like fish and meat do contain a lot of protein. But not all of those proteins contain the eight essential amino acids in the proportions of a "complete" protein. In other words, animal protein is not as complete as we have been led to believe. It's only about half high-quality protein.
- There are certain legumes and grains with a higher percentage of total protein, and a higher percentage of complete protein, than meat and fish.
- Most important, when I began to match foods containing a high proportion of only one amino acid with other foods for which that one is the limiting amino acid, I found not dozens, but *hundreds* of combinations of foods high in "complete" protein. Defining "variance" as the extent of difference in the proportions of each food's essential amino acid pattern from the proportions found in the egg, the computer has now spewed forth several thousand combinations of two and three foods with a "variance" of under 100 and over a thousand combinations with variances of under 20 (compared to most animal proteins, which have variances between 20 and 50).

I believe these are essential discoveries. Finding new sources of protein by combining foods whose protein content was thought to be negligible may help not only food-sensitive individuals in affluent countries but masses of hungry children all over the globe who lack adequate protein in their diets.

ABOUT THE BOOK IN GENERAL

This book is more than a list of possible new food combinations. Cookbook, menu planner, sourcebook and how-to guide, it should serve as a comprehensive resource for vegetarians and anyone concerned with personal health or the health of our ecology, or even of our economy.

COOKBOOK

With my research behind me, I rolled up my sleeves with a gourmet vegetarian chef to transform the lists and numbers into satisfying gourmet meals. Our new recipes feature many foods you may never have tried before, and other hitherto uninteresting staples you may not have imagined could taste so good.

MENU PLANNER

Taking into account that, whether they know it or not, *most* people ought to be following the clinical ecologists' suggestion to rotate their foods, the recipes and meals presented in this book are designed to fit into a diversified rotary diet: with these recipes and a bit of creativity you should be able to design a diet in which no food appears more than once in four days. We have given you a wide choice of food combinations that are guaranteed to give you enough protein.

SOURCEBOOK ON VEGETARIANISM

This book is meant to serve as a comprehensive statement on the value of vegetarianism, that sums up not only my own findings but those of several generations of vegetarians, researchers, and clinicians. I have sifted through the wealth of available material to present answers to your questions about vegetarianism from various points of view:

- Natural hygiene: What is the relation between diet and disease or health?
- History and anthropology: What kinds of societies have been vegetarian, and with what effects?
- Religion: What dietary restrictions and suggestions have some of the world's religions made?

- Ethics: What role can vegetarianism play in advancing human and animal rights?
- Economics and ecology: What are the potential effects on our social and biological environment of a change from a meat-dependent to a primarily vegetarian economy?

A GUIDE FOR NEW VEGETARIANS

I will show you how to change your diet so you will be able to sustain your new life-style. Psychologists and nutritionists agree that crash diets don't work, and new habits must be cultivated gradually. As you progress, making one small change after another, you will see for yourself the rewards of your new eating habits in better health, better looks, more energy—and a whole new world of foods to explore.

INTRODUCTION

I n making the decision to become a vegetarian or to shift your diet from one primarily composed of meat and dairy products to one that focuses on grains, legumes, fruits, and vegetables, there are a number of factors which you may want to consider.

The first is the moral issue surrounding the consumption of meat. Up until quite recently, this was the primary motivating factor for most people who opted for a vegetarian way of eating. There have been famous vegetarians throughout history, included among whom are such luminaries as Socrates, Gandhi, George Orwell, George Bernard Shaw, and Henry David Thoreau. Recorded in their works or biographies it is not uncommon to find moral objections to the consumption of meat. These objections include philosophical discussions as to the propriety of taking an animal's life, the effect that the eating of animal flesh has on physical, mental, and spiritual health, or the aesthetics of consuming flesh as compared, for example, to tree-ripened fruit.

During the 1960s, when vegetarianism started to gain in popularity in the United States, these types of philosophical and moral considerations continued to be the primary motivating factors in most vegetarians' minds.

While these moral issues are just as important for many people in the 1980s as they were in the past, today, the growing awareness of the health and medical problems associated with the consumption of meat and animal products are leading an ever increasing number of Americans to consider the vegetarian alternative.

For quite some time now, the American Heart Association, as well as the American Cancer Society and the National Academy of Sciences, have been warning the public to cut down on their consumption of meat and other animal products. These alerts are motivated by the rapidly accumulating body of scientific evidence linking excessive consumption of these products to the nation's most prevalent diseases, namely, breast, colon, and prostate cancer, heart disease and atherosclerosis.

While the health risks associated with animal products will be discussed more fully in the later chapters on protein, I will outline here some of the more important aspects of what may very well turn out to be one of America's most pressing health issues.

After years of scientific study and announcements concerning the link between high-blood-cholesterol levels and heart disease, *The New York Times*, in a front page article, unequivocally confirmed that "For First Time, Cut in Cholesterol Is Shown To Deter Artery Clogging." According to *The Times*:

> A team of scientists reported today the first "clear evidence" that a large reduction in blood cholesterol will slow and in some cases even reverse the formation and growth of fatty deposits that clog the arteries and cause heart attacks.
>
> The findings were endorsed by Federal health officials, who said a cholesterol-lowering treatment could benefit the six million Americans who suffer symptoms of coronary artery disease, the nation's leading cause of death. They said the study also reaffirmed the need to reduce cholesterol levels in some 40 million Americans who have dangerously high cholesterol but no symptoms of coronary disease.[1]

While the article touts the originality and dramatic evidence of its report, basically, it does not say anything new. It is however important, in that the link between diet and disease, which has for so long been belied by the conservative American medical establishment, public health officials, and the press, is finally so substantial that it can no longer be controverted even by its opponents.

This "significant new information" is particularly important for people interested in their health and considering a natural and safe alternative to such drastic and costly medical treatments as heart by-pass surgery. As the primary source of cholesterol in the American diet is from saturated fats contained in meat and animal products, switching your diet from one centered on these products to one that is mainly vegetarian may be an important step in preventing coronary and artery disease.

Furthermore, while the medical establishment still takes only a tentative stance vis-à-vis the role of diet in preventing disease, the most recent edition of *Cancer Facts and Figures* published by the American Cancer Society made the following health recommendations:

- Cut down on total fat intake.
- Eat more high-fiber foods such as whole grain cereals, fruits, and vegetables.
- Include foods rich in vitamins A and C in your daily diet. (Dark green and deep yellow fresh vegetables and fruits such as carrots, spinach, sweet potatoes, peaches, and apricots as sources of vitamin A; oranges, grapefruit, strawberries, green and red peppers for vitamin C.)
- Include cruciferous vegetables (cabbage, broccoli, Brussel sprouts, and cauliflower) in your diet.[2]

These recommendations reflect recent scientific findings that excessive consumption of meat is also one of the major contributing factors in colon and prostate cancer. Although the reasons for this are still sketchy, research has shown that in those cultures eating a diet high in fiber-rich fruits, vegetables, grains and legumes, and low in animal products, colon and prostate cancer are virtually nonexistent. On the other hand in cultures like that of the United States, where the diet hinges on fatty, fiberless foods, often of animal origin, these cancers abound.

The importance of fiber in a healthy diet and as a preventative measure against disease cannot be over-stressed. Fiber aids in the speedy digestion and elimination of our foods. It works like a scrub brush to scour our intestinal walls from accumulating deposits. Left to accumulate, these particles would otherwise decay and putrefy, sending toxins throughout the entire body and acting as a local irritant within the intestines. Foods of vegetal origin are naturally rich in high amounts of fiber and thus are easily digested, while promoting the health and cleansing of the intestinal tract. Meat and other animal products are almost completely without fiber. They are difficult to digest and can often remain in the intestines for three to four days.

In addition to these health problems, which are at last receiving the media and medical establishment attention they deserve, there are a number of other very serious issues associated with meat consumption which have, as yet, been relatively ignored. These issues center, either directly or indirectly, on the manners in which animals are raised for commercial production and sale.

Meat, poultry, and dairy production is big business in America. Gone are the days of the small farmer who grazed his cattle on wide open fields, or whose chickens were allowed to run freely. The meat, dairy, and poultry industries are no longer content to have their profits limited by the laws of nature. Today the animals which are destined for the slaughterhouse, or raised for their egg or milk production, are assailed from birth until death with a barrage of biotech chemicals, drugs, and hormones, designed solely to increase their profitability.

With economics as the guiding rule, these animals are raised in cramped and squalid conditions in which disease runs rampant. Calves, for example, are chained in stalls so narrow that they cannot turn around and are purposely rendered anemic in order to yield that tender, pale white veal so coveted by gourmet chefs. Cattle in general are likewise closely quartered as exercise makes their meat tough and causes them to require more feed.

Many of the drugs and chemicals administered to these animals to combat diseases arising as a result of these unnatural living conditions have never been approved for human consumption. They are, needless to say, *not* listed or disclosed on any packaging of these animal products. Yet, they are there and we consume them every time we eat the animal itself, its eggs, or its milk.

A very informative pamphlet on the contaminants in our foods, published by the public interest group, Americans For Safe Food, summarizes this situation well:

> In the midst of the current concern over drug use, what if you learned someone was regularly slipping you small amounts of potentially harmful drugs without your knowledge or consent? Unless you're a vegetarian, that may well be the case.
>
> Large amounts of drugs, including substances never meant for human use, are given to livestock of all kinds, not just to keep them well, but to make them grow faster. Residues of these chemicals turn up in our food, sometimes at high levels if a drug has been misused. Unfortunately, testing for such residues is not a high priority with government inspectors, and the residues of some animal drugs cannot be detected.

In the case of antibiotics administered to livestock, the use is clearly creating new strains of "supergerms" that cause human disease and cannot be quelled by standard medical treatment. Just as disturbing is the unknown long-range effect of ingesting residues of hormones, which are also used for food ...[3]

What are these contaminants? Do they really pose a threat to human health? If so, why are they used? These are but a few of the questions that are raised by this little known aspect of agribusiness and its alliance with the multinational petrochemical industry.

There are approximately 2,000 different drugs and chemicals which are routinely administered to livestock, the most common of which include:

- antibiotics;
- hormones;
- pesticides;
- gentian violet, a fungicide and known carcinogen used as an additive to poultry feed; and
- clorsulon, a drug used to treat livestock with a parasitic infection called fluke. It has been linked to kidney tumors in some laboratory rats.[4]

Antibiotics today are given to some 80 percent of all American poultry, 60 percent of cattle, 75 percent of dairy cows and swine. In fact, antibiotics for livestock are so prevalent that approximately one-half of the entire annual production of these drugs by United States manufacturers ends up being used for this purpose. Even though the routine use of antibiotics entails subtherapeutic dosages, they can still present serious health problems for the meat and dairy consumer, the most dangerous of which is the emergence of the "supergerm." These are bacteria which, through the process of adaptation, have developed a resistance to a specific antibiotic. However, the process does not stop there. These resistant strains can transfer their immunity to other bacteria, and often, they tend to be resistant to other types of antibiotics as well. This can have a number of consequences. First, the resistant strains can be transferred directly to the consumer of the infected meat or milk.

Salmonella, a bacteria which can cause severe food poisoning, is one such example. It is estimated that about 20 percent of the 40,000 cases of salmonella infection each year are caused by resistant strains of the bacteria, and that almost 70 percent of these cases are attributable to animal sources. Additionally, the fatality rate resulting from these resistant strain infections is 4.2 percent, which means that an estimated 232 Americans will die each year as a direct consequence of eating animal products infected with resistant strain salmonella alone.[5]

Another serious health problem related to the widespread use of antibiotics in commercial livestock concerns the residues of these drugs that remain in the animal's flesh when you consume it. If you are allergic to a given antibiotic, you may be getting a continued dosage of it from the foods you eat. Routine consumption of meat, dairy, and poultry products causes the antibiotic to build up in your system and may be linked to your otherwise inexplicable medical complaints. Furthermore, there is reason to believe that these antibiotic residues may also be causing drug resistant bacteria to proliferate in your intestines.

This may present even further health consequences. When you take an antibiotic, it kills off all the susceptible bacteria in your body. Many of these are "friendly" bacteria, which actually comprise part of the body's natural defense system by keeping harmful germs in check. Therefore, when antibiotics eliminate the beneficial bacteria, the resistant strains can get a stronghold and proliferate unimpeded.

Antibiotics are not the only chemicals that may be finding their way to your dinner table when you least expect them. Hormones, given to increase growth and control fertility cycles, are also commonly administered to commercial animals. The residues from these hormones remain in the meat when you consume it and can produce the same health problems that these hormones cause when taken directly. Synthetic estrogens and progesterone, for example, are known to cause cancer in women, as illustrated by the increased incidence in breast, cervical, and endometrial cancer in women taking birth control pills. The hormonal residues in your foods, of course, provide lower than therapeutic dosages, but the health risks are nevertheless present. These hormones are particularly dangerous for children, who, because of their lower body weight receive proportionately higher doses. They can cause abnormal sexual development, precocious puberty, and premature breast enlargement.

Animal feed, and the animals themselves, are also highly doused with pesticides and fungicides which add to the unlisted chemical residues you consume when you eat meat. As was the case with the now-banned pesticide DDT, many of these pesticides become more concentrated as they move up the consumption chain. This can pose a particular threat to infants whose mother's milk may contain high concentrations of these substances.

Additional health risks are posed by meat consumption as a result of the lax inspection procedures by federal and state agencies, whose job it is to ensure the safety of our foodstuffs. In fact within one week, *The New York Times* ran two separate articles on precisely this issue. In a May 17, 1987 article entitled "U.S. Inspector Is Dubious About Quality of Meat," it cites an Agriculture Department inspector who says that beef, pork, and poultry product labels should read: "Eat at Your Own Risk." The inspector attributes the dangerously low quality of these products to laxity by the government in enforcing food inspection regulations, favoritism toward plant owners, and "petty corruption" within the Agriculture Department.[6]

In another article appearing on May 13, 1987, *The Times* reports that:

> The Government's program for inspecting chickens is inadequate to protect the public against such dangerous disease organisms as salmonella and campylobacter, a panel of scientists said today.
>
> The scientists, noting that under the current system an inspector examines 60 to 70 slaughtered chickens a minute, said consumers would be better protected with "more rigorous testing of a random sampling of chickens for both microbial and chemical contaminants."[7]

As long ago as 1910, Dr. Peyton Roux discovered that over 90 percent of the chickens offered for sale in New York City were cancerous and carried a cancer causing microbe. Since that time, Virginia Livingston-Wheeler, M.D., has done extensive research into this subject and believes that:

- There does in fact exist a cancer causing microbe.
- It is present in the majority of chickens offered for sale today, as well as in much of the beef.
- The microbe is capable of being transferred from one member of a species to another member of the same

species (i.e., from chicken to chicken, or from chicken to egg). It can also be transferred from one species to another (i.e., from chicken to cow, and from chicken to human).

- The microbe is not isolated simply at the site of the tumor, but is present throughout the body of the infected animal.

Dr. Livingston's theories raise several important considerations. First, it is possible that some cancers, at least, are transferred to us via the foods we eat, in particular chicken. Much beef may also be infected because chicken feces, which according to Dr. Livingston can transmit the germ, are often added to cattle feed as a source of cheap protein. The same is true of pork.

Secondly, a recent broadcast on "60 Minutes" (March, 1987) revealed that the laxity of government inspectors is not limited to their failure to detect unsafe levels of pesticides, drugs, or germs in the nation's livestock and poultry. The broadcast reported that chickens with actually visible and palpable cancer tumors were passing through governmental inspection unimpeded.

Additionally, Dr. Livingston believes that the cancer microbe is present not only in the tumor, but also throughout the body of the infected animal. Consequently, even if the cancerous tumors were being detected by poultry inspectors, the rest of the bird, if allowed to pass, would still be able to transmit the microbe to the consumer.

Evidence is mounting daily as to the health risks associated with excessive meat consumption. Some of that evidence is, at last, being made widely available to the public. The rest of it, however, still remains largely ignored by government officials and medical authorities. Safety standards for highly toxic drugs and chemicals are often set at ridiculously low levels or go unenforced altogether. As the laws and regulations concerning animal products stand now, producers are under no obligation to disclose the many harmful substances contained in these foods. Until Congress or the governmental agencies involved in regulating food production in this country decide to act to protect the public from the deleterious effects of these substances, avoiding the most polluted of our foods, among which animal products figure prominently, may be the only safe solution.

I

INTRODUCTION
TO
VEGETARIANISM

ONE

What Is Vegetarianism and Why Choose It as a Way of Life?

D espite its quirky, food-fad connotation of the past, vegetarianism has in the last twenty years become a way of life for hundreds of thousands of people in the United States.

Some people still think being a vegetarian means a life sentence of brown rice and broccoli. The truth is far from this boring image. As the origin of the word *vegetarianism* implies—from the Latin *vegetare*, "to enliven"—vegetarianism is a health-enhancing approach to diet and life.

Being a vegetarian means nothing more than abstaining from the flesh of warm-blooded animals. But there is more than one way to do it:

- *Total vegetarians* thrive solely on plant foods. They eat not only vegetables, but fruits, nuts, seeds, grains, and legumes as well. This regimen omits all animal foods, including meat, poultry, fish, eggs, dairy products, and honey.
- *Vegans* have an absolute commitment to vegetarianism, abstaining not only from all animal foods and dairy products, but also from using any products derived from animals, such as leather or even wool or silk.
- *Lacto-vegetarians* include milk and milk products in their diet in addition to vegetable foods.
- *Lacto-ovo-vegetarians* consume eggs along with milk products and vegetables.
- *Pesco-vegetarians* allow fish in their diets. Prime example: the hundreds of millions of Asians who live on the staples of rice, fish, and vegetables.
- *Pollo-vegetarians* eat poultry (chicken, duck, game, birds) while still omitting red meat.

Throughout most of the world, vegetarianism is the rule, not the exception. Over three-quarters of a billion people follow vegetarian diets.[1] A growing number of these come from Western industrialized countries where meat avoiding is not at all prevalent. The U.S. alone today has over seven million vegetarians![2] That this number is increasing is making it easier for vegetarians to maintain their healthy life-style. They are dining out in restaurants that offer vegetarian "gourmet" entrees, reading meat-less cookbooks, even tuning in to radio shows and subscribing to magazines produced for vegetarians.

All these people have been attracted to the vegetarian way of life by a wide range of rationales. Their reasons each deserve equal time.

HEALTH

Not only is health a major, perhaps *the* major, prod for most vegetarians, it's one of the reasons many people *stick* with it. Cutting out fatty meats and substituting lighter, plant proteins can have amazing effects on general health and well-being. Not only that, but vegetarianism can in many cases actually *prevent* disease. For example, saturated fats and cholesterol, found in meats in high quantities, have been linked to breast and colon cancer. These bad fats also contribute to hardening of the arteries and heart disease. And overconsumption of animal proteins has been associated with diseases such as osteoporosis, stroke, liver and kidney disorders, and arthritis. Vegetarianism isn't a cure for these life-threateners, but by deleting meat from your diet, you're taking a very smart preventive step.

As if it weren't bad enough as it is, meat is often contaminated with hormones, antibiotics, tranquilizers, preservatives, additives, and pesticides. These toxins can have negative long-term effects on health, and recently have been connected with cases of salmonella.

And it isn't only the elimination of meat that makes vegetarianism such a healthy life-style. Putting more fiber-rich vegetables and grains into meals can improve the functioning of the digestive tract. The result: less constipation and gas.[3]

ECONOMICS

The economics of vegetarianism are hard to beat. Ounce for ounce, plant foods are thriftier choices than meat, across the board. Heading for the produce stand instead of the butcher will leave your wallet fatter, while enriching your diet with fiber and more varied vitamins and minerals than a pot roast ever would.

On a larger scale vegetarianism can also produce beneficial effects. Agribusiness rules the meat industry roost. These enormous corporations rely on high-tech, high-cost methods of meat processing, making it virtually impossible for the small farmer to compete. A general switch to vegetables could provide the small farmer with a "new lease."

CONSERVATION OF NATURAL RESOURCES

The breeding and slaughter of animals, and the subsequent processing and packaging of the meat, requires an inordinate amount of land, water, energy, and raw materials. Many people opt for vegetarianism as a personal contribution to the necessary preservation of our fragile ecosystem and limited natural resources.

FOOD RESOURCES

Similarly, the ideal of eating simply so that everyone may eat, often leads people to an animal-free diet. The logic? Land is capable of supplying food for nearly fourteen times as many people when it is used to grow food for people rather than crops to feed livestock. Cows, for instance, consume approximately sixteen pounds of grain to yield just *one* pound of flesh![4] In contrast, it has been estimated that our current yield of plant foods could nourish more than double the world's population, perhaps even turning the world hunger problem around, if meat-consuming societies would curtail their meat demand and free grazing land for the more efficient purpose of growing food crops.[5]

RESPECT FOR ANIMAL LIFE

Many vegetarians are against animal slaughter, feeling that the breeding of livestock for food is inhumane. Their vegetarianism is a cry against cruelty, and is based on the belief they can help to save the lives of innocent creatures.

RELIGION

There are many religious disciplines, both contemporary and ancient, that incorporate a meat-free diet. Their reasons for endorsing vegetarianism may stem from a belief that human life may be reincarnated as animal life or vice versa; from ethical considerations against the taking of life; or even from considerations of its health benefits.

PERSONAL TASTE

For many, a taste for meat is an acquired one, starting in childhood; it is not due to an innate craving for protein. For those who choose to skip the steak and burgers for whatever reason, the taste for them usually fades fast. And no wonder, with the endless variety of protein-providing plant foods available and the tasty ways they're being combined, seasoned, and cooked in these modern vegetarian times.

Clearly, there are many sound reasons for adopting a meatless eating style. We will be discussing all these reasons in depth in part III.

TWO

Famous Vegetarians

Many people throughout the ages have made the decision to forgo red meat after much thought. It's fascinating to follow the evolution of the vegetarian life-style from ancient to modern times, noting the varied reasons famous vegetarians had for their eating styles. Gandhi, the Indian leader and pacifist, for example, felt such a strong kinship with animal life he couldn't bear the thought of using innocent creatures for food. Said he: "To my mind, the life of a lamb is no less precious than that of a human being. I should be unwilling to take the life of a lamb for the sake of the human body."[1]

In ancient Greece, Socrates and Plato taught that vegetarianism was the ideal diet. Buddha, in India, and Mohammed, in Arabia, also advised against meat consumption. This diet has also been embraced by many well-known artists, writers, and scientists, including Leonardo da Vinci, Leo Tolstoy, Sir Isaac Newton, Ralph Waldo Emerson, H.G. Wells, Upton Sinclair, and Charles Darwin.

Another legendary figure who was a vegetarian is Albert Schweitzer. Schweitzer echoed Gandhi's philosophy when he wrote, "There slowly grew up in me an unshakable conviction that we have no right to inflict suffering and death on another living creature unless there is some unavoidable necessity for it, and that we ought to feel what a horrible thing it is to cause suffering and death out of mere thoughtlessness."[2]

George Bernard Shaw viewed meat consumption as "cannibalism with its heroic dish removed." He attributed his long, productive life as a socio-political analyst and writer to this healthful diet. "I flatly declare that a man fed on whiskey and dead bodies cannot do the finest work of which he is capable," he wrote. "I have managed to do my thinking without the stimulus of tea or coffee." Shaw boasted that he felt "seldom less than ten times as well as an ordinary carcass eater."[3]

Shaw felt so strongly about his vegetarian way of life that he published, in 1918, *The Vegetarian Diet According to Shaw* in order to dispel the misconceptions about this dietary style. "An underfed man is not a man who gets no meat, or gets nothing but meat. He is one who does not get enough to eat, no matter what he eats. The person who is ignorant enough to believe that his nourishment depends on meat is in a horrible dilemma." Shaw further believed that naturally harvested foods continually nourished the life force within him. He wrote, "Think of the fierce energy concentrated in an acorn! You bury it in the ground, and it explodes into a giant oak. Bury a sheep and nothing happens but decay."[4]

Philosopher Henry David Thoreau dedicated pages to the ideals of vegetarianism. He felt that "it is a part of the destiny of the human, in its gradual improvement, to leave off eating animals, as surely as the savage tribes have left off eating each other when they came in contact with the more civilized."[5] Thoreau, like Shaw, felt that avoidance of meat improved his artistic endeavors.[6] In his masterwork, *Walden*, he wrote, "I believe that every man who has ever been earnest to preserve his higher or poetic facilities in the best condition has been particularly inclined to abstain from animal food." His personal abstinence from meat as well as coffee and tea was not so much for health reasons, but because "they were not agreeable to my imagination."[7]

Perhaps the best inspiration for a person on the brink of "going" vegetarian is a pair of well-known modern-day meat-shunners, Helen and Scott Nearing. They wrote several books in which they recount their experiences with the vegetarian life-style with much joy and reverence for life. And no wonder: Both reaped the health benefits of the practice, living long and productive lives (Scott lived to be a hundred; Helen is now in her eighties). Their meals consisted of wonderful concoctions of fresh fruits, whole grains, vegetable soups, nut butters, and molasses. Their story is more than a tale of amazing longevity, however. As newlyweds in the thirties, the Nearings left busy city life and settled in the peaceful atmosphere of Maine. Here they worked hard together to become monetarily independent, self-sufficient and rich: "rich in fresh air, fresh water and sunshine," Scott exalted. Growing themselves most of what they ate, the Nearings enjoyed a freedom that no one dependent on commercially packaged meats and other foods could imagine: the freedom of "being master of your own destiny."[8]

More recent vegetarians include well-known athletes, actors, and musicians. Oscar-winning Cloris Leachman, for example, attributes her youthfulness and vibrant health to her vegetarianism, which she describes as her "life-support system." Leachman, who switched to meatless eating when she began "to read about what's wrong with meat" is particularly outspoken about the political system that foists meat on unwitting consumers. The meat industry, she points out, has a very powerful lobby in Washington, and its effects reach even our schools; you'll rarely hear about the value of vegetarianism in school. Moreover, poor people have been led to feel that a steak on the table is a symbol of prosperity. Why? "Because they have been indoctrinated to believe this by the meat industry."

Leachman isn't all politics. One reason she chooses a natural-foods meal plan, consisting of wholesome, colorful, low-fat fresh foods, is to do away with the necessity of dieting. Relying on calorie counting to control weight leads to unhappy experiences, and to certain diet failure. "I'm interested in an approach to eating that is a way of life, where the road just unfolds before you and leads you into good feelings and uplifting experiences."[9]

Other vegetarian actors have included Dennis Weaver, a veteran vegetarian of over twenty years; James Coburn; Paul Newman; Cicely Tyson; Gloria Swanson; and Susan St. James. Musicians include Bob Dylan; George Harrison; Paul McCartney; Ravi Shankar; John Denver; the now-slim Chubby Checker; Gladys Knight; and the members of the "new wave" group the B–52s.[10]

Susan Smith Jones, a health writer, lecturer, and physical education instructor, incorporates vegetarianism into a holistic life-style including a ten-mile morning run and an hour of meditation every day. She believes that "the tangibility and reality of a full life is not only what you know, but how you apply it to every day.... We are not victims of circumstance or fortuity, but rather architects of our lives, ourselves and our feelings." Most people believe that a well-thought-out regimen of healthful living is too time-consuming. To this, Susan replies, "if we don't take time for health, in whatever capacity that might be, we must take time for sickness."[11]

Even athletes who once believed that top performance required them to "pump" iron into their bodies with massive amounts of red meat often end up turning to vegetarianism. These include vegetarian body builders like the legendary Gilman Low, who set nine world records in 1903 for his strength and endurance; Roy Hilligan, the first vegetarian "Mr. America"; and more contemporary competitors including Ron Gleason, a contender in the 1972 Olympics.[12]

Besides these celebrated muscle men are other star athletes. John Marino set a transcontinental bicycling record in August 1978—riding after three years of training from Los Angeles to New York in just thirteen days, one hour, and twenty minutes! Marino maintains that his vegetarian diet was the primary factor for his athletic achievement.

Describing his training he explained, "the first step is detoxification of the body. Unnatural foods, chemicals, drugs, alcohol, artificial flavorings, and preservatives bring on a toxic buildup in the body, which can lead to disease, lethargy and, in extreme cases, death. Our bodies are designed to consume organic foods in the natural state."[13]

Another athlete who renounced meat is Norwegian skier Arden Haugen, elected to the Skiing Hall of Fame after winning four national and three world skiing championships. Turning away from meat toward a diet of whole-grain cereals and breads, vegetables, fruits, and soy milk, he asserted, cleared his skin, upped his stamina, and made breathing easier.[14]

Longer life, clearer thinking, optimum body performance, and even creative inspiration have all been attributed by famous vegetarians to their eating style. Follow their lead. You may not become as famous as these celebrity vegetarians, but chances are you'll reap similar physical, mental, and emotional benefits.

THREE

A
Brief History
of Vegetarianism

Vegetarianism has been around a long, long time. In fact, the book of *Genesis* advocates a diet of fruits, seeds, and nuts[1] that's decidedly vegetarian.

Other roots of vegetarianism date to the early history of Eastern nations. Here, ancient religious beliefs in the transmigration of the human soul to "lower" life forms led followers to maintain a vegetarian diet out of respect for animal life. Buddha later commanded, "Do not butcher the ox that plows thy field," and "Do not indulge a voracity that involves the slaughter of animals." Buddhism quickly spread eastward from India, became the state religion of China around 500 A.D., and finally flowed to Japan a century later. Vegetarianism for the Japanese Buddhists included the belief that eating animal flesh polluted the body for one hundred days.[2]

Vegetarianism in the Hindu religion of India is founded on health standards formulated in the Hindu epic poem, The Mahabharata:

"Those who desire to possess good memory, beauty, long life with perfect health, and physical, moral and spiritual strength, should abstain from animal foods."

Jainism, more a philosophy than a religion, is based on the principle of nonviolence and abhors the killing of animals, fish, or fowl for food.

Yoga, another Oriental discipline, follows the vegetarian beliefs of the Hindus and Buddhists, teaching that all life is formed and sustained through *prana*, or the "life force." The ideal foods, according to this philosophy, are those containing life energy, including vegetables, fruits, nuts, legumes, and grains. Accordingly, the meat of dead animals, which have lost their prana, is useless and should be avoided.[3]

Analysis of the intestinal contents of mummies have unearthed yet another race of vegetarians, the Egyptians. These ancients have earned the modern nickname "the eaters of bread."[4] Much later in the Middle East, Mohammed's holy book of Islam, the Koran, prohibited the eating of "dead animals, blood and flesh."[5]

But it's ancient Greece that boasts the beginnings of the "real" vegetarian movement, founded by Phythagoras and supported by the likes of Plato and Socrates. What began as religious policy grew into a feeling that vegetarianism was natural and hygienic, and therefore necessary to healthy living.[6]

An unlikely vegetarian race were the Romans, who conquered the known world with an army fed on bread and porridge, vegetables, wine, and sometimes fish. Says historian Will Durant, "The Roman army conquered the world on a vegetarian diet. Caesar's troops complained when corn ran out and they had to eat meat."[7]

But after the fall of the Roman Empire, vegetarianism fell out of popularity for some twelve hundred years. Only the devotion and dedication of a few cloistered orders of the Catholic Church, the Benedictines, and the Cistercians kept vegetarianism alive until the Renaissance revived the ancient teachings and modern vegetarianism got under way. The "new" ideologies had the same support from many influential people as the "old." Among the famous vegetarians in the political, literary, and scientific arenas were Sir Frances Bacon, Shakespeare, Voltaire, and Benjamin Franklin.[8]

Despite—or perhaps because of—the increase in meat eating by the nineteenth century, most European countries saw the organization of whole vegetarian movements. It was one of Great Britain's most revered vegetarians, Reverend William Metcalf, who carried the movement across the waters to America in 1817. Also John Wesley, the founder of Methodism, who promoted the idea that vegetarianism was a more healthful way to live. The result: a convention in 1850 which established the American Vegetarian Society. The cause was furthered by Anna Kingsford, a nineteenth-century medical practitioner who dedicated much of her scientific writing to the subject of vegetarianism. She reported that the strongest animals in the world, including the horse, elephant, and camel, were herbivorous, eating only plant foods, and paralleled this fact with the amazing athletic prowess of the ancient Greeks, who avoided meat.[9]

Real strides in scientific vegetarianism came out of World War I, when food scarcity prompted scientists in the U.S. to re-evaluate the national diet. Forced to find alternative sources of protein, they discovered the healthy benefits of non–meat eating at the same time. The American way of handling meat shortages was adopted by other countries as well: Denmark in 1917 adopted a simple, meatless wartime diet based on whole grains, vegetables, and dairy products. The result was overall improved health and lowered mortality rates.[10] During World War II, Norwegians drastically cut their meat consumption, depending on cereals, potatoes, and other vegetables. Once again, vegetarianism improved the country's health and lowered mortality rates! Not surprisingly, these health statistics flipped over when the war ended and "normal" meat consumption resumed.[11]

Around the early forties, the number of vegetarians living in the United States was estimated to be between two and a half and three million. Since then, the ranks have swelled to over seven million, and vegetarianism has taken on new meaning. No longer is it strictly a religious or counterculture characteristic. The recent rise in health consciousness has inspired many Americans to improve their lifestyles by becoming vegetarian. Concerned about the health damage that eating meat can cause, more people are now enjoying the benefits of eating more fresh foods. But relative to the size of the general population, the number of vegetarians is still small. The vegetarian movement has only one way to go: up.

11

PROTEIN:
THE
LARGER
PICTURE

FOUR

Protein: Unraveling the Myths

As a longtime advocate of the benefits of a vegetarian diet, I was pleased to see an article in *The New York Times* entitled "Vegetarianism: More Popular, if Less Pure" (March 25, 1987). The article announced:

> Vegetarians no longer need to defend their diets at parties. While some unrepentant carnivores may sneer at their victuals as assorted seaweed with an occasional foray into nuts and berries, there is clearly a growing interest in the vegetarian way of eating.
>
> Vegetarian magazines, organizations and cooking classes are thriving. Tofu, a soybean curd that once seemed exotic, is sold in smalltown supermarkets. Mexican, Indian and other restaurants that use grain and beans are more popular. Consumption of fresh vegetables has grown 12 percent since 1980, according to the Agriculture Department.[1]

When *The New York Times* prints an article about changing trends in the health and nutrition field, you can be pretty sure that the latest trend it is covering has been around for a good five years. This is not a put-down of the *Times* per se, but it merely reflects the tendency of the establishment press to cover controversial dietary issues only when most of the controversy has dissipated. What is exciting in this article then is not the newness of the ideas it presents, but rather that many Americans are now making the conscious decision to move toward a healthier diet.

Some of my purist vegetarian colleagues would find fault with *The New York Times* article, and contend that the new "vegetarianism" it is heralding is not "real" vegetarianism. As the same article itself states:

> Now, however, vegetarians have something new to defend: their name. More Americans are adopting some of the principles of vegetarianism and may even proclaim themselves to be vegetarians, associating a diet of vegetables, beans and grains with wholesomeness, healthfulness and nutritional enlightenment. But while many of these people eschew meat, they continue to eat fish or chicken, which rules them out as bona fide vegetarians.[2]

I do not find it particularly useful to bicker over the semantics of what this new diet should or should not be called. What is important is that at long last Americans are beginning to realize that optimal health and well-being comes from a diet rich in fruits, vegetables, grains, and legumes instead of products like meat, cheese, and eggs. The American Cancer Society and the American Heart Association have been telling us that for years. Their message is clear. The high-fat, high-calorie, high-protein diet of Americans is directly related to the ever increasing incidence of obesity, heart disease, and cancer in the country. In the face of all this disease, the fact that these new "vegetarians" are not true vegetarians in the strict sense of the word, does not trouble me in the least. At last, we are seeing some movement in the right direction. Not only that, but it is a large-scale movement and its momentum is the power of personal awareness, responsibility, and decision making instead of mass advertising. This, too, is something new.

A LESSON IN PROTEIN MYTHOLOGY

The myths about protein abound in the Western world, making it one of the most misunderstood areas in nutrition. Many of these myths are so entrenched in our psyche, we find it difficult, if not impossible, to let go of them, even though the recent scientific data shows them to be false. Concepts of what protein does, where it comes from, what will happen to us if we don't get enough, are all part of these myths. If you have thought about becoming a vegetarian, chances are that you've been discouraged by the believers of these myths who have told you that you will not be getting enough protein.

Over the years, this nation has become one of protein fanatics. Athletes have been led to believe that they had to eat massive amounts of protein for strength and endurance. They were told that protein was stored up in their muscles and that without lots of meat, milk, and protein powders to "beef-up" their muscles, they would become like Samson shorn of his hair by Delilah. As will be discussed later on, this is simply not true. In fact, today's athletes, the ones who are winning the races and sports events, are not loading up on protein, but rather, on carbohydrates.

You may also remember being in science or health classes as a youngster and being shown the different food groups. In these classes, I, at least, was led to believe that protein was synonymous with meat, dairy, and egg products and that fruits, vegetables, and grains may have been good as sources of vitamins, but were certainly not reliable as sources of protein.

This same message has been promulgated by the animal-foods industries via their massive advertising campaigns. The ad run by the beef producers now has actress Cybill Shepherd face-to-face with a hamburger, telling the audience that she's heard of people who don't eat burgers, but that she doesn't know if she can trust them. The slogan is that beef is the "real food for real people." The milk ads, for years now, have exploited the health and vibrancy of American youth in order to extol the benefits of milk. What these ads do not tell us is that beef and dairy products are filled with all sorts of chemicals and drugs, are high in cholesterol, are not easily digested, and that the excessive consumption of these products may be responsible for much of the disease in this country.

Even though both science and common sense would dictate otherwise, the misconceptions surrounding protein are still promoted as truth in this country.

The most commonly held beliefs about protein are:

1. Animal products are our only source of protein.
2. If you go on a vegetarian diet, you will become protein deficient, and then weak, sick, and anemic.
3. Meat promotes virility and sexual potency; "real" men need meat.
4. We cannot get too much protein; any excess will be stored in the muscles.
5. Animal protein is low in calories and will keep you slim; carbohydrates are fattening.
6. Man was made to eat meat.
7. Animal products are our only source of vitamin B_{12}.

You may be surprised to learn that every single one of these statements are false. Let's look at them one by one:

1. Animal products are not our only source of protein. Soy products like tofu and tempeh, as well as spirulina and chlorella, which are single-celled algae, are very high in protein. In addition, almost every grain and legume provides us with protein that is often more fully utilized than that of animal products. Certain combinations of nonanimal products such as rice and beans, chick peas and sesame seeds, or peanut butter and wheat, not only provide protein that is more easily absorbed and utilized by the body, but they provide as much protein as animal products.
2. The recent scientific literature in this country is revealing what other civilizations, such as the Hindu and the Japanese, have known for thousands of years, namely that we do not need meat or dairy products in order to sustain human life and health. In fact, it is becoming increasingly apparent that the healthiest civilizations are those eating little or no meat and leading essentially vegetarian life-styles.

   The truth of the matter is that meat probably saps more energy than it imparts. It is very difficult and time consuming to digest, remaining in the stomach for upward of six hours and in the intestine for about three days. Just the digestion of meat is an energy-consuming procedure for the body that can leave you tired and sluggish. Meat also tends to putrefy in the intestines and send toxins through the body, further weakening it. Constipation caused by meat can mean exhaustion.

   Furthermore, because of excessive meat consumption, many people are allergic to it, which can cause tension-fatigue syndrome.

3. As to virility and potency, "real" men, and women, need meat about as much as they need prostate cancer, gout, liver and kidney failure, and heart disease, which are all promoted by the eating of meat.

4. Excess protein in the body is now believed to cause an increase in the rate that protein is replaced in the body. This increase can lead to cell damage and thus speed the aging process.[3] Furthermore, protein metabolism produces a by-product called urea which is filtered through the kidneys. Excess protein causes excess urea which, in turn, can lead to kidney stress. This is especially serious for those who have pre-existing kidney damage.

5. Animal protein is extremely high in calories because it is usually accompanied by a large amount of fat. An average 16-ounce steak, for example, is about 1,500 calories. There is little doubt that excess meat consumption is one of the major causes of obesity in this country. Carbohydrates, other than refined carbohydrates and sugars, are much lower in calories than animal products and have the added advantage of being full of fiber.

6. Physiologically, man was made a vegetarian. He has a long digestive tract, measuring some 22 feet. Carnivorous animals have very short intestinal tracts, so that meat remains within their bodies only for a short time. With man's long, alkaline intestines, meat can stay within

the body for three to four days, during which time it begins to decompose and putrefy, at our constant 98.6 degree body heat. This putrefaction sends toxins throughout the body and may be one of the major causes of colon and prostate problems.

7. Vitamin B_{12} is manufactured by micro-organisms, so it is not normally found in the fruits and vegetables that you eat. However, it is present in fermented foods like miso, soy sauce, tempeh, and of course yogurt, if you eat dairy products. While it is more difficult to get this vitamin if you do not eat animal products, it is by no means impossible. I, personally, have never known a vegetarian who planned their meals properly, to be B_{12} deficient. If you are worried, a supplement is simple enough to take.

WHAT IS PROTEIN?

With all these misconceptions floating around, you may wonder what protein is and why there seems to be such a fuss about it.

There is no question that protein is a very essential nutrient. It helps to build, maintain, and repair just about every part of our bodies; it makes up our hair, finger and toe nails, skin muscles, cartilage, and tendons. Many of our hormones, antibodies, and enzymes are made up of protein. Basically, you can think of protein as building blocks; it is the stuff from which we are made. Only in the unusual situation, like starvation or in some of the high-protein, low-carbohydrate diets, is protein broken down and used as energy. It is primarily fats, carbohydrates, fruits, and vegetables that are used for that purpose.

Chemically, proteins are long chain molecules made up of individual links called amino acids. There are approximately twenty-two amino acids that make up the protein we use. These are the same amino acids that make up all other protein in nature as well, be it plant, animal, viral, or human. There are eight of these amino acids—nine in children—that we cannot manufacture, which is why we call them the essential amino acids. They are: valine, leucine, isoleucine, lysine, threonine, tryptophan, methionine, phenylalanine, and histadine. This last amino acid is important for the growth and development of children.

Foods that contain all of these amino acids in about the right proportions for human utilization are called "complete proteins." They include meat, eggs, and dairy products, and also nonanimal foods like peanut butter and whole wheat, rice and other grains and beans, corn and beans, and chick peas and sesame seeds. Foods that do not contain all of the essential amino acids in the right proportions are called "incomplete" proteins. As we will see later, there are really very few foods that fall into this category, hence the concept of "complete" versus "incomplete" protein is actually obsolete.

UNRAVELING THE MYTHS

Much of the confusion surrounding protein can be traced back to the earliest studies on protein done in 1914 by two scientists by the names of T.B. Osborne and L.B. Mandel. These studies, which were performed on rats, basically showed that these rats grew better on animal protein than on vegetable protein. From this it was extrapolated that human beings needed animal protein to grow and develop properly.[4] John A. McDougall, M.D., a leading nutritional physician and author of *The McDougall Plan for Super Health and Life-Long Weight Loss* (New Century Publishers Inc., 1983), has done extensive research on the scientific history of the study of protein. He comments on this rather amazing bit of scientific deductive reasoning as follows:

> What came about was a classification which stuck with us. That classification was that animal protein was called class "A" protein or superior and vegetables were called class "B" or inferior protein. Nobody bothered to recall that these studies were based on rats.
>
> Now in the 1930s they discovered the amino acids, or the building blocks, and they tried to fit [the old data on the] poor growth of rats [with] these new findings of amino acids. When they started analyzing the various needs of different animals of these building blocks, in the case of the rat, they found that the rat could make 10 amino acids out of the 20, but that there were

10 amino acids that the rat could not make and had to get from its diet. So they called those the essential amino acids. What they theorized, again looking back on Osborne and Mandel's work showing inferior and superior proteins, was the reason some of these proteins were inferior was because their essential amino acids were not great enough in quantity to supply the need of the rat. That is how those two theories were tied together.[5]

What is important in these early works is that the conclusions, which were later taught in U.S. high schools or junior high schools as fact, were nothing more than conjectures and educated guesses —educated guesses, which, it turns out, are wholly unfounded.

It was not until the late 1940s that experiments on man's protein requirements were performed. Dr. William Rose, who conducted these experiments and recorded their results in 1952, to date remains the definitive authority on protein requirements for human beings.[6]

What Dr. Rose did was to feed healthy young men restricted diets of corn starch (maize), sucrose, butterfat, vitamins, and purified amino acids. This part of the experiment was to determine the protein requirements of the men. Amazingly, Dr. Rose found that they required a mere 20 grams of protein daily.

The second part of his experiment was to find out which of the amino acids were essential. He knew that for rats ten were essential and he assumed the same was true for humans, but he discovered that adults could synthesize both histidine and arginine, which the rat was incapable of synthesizing. In determining which amino acids were essential, Dr. Rose withdrew the amino acid he was testing for from the diets of the young men. He found that if it was an essential amino acid, the men would become very debilitated within two days. They would lose their appetite, become nervous, irritable, and depressed. In fact, the men were in such distress that Dr. Rose recorded in his research papers that he felt obligated to discontinue the experiments.[7]

It is obviously true that these amino acids *are* essential. But what quantities do we require? And what are our best sources of the essential amino acids? These questions will be discussed in the next chapters.

FIVE

Protein Requirements

Since protein plays such an important role in building, repairing, and maintaining our bodies, we want to make sure that we get enough. Our bones and hair and almost every other part of our body are made of protein. In addition, protein is what makes up collagen, the gluelike material which connects all of our tissues; quite literally, without protein we would fall apart. So, we certainly want to make sure that we get enough. But just how much protein is enough?

HOW MUCH PROTEIN
DO WE REALLY NEED?

Because of the importance of protein, almost all of the statistics we receive concerning protein requirements are inflated with "safety margins"; some to greater, some to lesser degrees.

Ideally, the most precise way to measure your protein requirements would be to measure the amount of nitrogen you use and lose in a given day, since protein is the only nutrient that supplies us with nitrogen. This is not really practicable on any large scale or regular basis, although there have been scientific studies measuring the body's "nitrogen balance." Some of these studies were conducted over thirty years ago and concluded that a mere 20 grams of protein, only 70 percent of which was high quality, was adequate to maintain the body's nitrogen balance.

Since measuring your nitrogen utilization is not a practical way of determining protein requirements, what has been done instead is to establish tables of "guess-timations" as to our required protein.

Dr. McDougall bases his protein-requirement calculations on the scientific research that has been done in the area. His figures are on the low end of the protein-requirement scale. Dr. McDougall believes that an average person's protein requirements are somewhere around 2½ percent of his or her total calorie intake. The calculations work like this: You take your total calorie intake for a day. (Those calories can come from three sources: proteins, fats, and carbohydrates.) If, for example, you burn 3,000 calories per day, you take 2½ percent of these calories—75 calories—and then divide by 4 (calories per gram—1 gram of protein has 4 calories), which gives you 18.75. You will need only around 19 grams of protein per day, according to Dr. McDougall.[1]

Even though these figures are based on reputable scientific research, I personally believe that they are too low and should be doubled. Dr. McDougall's calculations coincide more or less with the "minimum requirements" determined by Dr. Rose back in the 1940s, but are about half of Dr. Rose's "recommended requirements."

Dr. McDougall discusses how Dr. Rose arrived at his figures: "William Rose determined that we needed eight essential amino acids and he determined the level of each amino acid. Because he didn't want to make any mistakes, he took the largest requirement from any single individual and he called that his *minimum* requirement for that particular amino acid. Then he took that requirement and he doubled it and called it his *recommended* requirement which he also declared to be a definitely safe intake of that particular amino acid."[2] (*italics added*)

Dr. Rose's "recommended requirements" now fall in the middle range of recommended figures. And they correspond with those published by the World Health Organization, which essentially doubled Dr. McDougall's figures in order to provide a safety margin for people who are under stress, or suffering from infection or injury. The World Health Organization recommends 5 percent of calorie intake as protein, 6 percent for pregnant women and 7 percent for women who are nursing. By these figures again, if you are burning 3,000 calories per day, you will need around 37 grams of protein. If you are using 2,300 calories per day, you will need around 29 grams of protein.

On the upper end of the recommendations for protein are the "beefed-up" figures of the National Academy of Science. The Academy recommends that you should be taking about 10 to 15 percent of your total calories in the form of protein. The way that the Academy calculates its figures is based on its estimate that we need approximately .9 grams per each kilogram of body weight. It comes up with this table:

The requirement for newborn babies up until six months old, based upon a diet with human milk as the source of protein, is calculated by multiplying kilograms of body weight by 2.2.

Six months to 1 year:	kilograms of body weight times 2
Children, 1 to 3 years:	Require 23 grams
4 to 6 years:	30 grams
7 to 10 years:	34 grams
Males, 11 to 14 years:	45 grams
15 to 51 years and over:	56 grams
Females, 11 to 18 years:	46 grams
19 to 51 years and over:	44 grams

Pregnant women need 30 extra grams per day

Lactating women need 20 extra grams per day

As you notice from the above figures, certain conditions will require increases in protein. Children in their formative years require more than adults because they are building bones, muscles, teeth —in short, their whole bodies—"from scratch." Adults normally require protein primarily for maintenance and repair. Pregnant and lactating women, however, also have higher protein requirements. If you are engaged in a regular exercise program, especially if it includes bodybuilding, you will also require 10 percent more protein than you would normally need (i.e., if you would normally need around 40 grams, then you need an additional 4 grams).

With all of these different protein requirements floating around, it is confusing for you to know how much protein you actually need. I have presented these different views on protein requirements in order to give you a framework in which to determine your own unique needs, and also to illustrate that even with the inflated figures of the National Academy of Science, we really require very little protein—protein, which I will show later, is easily available from nonanimal sources.

If you want to know if you are getting enough protein, you may want to go through the calculations above, figuring out your total protein intake and then comparing it with the various recommendations. Many foods have their nutrient breakdown on their packaging, so you can add up the protein in grams on those foods. You may also want to write to the federal government and ask for the United States Department of Agriculture (U.S.D.A.) Handbook #8, a publication which gives the breakdown of various nutrients. For those of you who will be following the program I am setting forth, you will find an appendix in the back of this book of over a thousand high-protein food combinations.

CALCULATING YOUR REQUIREMENTS

No matter whose recommendations you follow—whether it's the World Health Organization's 5 percent of calorie intake, or the more conservative National Academy's view of 10 to 15 percent, you can easily calculate two important factors that relate to protein requirements: the percentage of calories your body requires from protein, and how much of your diet's total calories are being derived from proteins. Looking at the National Academy of Science figures, for example, an average adult male needs to obtain 56 grams of protein, from a daily intake of 2,700 calories. Since each gram of protein has 4 calories—no matter what the source of the protein—it's easy to calculate what portion of your calories should be coming from protein:[3]

56 grams (protein) × 4 (calories per gram) = 224 calories

$$\frac{224 \text{ protein calories (required)}}{2,700 \text{ calories (total intake)}} = 8.3 \text{ percent}$$

In this diet, about 9 percent of the calories need to be in the form of protein. To insure that we are getting this amount, we can calculate what percentage of the food we eat is protein of some kind. It's another easy calculation. All we need to know is how many grams of protein and how many total calories a particular food contains in order to figure out its protein-calories contribution. For example, 100 grams of uncooked lentils will provide 340 calories and 24.6 grams of protein. You can see that by looking on the bean package's label or checking any nutrition book. As we know, there are 4 calories in a gram of protein. We then multiply 24.6 grams of protein by 4 calories/gram to arrive at 98.4, or the amount of calories we receive from the protein portion of the lentils alone. To get our percentage, we divide 98.6 by the total caloric content of the lentils, or:[4]

$$\frac{98.6 \text{ calories}}{340 \text{ calories}} = 29 \text{ percent}$$

All of this basic arithmetic allows us to analyze any food so that we can evaluate its protein contributions to our diet. When you take the time to do these simple calculations, you will probably be surprised at the high protein content of many plant foods.

Research done over thirty years ago concluded that 20 grams a day of protein—of which only about 70 percent was of high quality—kept humans in "nitrogen balance."[5] Nitrogen is the main constituent of protein, and a person maintains this equilibrium when his protein intake is adequate. To calculate this, we say that the amount of nitrogen in the foods we eat is comparable to the amount we excrete through our feces, urine, and sweat. If the result reveals an equal or lesser amount, then a person's protein intake is adequate. When the amount excreted exceeds our dietary intake, we are said to be in "negative nitrogen balance." This means that our protein intake is way below par, and that we're breaking down fat or muscle tissue in the body to release extra nitrogen.

Eating an inadequate amount of high-quality protein will create a state in which our bodies will break down more molecules than it can build up, resulting in an overall deterioration of our bodies. Some symptoms of a protein deficiency are muscle weakness, loss of endurance, fatigue, growth retardation, loss of weight, irritability, lowered immune response, poor healing, and anemia. Pregnant women must be extra careful to avoid such a situation, as it will not only affect their health but their unborn baby's as well. A protein deficiency can promote a miscarriage, premature delivery, or toxemia, and its effects on the baby's development may set the stage for chronic diseases later in life.

But then, experiments in which only plant sources of protein were given to subjects showed that these individuals maintained proper nitrogen equilibrium.[6] Therefore, it is not scientifically proven that it is necessary to eat any animal products in order to get your required daily amount of nitrogen. Eating a variety of vegetables, grains, legumes, seeds, and nuts will provide adequate amounts of high-quality protein, even if you look at protein from the point of view of nitrogen equilibrium.

But no matter how you measure it, researchers now agree that American meat eaters and vegetarians alike are getting more than their needed share of protein.

Dr. McDougall points out that this concern about adequate protein has become a sort of national obsession.

> For so many years we've worried about getting enough protein and the right kinds and all the essential amino acids. But think about it. How many people have you met in your lifetime who have suffered from protein deficiency, amino acid deficiency. I mean, talk to your doctor, ask how many cases of amino acid deficiency your doctor has treated over the past decade. The answer is essentially none. The problem is not a deficiency of protein, the problem is an excess of protein.[7]

With the abundance of protein in the American diet, especially if you eat animal protein, it is not easy to have a protein deficiency. According to Dr. McDougall even if you consumed only a single food like potatoes, which are not ordinarily associated with protein, you would get 80 grams of protein in 3,000 calories of potatoes; or 60 grams of protein in 3,000 calories of rice—all of which is highly usable protein. In his book *The McDougall Plan*, Dr. McDougall has a very interesting chart that graphs amino acid levels in different vegetable foods.[8] About this he says:

In that chart I put down Rose's minimum requirements, then I put down double his minimum requirement which were his recommended requirements and then I put down how much of each essential amino acid would be provided by a single starch such as corn, brown rice, oatmeal, beans, wheat, potatoes, sweet potatoes and so on. What I found when I sat down and calculated the amount of each essential amino acid is that *all* the starches and vegetables provide *all* the amino acids an individual would need. What I mean by "all" here is that they met easily, in fact in most cases doubled and tripled Rose's recommended requirements, which you will recall was twice his minimum requirement, which was the maximum of any subject in his experiment.

You see, nature put the foods together so that they would be complete a long time before they hit the dinner table. After all plants require protein in their makeup and the proteins in plants have to have all those amino acids to make a variety of proteins that allow the plant to be what it is. So it would make no sense at all not to have all these essential amino acids in your plant foods.[9]

Accordingly, Dr. McDougall does not believe that vegetarians need to worry about combining their foods in order to obtain adequate protein. On this point I disagree with Dr. McDougall. Different people may metabolize foods in different ways. They may have different absorption rates, or different amino acid requirements from those provided by a particular food. While I do not believe that knowledgeable vegetarians have to fret over exact food combining, I do believe that it is important for them to understand its basic concepts. Practically speaking, once you start to eat a vegetarian diet, food combining becomes second nature. The combinations that are the best for you are usually those that taste the best.

One other point of disagreement I have with Dr. McDougall is where he asks "how many cases of protein deficiency has your doctor seen in the past decade?" None, said Dr. McDougall; yet several years ago several doctors, namely Harry Rudolph Alslebens, M.D., and William H. Philpott, M.D., reported that in testing patients for amino acids, every single sick person had severe amino acid imbalances. This contradicts Dr. McDougall's contention. Unless and until you run amino acid assays, you cannot be certain that there is no deficiency because you have not looked for it.

SIX

What Are Our Best Sources of Protein?

Protein can come from any number of sources: meat, fish, milk products, eggs, legumes, nuts, cereals, and even vegetables, or combinations of any of these foods. Where you decide to get your protein then becomes an issue of personal choice and responsibility.

Let's look first at animal products: meat, fish, dairy, and eggs. As a protein source, the egg has the highest degree of utilization by the human body. What this means is that while eggs may not have the highest protein content of any food, the protein that they do have is the most efficiently used. This is because the egg, in addition to having the eight essential amino acids, also has these amino acids in the proportions most suited to human protein metabolism.

While the protein in eggs is 95 percent utilized by our bodies, this high degree of utilization is not found in other animal products, whose "net protein utilization" (NPU) rates are:

Milk	82 percent
Fish	80 percent
Cheese	70 percent
Meat and Poultry	67 percent

The NPU of meat and poultry is only slightly above that of tofu (soybean curd), at 65 percent. So while meat products may be fairly high in protein (about 20 percent) only some two-thirds of that protein can actually be used by our bodies.

The concept of "quality" of protein, as determined by the utilization of the protein by the body, sheds a different light on animal-source protein. Is it really the wonder food it's been made out to be?

A CLOSER LOOK AT MEAT

For many in the U.S., the entire diet pivots around meat. They believe that meat is synonymous with protein, health, strength, and, for men, virility and sexual potency. Their eating habits may include eggs and bacon, sausage, or ham for breakfast, a hamburger or roast beef sandwich for lunch, and a meat and starch food like rice or potatoes for dinner.

Within the last five years, the major medical associations like the Heart Association and the American Cancer Society have begun to warn us that this type of meat consumption is not in our best interests; but after decades of hearing otherwise, it is hard for many people to really believe this. Besides, these associations are not the vehement spokesmen that the advocates for meat consumption are. Telling us how good meat is for us are the beef, pork, and poultry producers, and the fast-food restaurants like McDonald's, Burger King, and Wendy's. And adults still tend to associate meat with health, and children to look at meat as "fun food," the "in" thing to eat.

So what is the truth about meat?

First, it is true that meat supplies protein, but not in the quantities or of the quality that most people think. Beef for example is only 20 percent protein; the rest is fat and water. Nor is beef a low-calorie food. Its high-fat content makes it one of the highest-calorie foods around. A 16-ounce steak alone is about 1,500 calories. Couple this with a baked potato with butter and sour cream, and add a dessert, and you've eaten around 2,500 calories before bed.

Not only is beef much lower in protein than is normally believed, the protein that it does contain is not the highest quality protein. Only 67 percent of it can be utilized by our body.

Furthermore, the fat in beef is saturated fat. This builds up in your arteries as cholesterol and is now thought to be one of the major culprits in arteriosclerosis and heart disease.

CHEMICALS IN MEAT

Meat is also one of the most chemical-ridden foods in the U.S. diet. Currently some twenty to thirty thousand different drugs are administered to animals![1] Of these, it is known that four thousand may be transferred to the human population via meat, dairy, and egg products. Many of these drugs, because they are initially administered to animals and not humans, do not require or have FDA approval. Even those drugs that are FDA approved are not necessarily safe.

Antibiotics are perhaps the most widely used (and abused) of these drugs. Since they were first introduced into animal feed in 1949, the use of antibiotics has grown from 490,000 pounds in 1954, to 1.2 million in 1960, to around nine million pounds per year today. The cost of these additives exceeds $300 million dollars annually.[2] These antibiotics are primarily administered to stave off disease that would otherwise be rampant in the close, unsanitary conditions in which meat animals are forced to live. They are fed to veal because these calves are purposely made anemic by iron deprivation in order to yield the white, pale meat preferred by many chefs. In this anemic condition the calves are prey to all sorts of infection.

These high levels of antibiotics have numerous side effects on the people who eat these drug-ridden animals. First, after a while bacteria become resistant to antibiotics. It is now recognized that these resistant strains of bacteria can be passed from animal to man and that they may not be treatable by other antibiotics. Second, the antibiotics themselves remain in the animal flesh after it has been slaughtered and is then passed on to the consumer. Over time these drug residues can build up and make your own body resistant to antibiotics when you really need them. Third, people who are allergic to the antibiotics fed to the animal may suffer very serious adverse reactions when eating meats full of drug residues.

Other drugs and chemicals which are routinely used on animals include hormones to regulate breeding, to tranquilize, and to promote weight gain. These synthetic hormones can cause cancer in the animals given the drugs, which in most cases does not affect the marketability of the meat. We do not yet know the degree to which cancer is viral in its origins, but recent studies have found viruses to be responsible for some cancers. So, apart from the unappetizing aspect of eating cancerous meat, this meat may actually be the vehicle for cancer viruses to enter our bodies. Additionally, the residues of estrogen, one of the hormones commonly fed to these animals, may also increase women's chances of contracting uterine and breast cancer. Also, children exposed to estrogen may enter puberty prematurely. Androgen, a growth-promoting hormone, may cause liver cancer. DES, a hormone which was banned from human use in the 1960s, remained in use on animals until 1979. Other drugs which are used are Ralgro, an estrogen-like compound; Synovex, a naturally occurring hormone which affects weight gain; Lutalyse, a prostaglandin, often given to an entire herd so that they will ovulate at the same time. This drug can affect the menstrual cycle of women and can also cause pregnant women to miscarry.

Cattle are also commonly and frequently sprayed with pesticides such as Vapona, which is in the same family as nerve gas. This is the same chemical used on the "No Pest Strips" and is considered so toxic that the World Health Organization set the daily allowable limit of .004 milligram per kilogram. You could exceed this limit by merely staying indoors with one of these strips for nine hours.[3]

Unfortunately meat is not the only animal product which is filled with chemicals. The chemicals fed to milk cows or sprayed on them is passed into their milk; chickens are given the same assortment of drugs that beef cattle are given, which in turn shows up in eggs. Chickens are given additional drugs to promote shell hardness and uniformity of yolks in their eggs.

HOW IT ALL BEGAN

The popularity of meat and other animal proteins in the U.S. diet can be traced back to the early 1940s when the concept of "complete" and "incomplete" proteins was popularized. You may even remember being taught this concept in health or science class, where you were shown charts of meat, dairy products, and eggs and told that those were "complete" proteins—usually the connotation being that complete is equal to good. Then there were all the other foods, namely vegetables, grains, legumes, and fruits, which you were probably told were "incomplete" or bad sources of protein. According to the original theory, complete proteins had all the essential amino acids in the right proportions, while incomplete proteins lacked certain amino acids and did not have them in the right proportions.

This theory was music to the ears of the meat and dairy producers. It was not long before their products began to be advertised in dietetic journals and on television as the "right" kind of protein. An advertisement for the Armour Beef Company in a 1949 issue of the *Journal of the American Dietetic Association* stated that fine beef is "a rich source of complete protein, various minerals essential to a normal blood picture, and fuel-supplying calories. And its satiety value and thorough digestibility make it an important addition to virtually every balanced diet."[4] That journal soon became chock-full of various ads supporting the meat industry. The American Meat Institute of Chicago, for example, ran full-page ads resembling scientific reports of the kind usually found in medical journals.

This was all geared at getting more meat into the stomach of the American consumer. These ads all tried to lend scientific credence to the idea that meat was a great food. Another ad, called "Meat . . . and the Dietary Fallacies in the Public Mind," run by the American Meat Institute, labeled the scientific findings on the connections between high dietary uric acid intake and degenerative diseases "erroneous." They assured the public that meat did not aggravate such disorders as gout, rheumatism, and hypertension. Furthermore, they stated that high-protein diets were not harmful.[5] A 1948 ad still advertised meat as "Man's preferred complete protein food." It stated that "meat provides protein of biological completeness. Requiring no protein supplementation from other sources, it instead enhances the nutrient value of the daily diet by supplementing incomplete protein foods to full biological adequacy."[6] Poultry, on the other hand, was pushed as being "rich in protein—relatively low in calories."[7] The message became clear: eat meat, or if you want to lose weight, eat poultry.

This kind of advertising was soon being done by other industries whose foods were protein rich. The Dairy Council, for instance, hailed milk as a high-protein food, especially necessary for children and teens. A 1964 ad, paid for by the National Dairy Council, pictured carefree teenagers romping on the beach and read, "Teenage nutrition: Protein? They couldn't care less!"[8] But not to worry, the Dairy Council added that as a prime source of readily available, high-quality protein, milk is particularly well endowed to help meet the unique nutritional needs of teenagers.

The American Dietetic Association went so far as to endorse ice cream as a good source of protein. They recommended it, particularly, for difficult appetites, the convalescent and the elderly.[9] Ice cream only contains 3.85 grams of protein per 100 grams, but it does have 12.06 grams of saturated fat, which, as we now know, can clog the arteries.

The practice of biased and deceptive advertising by special-interest groups still prevails today. The pork industry, for one, has recently been running a pro-pork campaign. They're promoting pork as a lean meat, ideal for dieters. They're also saying that it is a great source of protein—despite the fact that pork is high in saturated fat, cholesterol, and calories.

These ads can currently be seen on television and in magazines like the *Journal of the American Dietetic Association*. This organization has helped to perpetuate the notion that meat and other animal products are the superior sources of complete protein.

What is so amazing about this "complete" versus "incomplete" protein theory is that it remained intact and unchallenged for so many years. The truth is that it is wholly unfounded. Animal products are not our only sources of protein, and aside from the egg, they are not even high-quality sources of protein.

Modern nutritionists have abandoned the theory of complete and incomplete proteins, now evaluating protein in terms of its quality. Quality is determined using a formula that evaluates the utilization of a protein food. Researchers call this the "net protein utilization," or NPU, and it tells how much we use of the protein in a food.[10] We also need to take the amino acid content and digestibility of the food into account when assessing it. The highest-quality proteins contain the most complete set of essential amino acids. Due to their ideal protein patterns, they are utilized with maximum efficiency by the body. The digestibility of the protein-containing food is also very important because if we cannot thoroughly digest something, we cannot utilize its protein. One factor in increasing the digestibility of a food is a high fiber content. Our richest sources of fiber are from the plant kingdom, including whole grains, seeds, fruits, and vegetables. The undigested fiber portion of the food sweeps quickly through the intestinal tract, inhibiting much bacterial action and insulating the protein molecules within the food from the destructive chemical action of digestive enzymes.

While the American Dietetic Association still supports the old theories on protein originated by the meat, poultry, and dairy industries, nutritionists and biochemists from the United States Department of Agriculture and the Food and Drug Administration support the more current view of protein. According to the Food and Human Nutrition Information Center, a division of the U.S. Department of Agriculture, total protein refers to the amino acid composition of a food rather than to its completeness. For example, animal sources have a higher quality of protein than most individual vegetable or grain sources. However, the total protein figure for an animal product such as beef is not synonymous with its quality or, more accurately, its net protein utilization. Simply put, what matters when you're eating a protein is if it has in it all the amino acids you need to sustain life, and whether those amino acids are in the right proportions for you to absorb them.

As Dr. McDougall has pointed out, with the exception of only a very few foods all of the vegetable foods (which includes vegetables, fruits, grains, and legumes) contain all of the essential amino acids. Some of them contain very large amounts of these amino acids and all have a very high net protein utilization (i.e., they contain these essential amino acids in the proportions the body needs to properly use them).

THE CHOICE IS YOURS

There is no question that we all need protein. Men need somewhere between 30 and 60 grams; women 25 to 50 depending upon which "guess-timation" you use to calculate your protein requirements. However, contrary to what you may have been led to believe, where you decide to obtain that protein is a matter of personal choice and responsibility.

Up until recently when people thought "protein," they thought of meat, cheese, milk, fish, or chicken. Red meat had top billing for most people. With the increasing awareness of the disadvantages associated with red meat and with animal products in general, many people are beginning to reassess their alternatives. And there is no shortage of suggestions for those alternatives. *The New York Times* article I cited at the head of chapter 4 suggests one such alternative: a diet centered around grains, legumes, fruits, and vegetables but which is flexible and relatively easy to follow in that it includes some dairy products, chicken, and fish. There are of course many variations on this theme. You may want to eliminate the dairy products because you are allergic to them and know that they cause excess mucus to build up in your system. You may eat fish only when you are assured that it is fresh. You may eat chicken once a week or only when you dine out. It is really up to you to decide.

Or you may decide that you really do not want to eat any types of animal flesh, including fish. If you continue to eat dairy products and eggs your diet would be called lacto-ovo-vegetarian.

If you eliminate all animal products then you fall within the traditional definition of a vegetarian.

I feel that being a vegetarian is a whole way of being, that includes harmony with one's environment, cooperation, and flexibility. These factors were often lacking in vegetarians who believed that their dogma was more important than their way of being. This is why I welcome the new "vegetarianism" heralded in *The New York Times*. It offers a flexibility not found in the stricter forms of vegetarianism. It allows you to eat out without being a burden on a host or hostess, or without having to drag your friends to eat at macrobiotic restaurants which often seem unappetizing to nonvegetarians. It also serves to make the benefits of a vegetarian diet accessible to many people who may have found the rigid dogma of strict vegetarianism forbidding.

NONANIMAL PROTEINS

Thirteen years ago I became interested in the idea of using the egg as a blueprint against which I could match vegetable-source foods in order to derive high-quality proteins of nonanimal origin. (Remember, the closer the range of amino acids comes to what the body needs, the better the protein is utilized and the higher its quality.) This led me to formulate what I called the "Protein Combination Project." In this project I looked at the distribution of amino acids in the egg and with the help of a computer and a very knowledgeable programmer, began to match various combinations of two or three foods. In the appendix, I have included more than a thousand of these combinations, the protein quality of which is often very close to that of the egg and by far surpasses that of meat, poultry, and dairy products.

The main advantage of vegetable protein over that of animals is that it contains fiber which aids in digestion, and gives a feeling of fullness without the calories. Meat, which is fiber free, can easily remain in your digestive tract for three days. As I mentioned earlier, this can cause constipation and the release of toxins, and may be a major factor in some forms of cancer. Vegetables, grains, and legumes, on the other hand, are full of fiber, which has become an especially important commodity in this day of refined sugars and starches. At one time, people used to easily get all the fiber they needed from their diet of whole-grain breads, legumes, fruits, and vegetables. With the advent of food refining and high-protein diets, fiber became all but nonexistent in many people's diets. Fiber works something like a scrub brush on your intestinal walls. It absorbs fluids like saliva and gastric secretions, expands and scours the walls of your intestine as it moves through, removing some potentially toxic agents which would otherwise accumulate there. Fiber is now recognized even by the traditional medical establishment to play a large role in preventing colon and prostate cancer.

Another benefit of fiber is that it works as a natural laxative, as opposed to meat which generally leads to constipation. Fiber can help you to lose weight by making you feel full and satiated by your food, where meat, being much higher in calories but without fiber, can cause you to gain. Fiber, a non-nutritive substance, also works to provide a slow, steady release of energy from the foods you take in, rather than the sudden spurt and the subsequent slump you get from high-sugar, refined foods.

EGGS AND DAIRY PRODUCTS

As mentioned before, eggs provide the highest-quality protein of any food you can eat. Unfortunately, you probably would not feel very well if you relied solely upon eggs for your protein. Any food which is eaten routinely may begin to cause you food allergies in time. Clinical ecologists, medical doctors who specialize in environmental allergies (i.e., those resulting from things in your environment or foods you eat), have shown that the foods most frequently eaten by Americans are the foods most frequently causing allergic reactions. Among these foods are beef, eggs, dairy products, wheat, and corn. Food allergies are highly individualized and can take on totally different symptoms in each person. For example, your allergy to eggs may be the cause of your arthritis, while an allergy to eggs may be causing your child's hyperactivity. Clinical ecologists have seen food allergies to be responsible for such diseases as diabetes, arthritis, hyperactivity, schizophrenia and other mental disorders, migraine headaches, obesity, and tension-fatigue syndrome—which is characterized by a chronic fatigue which is not alleviated by rest.

Because you may be allergic to eggs (and not even know it) or because you want to avoid becoming allergic, you should not consume them much more often than once every four days. Any more often and you are "abusing" them and potentially setting yourself up for allergy. Additionally, eggs are high in cholesterol and should be limited to prevent or control the advance of atherosclerosis and heart disease.

Milk and other dairy products like cheese, yogurt, and butter have the same drawbacks as eggs in that many people have also abused them to the point of becoming allergic to them, and in that these products are also high in saturated fat. Skim or low-fat milk is better than cream or regular milk from the point of view of cholesterol. Even though butter is a saturated fat, I recommend that you use it as opposed to margarine, unless you are allergic to dairy products. Butter is a naturally occurring substance, whereas margarine, which also is a saturated fat, is a purely chemical concoction. (It is made from an unsaturated oil, but in order to give it its hard consistency the oil is hydrogenated, which thereby saturates it.)

Once again, if you are not allergic to them, eggs and milk products in moderation can be used to supply good protein. Milk products often work well in combination with certain grains and legumes to increase their protein content as well. The best way to do this is to follow the Middle Eastern example and use plain yogurt as a sour cream –like garnish. I also recommend that you try to buy your eggs and even your dairy products from a reputable health food store to avoid the drug and pesticide residues usually found in these products.

SEVEN

Excess Protein

Since protein is such a good thing, you may be wondering whether you can get too much and if so, what will happen to you if you do.

Unlike certain other nutrients such as the water-soluble vitamins for instance, which can be consumed in fairly large quantities with no adverse effects, overconsumption of protein can be extremely hazardous to your health. This is due to a number of factors, the most dangerous of which is a by-product of protein metabolism called urea. Urea is formed in the liver and excreted via the kidneys. The kidneys have to work overtime to eliminate the excess urea which has built up in the blood. This can lead to kidney damage and is especially serious for older people whose kidneys function less efficiently, or for people with preexisting kidney damage. Remember that the primary treatments which modern medicine has for kidney disease are dialysis or a kidney transplant.

Speaking about excess protein Dr. McDougall says:

The real issue when you come to protein is not getting too little, it is a problem of getting too much. You can even do that on a vegetarian diet, but you primarily run into the problem on a diet that includes animal products . . . if you consume too many beans, peas, and lentils, then you can run into a problem where you're getting too much protein. But I have to qualify that statement with the fact that the vegetable protein is far less damaging to the body even in equal amounts.

If you take in more protein than is needed it is excreted (because remember, it is not stored). The way it is excreted through the body is through the liver. The liver has to increase its activity because of that increased work load and it changes that protein into urea (blood urea nitrogen we call it). That goes to the kidneys which filter out this urea and they also filter out the protein unprocessed. As a result of the filtering of the urea and the protein, the kidneys enlarge under this high protein load that we eat.[1]

In addition to enlarging the kidneys, the excess protein causes pressure to accumulate inside the kidneys, causing damage to the tubeoles, the filtering apparatus in the kidneys. For most people, this presents no real threat since we have much more kidney tissue than we actually need. Most people still have around 80 percent of their kidney tissue left by the time they reach old age. Even so, the blood filtering capacity of a seventy-year-old man is about half that of a twenty-year-old man. But if you have had an accident which caused damage to one or both of your kidneys, or if you have donated a kidney, or have suffered kidney damage due to diabetes or high blood pressure, the extra stress placed on your remaining kidney capacity can severely overtax it, and eventually lead to destruction of the remaining kidney tissue.

The risk of aggravating existing kidney damage by a high-protein diet is well recognized by medical authorities throughout the country. One of the first preventive measures given to a kidney patient is to put him on a low-protein diet, often as low as 2½ to 5 percent of total calorie intake. Dr. McDougall gives an example of how this diet may work.

A young girl came into my office with another member of her family. The girl was gray. She looked very sick. After I was through taking care of the one family member, I asked "What's wrong with this little girl?" He said "She's got kidney failure and she's going to have some shots put in and they are going to put her on the kidney machine in a couple of months." I said "Try something different. Let me teach this little girl a diet very low on protein, all vegetable protein, and we will see how it works." They agreed. Now that was seven years ago and that little girl's progressive kidney failure stopped and to this day that child is still off the kidney machine.[2]

In order to flush excess urea from our bodies, we need to drink plenty of water. Unfortunately, many people, especially the elderly, do not consume sufficient water for the kidneys to filter urea out of the bloodstream. This can result in dehydration. Infants are especially at risk when fed high-protein diets.[3] Many babies are receiving cow's milk, which has twice the protein of human milk. An unrestricted amount of this protein can be excessive, leading to hypernatremic dehydration. This occurs in infants when their small bodies have used up inordinate quantities of water during the urea filtration process. Hara Marano, executive editor of *American Health* magazine, says that "hypernatremic dehydration is four times more deadly than the water loss that accompanies diarrhea in infants, and can lead to brain damage, shutdown of the kidneys and death within hours."[4]

Dehydration from excess protein intake, or protein loading, can also present a serious problem for athletes. Not only are these athletes losing large amounts of fluid from perspiration, they also require extra water to filter urea from the blood. For a marathon runner this can lead to a serious heatstroke.

Another nitrogen by-product of protein metabolism is ammonia, which builds up in our intestinal tract and can cause cancer. Dr. Willard Visek, of the University of Illinois Medical School, explains, "in the digestion of proteins, we are constantly exposed to large amounts of ammonia in our intestinal tracts. Ammonia behaves like chemicals that cause cancer or promote its growth. It kills cells, increases virus infections, affects the rate at which cells divide and increases the mass of the lining of the intestines. What is intriguing is that within the colon, the incidence of cancer parallels the concentration of ammonia."[5]

Ironic as it may seem, another major problem associated with excess animal protein is calcium deficiency. Yes, calcium deficiency can come from drinking too much milk, even though we have been told for years that milk was our best source of calcium. The deficiency occurs in several ways. First, although milk is high in calcium, it is difficult to digest and much of its calcium never gets into our bloodstream. Milk is also high in phosphorus, which binds to the calcium and makes it less absorbable. Much of this calcium is then excreted in the urine. Hence, while the calcium is there, we cannot use all of it.

Another thing that happens is that when the kidneys begin to work overtime to rid the body of excess urea, they also begin to excrete large amounts of minerals, one of the most important of which is calcium. The result of this calcium excretion is twofold. First, the high concentrations of calcium mix with uric acid in the kidneys and form kidney stones. The second thing that can happen is that the body becomes depleted of calcium and draws it out of the bones, rendering them porous and weak; the end result can be osteoporosis. This disease has become so prevalent among elderly women that it is almost a household word. Most women in the U.S. are terrified by the thought of contracting this disease, which can leave them shortened in stature, stooped, and crippled. Its direct cause is a severe calcium deficiency, however in many cases its root may lie in excess consumption of animal protein.

"Unfortunately," says Dr. McDougall, "the people in this country have the wrong message as to what the cause of this disease is. They believe (for a very good reason: multi-millions of dollars are spent convincing them) that osteoporosis is due to cow's milk deficiency. Sounds like nonsense doesn't it?"[6]

Fortunately for women, milk is not our only source of calcium. There are many natural vegetable sources that are very good suppliers of calcium as well. They include leafy vegetables, cauliflower, sesame seeds, soy beans, carob flour, fresh and dried fruits, and sea vegetables. You can also get your calcium from a good supplement. Chelated calcium lactate, calcium citrate, and calcium gluconate are the best; bone meal is not as good.

VEGETABLE VERSUS ANIMAL

If you eat a mainly vegetarian diet, it is unlikely that you will be taking in excessive amounts of protein unless you eat large amounts of legumes. Even if you do take in excessive protein from these sources, there will be a number of mitigating factors. You will be getting a diet high in fiber which will cleanse your intestines from ammonia buildup. The fats that you will be getting will be mostly in the form of unsaturated oils, many of which include lecithin, a fat solvent which actually works to dissolve cholesterol, rather than develop it like the saturated fats in animal proteins do. With the fiber you will also get that full feeling without the excess calories. Vegetable proteins are easily digested and will provide you with calcium that you can actually use rather than depleting your body of it.

Animal protein, on the other hand, is where the problems of excess protein begin. First, a typical U.S. diet, say of eggs and bacon in the morning, a hamburger or meat sandwich with a glass of milk for lunch, and a meat dish for dinner can add up to over 200 grams of protein, or about four times higher than the highest recommended requirements. This means massive amounts of urea and ammonia, fat, drug and pesticide residues, and very little fiber (as most wheat products will probably be refined, while meat, dairy products, and eggs have little to no fiber). With this kind of diet for any extended period of time, the entire body is under assault. The result can be just about any of the major killer diseases which plague this country: heart disease; breast, colon, and prostate cancer; obesity; osteoporosis; kidney and liver damage. With health care now costing this nation over $400 billion annually, making it the second largest industry, next only to defense, it may be time for us to reconsider the way we think about what we eat.

EIGHT

Animal Protein and Added Chemicals

For all the risks involved in getting too much protein, protein is, after all, a necessary nutrient. But is it true or false that some proteins are worse for you than others?

THE DANGERS OF ANIMAL PROTEIN

Here's a hint: the "complete" proteins found in meat, poultry, fish, eggs, and milk can be associated with saturated fat, cholesterol, nitrates, hormones, pesticides, herbicide residues, antibiotics, preservatives, and countless additives. So the answer is true: animal proteins can be worse for you than vegetable protein, even though the meat industry would have us think otherwise. Unfortunately, the U.S. population is toeing the meat-industry line: on average, individuals in the U.S. eat about 200 pounds of red meat, 50 pounds of chicken and turkey, 10 pounds of assorted fish, 300 eggs, and 250 pounds of various dairy products a year. That's some feast!

What's the problem? Biochemical nutritionist Dr. David Kritchevsky gives one: "The best correlation with heart disease is animal protein." He found that animal sources contributed to more cases of atherosclerosis than vegetable sources.[1] Cross-cultural studies have also shown that there is a greater incidence of cardiovascular disease and colon cancer among people consuming diets high in animal products, i.e. protein and fat.[2] Research also indicates "a strong positive correlation between dietary protein and other cancers: breast, prostate, pancreas, endometrium, bowel and kidney," says T. Colin Campbell, a professor from Cornell University's nutritional science department.[3]

Digestion suffers too when bombarded with lots of protein. The high-saturated-fat content of animal products makes them hard to digest: these foods can "stick to your ribs" (in other words, settle in the stomach) for up to seven hours!

Confusion remains about whether it is the high protein itself or *its source* (namely animal products) that is to blame in cases of degenerative diseases. Arguments for the guilt of animal sources in the development of disease cite the ingredients they contain besides protein—food coloring, antibiotics, and hormones. These add-ins are introduced into livestock at the breeding phase. Unfortunately, it's no easy task to determine how much contamination reaches our dinner tables; meat is difficult to analyze, and there are over five hundred chemicals allowed by the government as additives. For starters, livestock and dairy cows consume large amounts of chemically treated feed. One of these chemicals is the well-known insecticide DDT (dichloro-diphenyl-trichloro-ethane). DDT became popular in the forties, and was used extensively for nearly three decades. How it gets to people is noteworthy, as it's first introduced into the food chain not through livestock but through farm soil. (In fact, since DDT was used virtually every year for decades, our soil has become saturated with it.) The crops absorb small amounts of DDT: livestock eat the crops and concentrate the chemical: we eat the livestock, DDT and all. Nor are we talking mere traces of the insecticide. Livestock need about 16 pounds of feed to produce 1 pound of flesh. And because DDT gets stored whole in body fat, a pound of beefsteak, say, may contain significant quantities of DDT residues. DDT may also be passed on in cow's milk. The DDT we ingest in our burgers and shakes is in turn stored in our body fat, where it sits idle until we diet or come under stress. When we begin to burn our fat, the stored DDT is catapulted into the bloodstream. DDT can even be passed on to babies through mother's milk. The long-term effects of DDT poisoning aren't completely clear yet, but in the short term, DDT has been shown to cause anorexia, tremors, and fever.

The two antioxidants BHT (butylated hydroxytoluene) and BHA (butylated hydroxyanisole) are added to livestock feed to keep fats in the feed from going rancid, to make feed handling and shipping easier and, ultimately, to improve the taste and appearance of the fat in the meat once the animal is slaughtered.

The food additive sodium nitrate, used as a color fixative in most processed meats—hot dogs, bologna, cured meats, bacon, meat spreads, sausage, and ham—is another ingredient detrimental to health. When eaten, nitrates form substances in the stomach called nitrosamines, which are potentially cancer causing. Vitamin C has been found to block the formation of toxic nitrasamines, and some bacon producers have added vitamin C to their products in an attempt to make bacon less of a cancer threat. Unfortunately, about two-thirds of C's power is destroyed during cooking.

Surprisingly, even certain substances, namely tranquilizers and antibiotics, which sound like perfectly innocuous meat additives (after all, doctors prescribe them for human consumption) have been shown to be responsible for many modern ailments. Tranquilizers have been added to livestock feed for twenty-five years now to slow down animal metabolism, so the animals will plump up quickly for slaughter. Antibiotics are used to keep animals disease-free and promote rapid weight gain in some livestock. As you might guess, the animals pass the drugs on to humans who eat their flesh. Humans who are allergic to antibiotics like penicillin may be aggravating their allergies by unknowingly eating meat treated with such drugs. The result: considerably lowered resistance to disease.

Unfortunately, you can't escape drug additions by eating poultry, or even eggs. Hens are often fed a combination of antibiotics, sodium bicarbonate, and terephthalic acid, a "three-niter mash" that assures a hard eggshell. Yolks are also manipulated through chicken feed additives to correct any pigmentation abnormalities. The consumers trusting in "premium," "jumbo," and "grade A" have no way of knowing how much of these toxic chemicals they are actually consuming.

Another nutritional area where animal sources fall short is cal-

cium. A 1983 study, for example, showed that the bones of postmenopausal women who were meat eaters were lower in mineral
content than those of lacto-ovo-vegetarians.[4] The significance of
calcium to bones is that, together with phosphorus, it keeps them
from becoming porous and brittle so that important minerals don't
easily leak out. Meat has a high phosphorus content, but it is very
low in calcium. Consequently, your burger, steak, or roasted chicken
may create an imbalance by loading you with phosphorus, detrimental without additional calcium. Calcium-rich foods must be eaten along with meat to keep the ratio of calcium to phosphorus even.
Otherwise, the body will take the calcium it needs to level the
balance—increasing the calcium levels in the bloodstream by weakening the bones. This rebalancing can put undue stress on the kidneys and lead to kidney stones. Studies show vegetarians are less
likely to develop stones than meat eaters.

The solution, however, is simple. To get enough calcium, vegetarians and meat eaters alike can turn to dark green, leafy vegetables
like spinach and kale; and to a variety of other nonanimal foods
such as cauliflower, sesame seeds, soybeans, torula yeast, carob
flour, dried fruits, sea vegetables (hijiki, nori, kelp); and also to
buttermilk, yogurt, acidophilus milk, kefir, and most other dairy
products. The idea is to take in 800 to 1,000 milligrams of calcium
a day, preferably through food, although there are supplements available. (These come in a number of varieties. Best choices: those made
of calcium lactate or calcium gluconate. But be sure, if you take
supplements, to use the kind that contains magnesium as well. The
Ca/Mg balance is important for the health of your heart.)

RAW VERSUS COOKED PROTEIN

By now the message is clear: A certain amount of protein is essential,
but we need less than we may presently be getting, and animal
sources are not the best choice.

There are plenty of plant protein sources, but to reap the protein
benefits, preparation is key. Specifically, cooking usually helps break
down the cell wall structure of vegetables, which makes them easier
to digest and allows for the complete release of their protein content.
(In some cases, cooking even lessens the chance of toxicity; beans,
for example, should not be eaten raw.)

Method matters too. Cooking food with water and steam protects protein value and preserves other vitamins and minerals. Certain classic meat-cooking techniques, on the other hand, can render animal foods carcinogenic: charcoal broiling, pan frying. (It should be noted that it's the cooking method that gives these foods cancer-causing properties: roasting, poaching, steaming, or stewing are perfectly safe methods of cooking meat.)

SOY PROTEIN

When meat eaters question the protein value of animal-free diets, vegetarians are quick to sing the praises of the soybean. In Asia, this bean has been used as a primary source of protein for over three thousand years. Only recently has it caught on in the U.S. Our soybean crop is used primarily in livestock feed and for pressed oil, but there are many delicious and nutritious culinary uses for soy products.

Tofu, or bean curd, is an easily digestible protein source made from coagulated soy milk. It has a cheesy consistency, and its mild taste and spongy texture allows it to soak up and absorb the flavor of other foods or spices added to it, making it the perfect foil for many dishes. "Burgers" made from tofu, for example, are as tasty as the originals, yet boast lower saturated fat and as much or more protein, depending on the recipe used. Tofu, like beef, is low in the amino acid methionine, but when complemented by any whole grain, like brown rice or wheat, becomes a total quality protein—certainly a healthy switch from a high-fat burger.

The protein content of tofu depends on how firmly it is pressed. The following standards have been set for protein concentration by the Tofu Standards Committee of the Soy Food Association of America:

Soft Tofu: 5.0–6.9 percent
Regular Tofu: 7.0–9.9 percent
Firm Tofu: 10.0–13.9 percent
Extra Firm Tofu: 14 percent or more

An even higher-protein soy product is tempeh. In this rendition, the beans are fermented and packed together by a type of favorable mold. Tempeh is usually packaged in ¾-inch-thick rectangular sheets or patties, and has such a meatlike texture that it can easily fool diehard meat eaters. Three ounces of tempeh contains 19.5 grams of protein, of which 8 grams are high-quality and contain adequate amounts of all eight essential amino acids.[5] Tempeh, unlike tofu, maintains the full nutrient content of soybeans—protein, fiber, and all.

In eastern Asia, one of the primary soy foods is miso—a fermented paste typically made from a mixture of soybeans, salt, and water. Some variations of miso contain barley, rice, or other ingredients like chick-peas or barley malt. Misos range in color from a tannish hue to a deep brown or red. The longer the miso is fermented, the darker its color and the stronger its flavor. Its adaptability makes it perfectly suited to add flavor to many recipes—soups, sandwich spreads, gravies, dressings, and dips. One of miso's claims to fame is its digestibility: it contains live lactobacillus culture and other digestive enzymes, and so it can be well utilized by the body. Beginning a meal with a cup of miso soup will prepare the stomach for the proper digestion of the rest of the meal to follow.

NINE

The Protein Combination Project

While the debate about the protein quality of plant foods rages on, the fact remains: the protein in plant foods comes from the same twenty-two amino acids found in animal protein. Protein quality is determined by the quantity and proportion of amino acids in a food, not by the food's source.

What about the practical implications? It is *easier* to get protein from meat: one filet mignon and you're covered. But it isn't better, necessarily. And plant foods in the proper combinations can provide a protein punch as powerful as a steak's. The Protein Combination Project should prove it.

Remember the concept of Net Protein Utilization? That tells us how much protein a food makes available to your body based on its amino acid pattern. Scientists use egg protein as a model for evaluating the amino acid composition and protein quality of other foods. Egg protein has the highest biologic value for humans—an

NPU value of 94 on a scale of 100. This means that for each gram of egg consumed, your body produces .94 grams of protein tissue. To meet a daily requirement of essential protein of 40 grams takes less than half an egg!

The Net Protein Utilization (NPU) concept has recently been elaborated upon by the Protein Combination Project, designed to come up with a listing of plant foods that, either individually or in combination, are similar in protein quality to the egg.

RATIONALE FOR THE PROTEIN COMBINATION PROJECT

For years, vegetarians were told that by forgoing meat consumption they risked protein deficiency. Vegetarians frequently overcompensated by taking very large amounts of particular single foods such as soy or dairy foods, in order to improve the protein in their diet.

Then, during the 1970s, the idea of complementing proteins—mixing, for example, a cup of rice with a cup of beans, a grain and a legume—was introduced. This certainly gave more substance to the idea that a vegetarian could obtain a full spectrum of protein in the diet.

But the idea of protein complementarity was developed before the calculating power of the computer became widely available. With the computer, we can look at how well *all* the other amino acids of the two foods fit together. In fact, we can look at combinations of three or even more foods and see which will provide the highest-quality protein with the least waste of protein and calories. We can analyze the *overall* composition of each and every food and let the computer figure out which are the most efficient combinations for protein.

And that's just what we did with the project. Working with mathematician Hillard Fitzky, Ph.D., we began the Protein Combination Project by developing formulas for setting the computer to the task of comparing the protein pattern of over one hundred commonly eaten foods to that of the egg.

The Protein Combination Project is thus a giant leap from the previous methods for evaluating protein quality. Instead of the vague advice to mix two foods, one of which contains high amounts of the other's limiting amino acid, the Protein Project ended up listing hundreds of food combinations in which the proportions of amino acids are very close to that of the egg.

PROCEDURE

First, we established a standard portion size. We chose an ounce and a half for nuts and seeds; 3-ounce portions, or approximately 100 grams, for all other solid foods; and 8 ounces for all liquids.

Then, for each of over one hundred commonly eaten foods, we measured the quantity of each essential amino acid present in one portion. Thus, for each grain, legume, vegetable, nut, seed, fruit, or tuber on the list, we measured the content of all eight essential amino acids.

Next, since the egg is considered the most perfectly utilized protein, the proportions of these amino acids were cross-matched against the perfection of the egg.

Once we had cross-matched all these foods against the egg-protein pattern, we assigned the computer the task of evaluating *combinations* of foods in the same way. What combinations make the most efficient mixes? Our computer threw together a huge variety of combinations, calculating for each combination how closely its protein pattern resembled that of the egg.

RESULTS

To our amazement, we came up with many combinations with NPUs higher than those for beef, chicken, veal, pork, and milk. That is, the protein in these combinations exceeded that of beef, chicken, veal, pork, and milk in quality (i.e., in utilizability by the body). And indeed, several of the combinations of twos and threes (meaning two or three food items together) actually equaled the quality *and quantity* of the protein of the egg.

This work sets a new standard for protein combining. The results of the Protein Combination Project makes it possible for a vegetarian, by combining foods scientifically and properly—and in edible quantities—to consume fewer total calories for better weight control; and to obtain higher-quality and more usable protein, avoiding excess protein consumption. These hundreds of combinations include a number of vegetables and even fruits usually thought of as devoid of protein, as well as some sea vegetables never before included on a food-combining list.

The concept of protein utilization is a far more precise way of defining the degree of "completeness" of a particular protein than the previous concept of the "limiting amino acid." Our work with the computer takes into account not merely the one or two amino acids in shortest supply in each food, but *all eight* essential amino acids, and the extent to which their proportions vary from the proportions found in the egg. (For the purposes of the Protein Combination Project, we took into account only the eight amino acids that are essential in the adult diet; the ninth, histidine, can be manufactured in the adult body.)

The Protein Combination Project clears the way for understanding how *all* the foods we eat—not just those we usually think of as protein foods, like meat, milk products, eggs, and beans—contribute to our protein picture. Until now, the quality of a protein was considered to be limited by the one, or perhaps two, amino acids in shortest supply—the "limiting" amino acid. Food complementing involved combining a food low in lysine, say, but high in methionine, with another high in lysine but low in methionine. The other amino acids were just presumed to fall into place.

By evaluating protein utilization for a particular combination, we can measure *exactly* how well all the amino acids work together. Again, the egg was used as the basis for comparison. First, foods were compared for their amino acid makeup, and each amino acid was accorded the same weight. So for two foods to be considered protein equals, they should carry equal amounts and proportions of the eight adult essential amino acids.

These comparisons were made on a percentage basis. For example, if a food contains 0.4 grams of the amino acid lysine, and the total amount of essential amino acids in that food is 4 grams, then the percentage of lysine would be 10 percent.

Second, foods were compared in 3-ounce quantities, except for nuts and seeds (1½-ounce measurements) and fluids (8-ounce measurements). Only the essential protein of each food counted, so for a food to "match" an egg, it would have to contain equal percentages of *every* essential amino acid. The closer a food comes to an egg, the more fully its protein is utilized by the body.

APPLYING THE RESULTS

Let's take another look at the significance of using the new "Protein Combination List" as a means of denoting the "quality" of a protein as opposed to the old way of the "limiting amino acid" approach.

With the "limiting amino acid" method, in order to insure that we consume enough of a particular food type to get our minimum requirement for one amino acid, we end up "overconsuming" other amino acids. The new Protein Combination List solves this excess consumption problem. It satisfies the "ideal" requirement, while seeing to it that the other amino acids are not consumed in excess, all through the intelligent use of protein complementation.

All of this is incorporated in the Protein Combination List. Combinations of food types have been scientifically analyzed such that several specific foods, when combined in one meal, will satisfy the requirements of providing all essential amino acids in the same proportion as the egg protein, while *minimizing* an excess of any one particular amino acid.

This is the basis of the Protein Combination Project. It is the first of its kind, and it should set a new standard for protein combining. The Protein Project enables knowledgeable vegetarians to save money, save their health, and get what they need—without extra calories, extra protein, or extra fats in their diet.

Our calculations show that the 3 grams of total protein found in rice is simply not synonymous with 3 grams of complete protein. But of the 5.6 grams of total protein contained in the rice, only 2 grams are made up of essential amino acids.

Most other vegetable proteins would be considered poor-quality alone, since they contain such small quantities of one or more of the essential amino acids. A low amount of lysine, for example, no matter how high the other amino acids, would act as the "limiting amino acid," making a particular food eaten alone a poor quality protein choice. For instance, the protein in whole-grain rye has only 58 percent isoleucine and leucine, although the other essential amino acids are present in complete amounts. Therefore, only 58 percent of its protein is usable by our body if it is eaten alone. More of that protein could be usable if the rye were eaten in combination with a food that has extra isoleucine and leucine. Thus, combining foods to complement their proteins creates a more efficient system of eating.

Besides thoughtful combining of foods, it is important to time their consumption carefully. Because the body is unable to store substantial amounts of protein, combined foods must be taken as close to each other as possible. The best way is to complement foods at the same meal—not lentils at lunch and rice at dinner, for example.

Nutrition is great, but what about flavor? We eat as much to taste as to fuel our bodies and keep them healthy. Check out the recipes at the end of the book based on food combining for proper protein, and you'll see: vegetarian eating according to the Protein Project can be tasty indeed!

THE PROTEIN COMBINATION LIST

The Protein Combination List is presented in the appendix. It provides combinations of food that, together, provide significant amounts of complete, high-quality protein. They are listed in general order of quality, starting with those whose protein is closest in quality to that of the egg. (It should be noted that their location on the list gives no indication as to the quantities the combinations will provide.) All you have to do now is develop interesting menus using these combinations.

III

REASONS
FOR
BECOMING
A
VEGETARIAN

TEN

Economics:
The Big-Bucks Bonus

I f you are like most people, you probably like getting a bonus from
your job, a tax refund from the IRS, or a payback from your insurance company. Switching from a traditional meat-based diet to
a vegetarian one offers big bonuses not only in terms of health, but
also in dollars and cents. It is estimated that consuming animal
products adds approximately $4,000 to an average household's an-
nual budget (including increased medical expenses). While this is
not a fortune, wouldn't it be nice to get a $4,000 IRS refund, insurance
policy payback, or job bonus?

And remember, the fact that vegetarian foods cost far less than
animal products is only a bonus. The most significant benefit is that
you are getting more of what your body needs in terms of nutrients,
roughage, and balance; and less of what it cannot tolerate in the
form of chemical additives, saturated fats, hormones, nitrates and
cholesterol. And all at a bargain price!

YOU PAY FOR THE MEAT YOU EAT

Most people would be shocked to discover how much more costly meat is than vegetables and grains. Five and a half ounces of steak, for example, supply the same 20 grams of protein that six and two-thirds slices of whole-wheat bread do. Yet, that amount of steak costs $1.17, compared to only twenty-one cents for the bread. You are paying five times more for a food that doesn't even rival its cheaper counterpart in terms of nutritional value and fiber content. About the same cost-to-value ratio exists if we were to compare bologna at eighty cents for 6 ounces with dried beans at fourteen cents a cup.[1]

Although hard to believe, the high cost of animal foods is fairly simple to understand. The nutrients you need to sustain life must ultimately come from plant foods. You can get these nutrients in one of two ways: either directly by eating the plant food itself, or indirectly by eating the animal that was fed on the plant food. When you consume meat, poultry, and dairy products, you are eating higher on the food chain than when you consume grains and vegetables.

It is far more economical to eat lower on the food chain, that is, to eat the vegetables and grains that are the source of your nutrients. To get them secondhand from the animal means you have to pay for them many times over. When you buy beef, you are paying for the grains fed to raise the animal, for the rancher's overhead on that animal, and for the slaughter of the animal, as well as for the processing, packaging and transport of the meat. And all for something you don't even need in the first place! Clearly it makes far better economic sense to eat the plant foods directly. If you had a chance to buy a sweater directly from a loom in your hometown, do you suppose it would be cheaper than to have the wool sent to a distant factory, to have it combined with synthetic fabrics, "designed," sent through an assembly line, then folded, pinned, transported to a wholesale distributor in yet another distant city, and finally bought by and shipped to a retail outlet right back in your hometown again? Now you can begin to understand how economically unsound and wasteful it is to get the nutrients you need to sustain your life and health "processed" through an animal rather than directly from the nutrient "loom"—the vegetable or grain itself.

To go a step further, consider this problem for just a moment as a matter of societal rather than personal economic concern. To satisfy the U.S. demand for animal foods, large amounts of meats and dairy products must be imported. Add to that cost that of supporting domestic animal agriculture with the importation of farm equipment, fertilizers, and petroleum, and you have an expense estimated as valued about the same as the national trade deficit of $40 billion! All for food items that we don't even need and are better off without. Think of what even a fraction of the resources represented by that money could do if released to work on our pressing problems and those of the world. Just as the bonus money a vegetarian lifestyle could save us personally to improve our individual standards of living, the same savings on a national level could help us to balance our trade deficit and still have excess funding to tackle the critical global issues of starvation and peace.

ANIMAL FOODS: YOU GET FAR MORE THAN YOU BARGAINED FOR

Most people eat animal foods because they believe it affords them a good complete source of protein. What they may not understand is that they are getting a lot more than just protein when they consume animal products. This misunderstanding is not too surprising when you realize that the powerful meat and dairy industries expend formidable advertising budgets to propagate information that is purely self-serving and without regard for the consumer's health. The National Livestock and Meat Board, for one, recently spent some $7.8 million to present to the public the notion that its products promote health and radiance even though their cost is exorbitant. The National Pork Producers' Council has unleashed a $4 million campaign aimed at making the consumer feel more comfortable about eating its products which have been much maligned, and correctly so, for their high fat content. It runs ads to reassure us that "pork has been on a diet," and that "America is leaning on pork."[2] Pork hasn't really changed, of course, but the industry's advertising pitch has, as it attempts to re-establish an undeserved credibility with a public that is becoming increasingly aware that it is getting more than it wants from pork as well as from other animal products.

Images and advertising hype aside, the fact is that you really are getting more than just protein from meat and dairy products. You are getting food products that are inordinately high in fat and cholesterol, elements that drastically increase your chances of developing atherosclerosis, heart disease, and other degenerative disorders. You may well be getting too much protein, since as a nation we tend to consume far more protein than we need. As a matter of economy, you already know that you are paying five times as much as you would to get the same amount of plant protein.

If you have just gotten up from the table after a meal that is high in animal and dairy foods you will know right away that you are coming away with more than you need. You will probably feel sluggish and tired; maybe you find it difficult to get right back to work or play, maybe you need to sit and catch your breath for a moment, maybe you hit the couch like a rock with your feet up and your mouth open and end up in a semi-comatose "snooze" for thirty minutes or more. What you have gotten from that steak or pork or cheesy, creamy entree—accompanied perhaps by a glass of milk, and maybe even topped off with some ice cream or whipped cream preparation—is a lot of empty calories in the form of saturated fat and cholesterol. You have gotten a lot more than you need or want of a lot of things.

Besides all the unwanted fat and cholesterol that slows you down and sets you up for heart and arterial disease, you can add to that a whole pharmaceutical array of antibiotics and hormones. Hormones are used by livestock raisers to stimulate faster growth in order to get the animals off the feed and into the slaughterhouse as quickly as possible. These same hormones are used to "bloat" the animal—make it grow bigger and fatter in order to create a maximum return for the raiser. After all, beef and pork are sold by the pound, not by the unit of quality. But what about the antibiotics? Don't they kill viruses and stem potential plagues? Of course they do. So what are they doing in our meat and dairy foods?

Antibiotics are big business when it comes to raising animals. Over one-half of the nation's annual antibiotic production goes to livestock and poultry. Antibiotics for livestock and poultry accounts for $800 million in annual sales in the major nations of the world. This figure is expected to rise steadily, as is the number of medicinal feed additives, now figured to be around fifty. The massive wealth being accumulated as a result of this brisk and flourishing enterprise has benefited only a few major companies, though. Nearly three-quarters of the feed-additive sales in the U.S. is generated by only three companies—Eli Lilly, American Cyanamid, and Pfizer.[3]

You probably consider very carefully how much of a particular antibiotic you take and make very certain that you are taking the right kind for your specific need. What may make one person well could kill another person, or simply be ineffective. Side effects from antibiotics, which can be considerable, vary widely from person to person. But you are probably not overly concerned because you would never take antibiotics unless your doctor prescribed them specifically for you—for *your* biochemistry, to treat *your* illness, and considering *your* specific reactions and possible allergies. But what if your doctor had no medical training at all, and just dished out the antibiotics indiscriminately because it helped him make money? In short, what if your doctor was not a doctor, but a cattleman or a pig farmer?

When you consume conventionally prepared meat, poultry, and dairy products you are consuming significant amounts of antibiotics. Who prescribed them? Agribusiness. Who pays for them in the form of inflated product prices at the food counter? The consumer! And who considered *your* specific drug requirements and indications? Nobody! The farmer only considered the requirements of the animals that he raises for slaughter. Because he raises them under such poor conditions—filthy, overcrowded quarters ripe for disease and plagues—he limits his losses from death and sickness of his herd by feeding it antibiotics on a regular basis.

As if it weren't enough that we come away with generous amounts of unwanted saturated fats, cholesterol, nitrates, hormones, and even antibiotics, Americans tend toward gluttonous overconsumption of foods—meat, poultry, and dairy products in particular. That is why more than a quarter of the U.S. population is overweight. (And a great many of us are constantly dieting and otherwise trying to avoid or stop being overweight; obesity itself does pose a major healthy hazard leading to disease and shortened life spans.) Still, for all our overeating, statistics show that the diet chosen by middle-class and wealthy Americans is less nutritious than it was ten years ago.[4]

Malnutrition, a close cousin of undernourishment, characterizes Third World people. They often traditionally have large families, in the belief that every new member of the family is another hand to contribute to the economy of the household.[5] But nowadays that new member of the family is more another mouth to feed than another hand. The subsequent increase in population thereby leads to even more malnutrition.

If poverty breeds malnutrition for lack of food, and wealth leads only to undernourishment despite an overabundance of food, perhaps we ought to start looking more carefully at *what* we eat and less carefully at *how much* we eat. We have already seen here that meat and dairy products give us far too much of what we don't want and certainly don't need. And to add insult to injury, we even get stuck with the bill! This is a good place for both individuals and nations to start cutting down on very expensive and unhealthy *quantity* and turn instead to a vegetarian life-style that provides superior *quality* for much less money.

THE VEGETARIAN LIFESTYLE: YOU GET FAR MORE FOR FAR LESS

With the cost of living increasing so greatly all around us, it would be nice to find a soft spot in the economic system . . . a place where we can cut costs for a change. Many Americans are now discovering that the vegetarian life-style offers us this opportunity. Per capita beef consumption dropped from 95.6 pounds in 1976 to 79.6 pounds in 1980.[6] Many observers believe that a prime cut of beef "may soon be a thing of the past for all but the most affluent."[7]

For the average consumer, the waning of the "Great American Steak Culture" is a blessing in disguise. Just as many people have turned away from high-priced beef and pork in favor of chicken and turkey, more and more people may be drawn away from even poultry and dairy products too, in search of more economical alternatives. Happily, there is a whole new world awaiting them in the form of leafy green vegetables, roots, whole grains, beans and fruits . . . and all for so much less. Have you compared the cost of a steak to the cost of dried beans? Or the cost of a baked cake to that of a bunch of bananas?

(Ironically, affluence may actually be a curse for the wealthy, as it allows them to continue to revel in their meat, dairy, and highly refined foodstuffs—pastries and the like. Of course they can afford the foods and the subsequent medical bills that come along with a diet like that. But can they physically afford to be sick and sluggish and to live shorter and less robust lives?)

While we may be lured into a vegetarian life-style for economic reasons, we find that we soon develop a taste for these foods. What at first tasted weird begins to taste rather delightful. Moreover, we can get up from the table with more energy than when we first sat down, instead of rolling over to the couch to regroup after an exhausting onslaught of fats and cholesterol. As the years roll on, we realize that we are getting sick less frequently, have shed past tendencies toward lethargy and lazy apathy, have become more lively and zestful participants in all the wonderful experiences that life offers us, and have seriously diminished the likelihood of heart disease, cancer, arthritis, diabetes, and other ailments that cut short our enjoyment of life if not life itself.

THE HIGH COST OF MEAT AND DAIRY: IT MUST BE GOOD FOR SOMEONE

You might wonder why we, as a nation, work so hard to market meat and dairy products if vegetable and grain foods are cheaper. It would seem to make perfect economic sense to raise, foster, and sell whatever is cheaper, easier, and more nutritious, especially in a world where rising costs of living and starvation pose such serious threats to our comfort and well-being and ultimately to our very survival. On the contrary, though, it is on animal products that we spend the most time, money, and resources. Obviously, what makes economic sense for the well-being of the population in general does not appear to make economic sense to certain groups within the population. The powerful meat and dairy industries are in business to further their enterprises at all cost.

If you thought that most of your meat and dairy foods are handled by rugged, hardworking farmers toiling on small plots in scenic valleys, walking their herds over picturesque pastures, and carefully selecting the best products for the marketplace—think again. Three percent of the farms in the United States control over one-half of farm sales. Presently, almost half of this nation's farmland is owned by nonfarmers, businessmen who have bought out the family farmer and forced the dedicated small-time farmer and farm laborer into retirement or into the unemployment lines. Only four corporations —so-called "agribusinesses"—control at least one-half of the sales of the entire food industry.[8] Swift and Pillsbury, for example, control an estimated 90 percent of the chicken market.

The huge conglomerates have the capital to keep competition a safe distance away while they appropriate megabucks on self-serving advertisements designed to look like public-service announcements. While small-time competitors are also free to advertise, it must be recognized that the large scale of the big corporation's advertising campaign is many times more effective than anything the competition can ever hope to muster. The National Egg Board and the American Egg Board, the United Dairy Industry Association, the National Livestock and Meat Board, and the National Pork Producer Council are a few of the major meat- and dairy-industry organizations that spend unheard-of advertising dollars that are passed on first to the actual farmer and then finally to you, the consumer, who pays not only for the product, but also to be persuaded to buy it.[9] So the next time you see a commercial "informing" you that a glass of milk, or a pat of butter, or a lean cut of beef is essential to a well-balanced diet, remember that it is not a public-service announcement, but strictly commercial advertising that would have you accept these products as healthful and even essential, without question or investigation. This type of advertising has become a major focus of the meat and dairy industries in recent years as they struggle to combat drops in sales that have resulted from their own inflated prices, a greater availability of vegetarian alternatives, and especially the rising public awareness of the severe health hazards of meat and dairy foods.

YOUR CONSUMER RIGHTS: WHO WILL UPHOLD THEM?

The government has been of little help to the consumer during this time. In fact, it has actually suggested that more wheat be raised for livestock than for people because, as one observer puts it, "It's cheaper to ship a pound of beef than it is to ship eight or ten pounds of grain."[10] The government has gone as far as to pay farmers *not* to grow wheat in a time of massive world famine.

It has also failed to protect the consumer from fraudulent advertising. The Federal Trade Commission has virtually ignored the advertising regulation field during Ronald Reagan's administration.[11] That means that when you see advertising that claims how lean pork is or how you need to drink as much milk as possible to strengthen your bones and prevent osteoporosis and other degenerative diseases of the skeletal system, you must take it upon yourself to weigh the validity of the information offered.

As long as the public is silent about its demands for regulation of advertising, disclosure of information, and so forth, its consumer rights will be disregarded. The powerful agribusiness monopoly is certainly vocal about its interests. When Jimmy Carter sponsored a meatless dinner at the White House in 1977, the President of the American National Cattlemen's Association immediately sent him a telegram. "The last thing we need is the President of the United States advocating a vegetarian diet for Americans," he wrote. Such an endorsement "could do great harm to the largest segment of American agriculture, the beef cattle industry," he added.

Just as the special interests voice their demands, so can you or I. Your congressman or senator will listen to *you* when you write or call concerning specific legislation that upholds your rights as a consumer. So let him know how *you* feel. Use your influence . . . those who have no interest in your welfare are using theirs!

If you wish to establish a good source of foods as alternatives to those offered by the meat, dairy, and processed-foods industries, there are several things that you can do very easily. For one, you can start or join a food cooperative to bypass the middleman retailer. All that is needed is a group of people that can place bulk orders large enough to be able to buy directly from wholesalers and producers at wholesale price. In this way you can not only get the quality types of food that you desire, but you can also get them as cheaply as possible by ordering at wholesale price. This can represent a discount of up to 40 percent.

On yet another level, the cooperative system of buying unites people with common interests and establishes a network that can serve as a catalyst for further group action in various directions.

Moreover, it gives everyone a hands-on actualization of their power as a group and as individuals. At this point there comes the realization that the large monopolies and agribusinesses are not the only special-interest group with demands and influences. Any properly motivated group can make its influence known and its demands acted upon.

You can still get even more actively involved in providing yourself with the kinds of foods that will promote health and prevent disease. You can grow them yourself. In this way you can maintain a fresh supply of organic produce. You don't need a lot of ground space, and you can learn how to do it from books on the subject and from magazines such as the popular *Organic Gardening and Farming*.

GROWING YOUR OWN FOOD INDOORS

Even urban and apartment dwellers can grow fresh produce, right indoors. Sprouts are high in nutrients and are easy to grow yourself anywhere. Here are a couple of methods.

The sprouting chart that follows details the amounts of dry seed, grain, or bean you should use, and their individual sprouting times.

1. In a jar. This is the simplest method. All you need is (a) a wide mouth jar, (b) a rubber band, (c) wire screen, cheesecloth, or an old clean nylon stocking and (d) a whole seed, bean, or grain.

   First, soak the seeds in plenty of water overnight. Use approximately twice the amount of water to the amount of dry seeds.

   Second, drain the water from the jar through the screen or cloth, and then rinse the seeds well.

   Third, turn the jar upside down at an angle; place in a bowl, pot, or wire stand; and put in a dark, temperate place.

   Rinse the seeds through the screen twice daily in cool-to-mild weather, and three times in the summer. During this time, keep the jar inverted (gently shake seeds to evenly distribute them around the walls of the jar).

   Most sprouts are ready to use when they are ¼–½ long. Alfalfa sprouts are best a little longer. After the

SPROUTING CHART

TYPE	SOAKING TIME	RINSE/DRAIN (TIMES PER DAY)	SPROUTING TIME	AMT. IN QT. JAR
Alfalfa Seeds	12 hrs. (overnight)	2	3 days	3 tbs.
Buckwheat	12 hrs.	3	5 days	5 tbs.
Fenugreek Seeds	12 hrs.	3	4 days	3 tbs.
Garbanzo Beans	12 hrs.	2	3 days	1 cup
Lentils	12 hrs.	2	3 days	10 tbs.
Mung Beans	12 hrs.	2	3 days	6 tbs.
Mustard Seeds	none	3	4 days	3 tbs.
Radish Seeds	12 hrs.	3	5 days	3 tbs.
Red Clover Seeds	12 hrs.	2	4 days	3 tbs.
Rye	12 hrs.	3	3 days	5 tbs.
Soybeans	24 hrs.	3	4 days	1 cup
Sunflower Seeds	12 hrs.	3	5 days	8 tbs.
Wheat	12 hrs.	2	3 days	5 tbs.

third day, place the alfalfa sprouts in the sun to enhance the development of chlorophyll (bright green in color) through the action of photosynthesis.

2. In a pan. First start the seeds in a pan using the above method. After the second day, spread the seeds thinly and evenly on the bottom of a glass or screen tray or even in a straw basket. Sprinkle generously with water two to three times a day. Cover with wet cheesecloth or a paper towel.

When sprouts have developed to their desired length, put them in a closed jar or plastic container and store in the refrigerator. They will keep a few days like any fresh vegetable if properly covered. The amount of seeds, grains, or beans to be soaked varies with the size of what you are sprouting and the size of the container. Allow enough room for an increase of from five to eight times the original size.

Sprouts are low in calories and easily digested. They are a good source of B-complex vitamins and provide a quick source of energy and protein, and can be used as a viable meat substitute when combined properly with other foods. Sprouting is extremely inexpensive, can be done right at home, and unlocks stores of nutrients. Sprouts are delicious as a snack food, or can be added to main dishes, casseroles, soups, and salads.

There are many reasons for adopting a vegetarian life-style. Some vegetarians feel very strongly about a single reason, while others have chosen their diet for a number of reasons. In any case, whatever your reasons may be, the chances are that as you go forward with this life-style, you will discover benefits that you had not anticipated when you first started.

As an economic issue, being a vegetarian can be quite beneficial—both individually and on a societal level, but we have already seen that there is considerable opposition on these grounds, primarily from the powerful agribusinesses. This brings us to a crossroads and a choice to make. Will we continue to support the interests of the concentrated economic power, or increase our personal strength and create change by becoming more self-sufficient?

ELEVEN

Natural Resources: In Search of Ecological Harmony

A vegetarian life-style makes as good ecologic as economic sense. Growing vegetables and grains makes much more efficient use of our natural resources than does raising livestock. Even growing plant foods cost us dearly enough in terms of land, water, energy, and raw materials—resources that will not last forever and so must be conserved in every way possible. To use a substantial portion of those foods to feed animals instead of people is wasteful. When we finally eat the animal, we get no more nutrients than the plant could have supplied us with from the beginning. The whole middle process of feeding, raising, slaughtering, marketing, and eating the animal could be eliminated. Then there might be more peaceful coexistence between man and animal, and far less of a drain on our finite natural resources.

Raising livestock has upset not only man-to-animal harmony, but also the man-to-man and animal-to-animal balance. The clearing of vast tracts of forest lands, and the appropriation of grasslands, for use as livestock grazing grounds has left large numbers of wildlife homeless. As they scatter in search of new shelter and hunting grounds, a high percentage are trapped or poisoned. One inevitable result of the growth of the meat industry has been to push out and even drive into extinction much of our wildlife.

As lifestock is pitted against wildlife, so man is also pitted against man. The raising of animals for slaughter may serve to feed those wealthy enough to buy meat, but it also wastes our natural resources and helps increase the price of farmland, to the point of undermining our ability to grow plant foods economically. This creates tension between the affluent countries of the West and those Third World nations besieged with starvation. (We should be reminded that while dietary habits and preferences may be local or national, natural resources are ultimately global and international. When we choose to support an industry that carelessly wastes "our" natural resources, we should realize that these resources are not really ours. Nobody can own the air, water, or soil. You might buy a piece of property and be called the "owner," but what you do with that land will affect every one of the earth's inhabitants. If you dump chemicals on "your" land, for instance, those toxins, via seepage, runoff, or precipitation can end up in people's drinking water virtually anywhere in the world.)

As we continue to carelessly waste these natural resources, their value continues to increase. This causes an increase in the cost of raising livestock, and hence diminished profits for agribusiness (or skyrocketing prices for meats). It would seem rational to change our pattern of food production so that vegetables and grains are grown for people instead of for animals. But this would decrease our dependence on meat, so a threatened meat industry has effected its own solution to the problem. Instead of raising fewer animals for slaughter it has stepped up sales pressure on consumers and increased its output. To feed all this livestock, farmers cultivate even more of our dwindling acreage for the production of feed crops. These crops—primarily corn, soybeans, and alfalfa—are among the villains in the soil-erosion story. The meat industry is little concerned; as one researcher noted, "The most erosive production system—continuous corn—produces the highest net income."[1] As long as profits are forthcoming, little else seems to matter, least of all ecological harmony.

HOW SHOULD WE USE OUR LAND?

Land used for meat and dairy production provides food for fewer people than land used only for plant foods. According to one estimate, up to fourteen times as many people could be fed using the same land exclusively for plant foods.[2] Land use is a critical issue. In a world where malnutrition and starvation are prevalent, we should be doing everything possible to eliminate inefficient and outmoded land use. If a single acre of land now supporting one hundred people could support fourteen hundred, shouldn't we investigate how?

At this time, there exists approximately one acre of fertile land in the world per person. That seems to be a safe enough ratio. Research shows that only one-third of an acre is needed to supply enough protein for one person for one year. But that estimate holds true only if the protein is derived from vegetable sources. Once we begin using animals as our source of protein, a full three and one-half acres are required![3] There is simply not enough fertile land to sustain the world's population on meat. To use our precious fertile land for livestock is to misuse it.

How much of our land is being misused in this way? In the United States, over one-third of our farmland is used for animal grazing, and almost 80 percent of our grain is livestock feed.[4] To make matters worse, the land on which livestock feed grain is grown is typically worked without regard for the essential principles of crop rotation: the land is being abused to support an abusive industry. This land misuse supports the meat and dairy industries. They can keep their products on your table; you don't have to change your traditional dietary habits; and, because Americans are willing to pay more for these items than ever before, agribusiness can see nothing but increased profit from increased production.

But look a bit closer at what is really happening. The president of the Worldwatch Institute in Washington concludes that the whole system is "creating an illusion of progress and a false sense of security."[5] The cost of agribusiness's immediate profits is the gross wasting of our earth's natural resources and the compromising of the integrity of our arable land for future use. When we buy that steak or cheese, we reward these industries with profits that encourage them to continue in their pursuit of illusory progress. Without our money, they would be forced either to find more efficient ways to use the land, or to convert to vegetable and grain production for people.

Even if we affect a callous indifference to the rape of our own land and to the stripping of our natural resources, have we the right to deny other peoples their share of the earth's resources? We have not yet felt the disastrous repercussions of soil erosion and land misuse, but people in other countries have. In many poorer nations, not only has the meat industry monopolized the land, but the foods that are produced for people frequently end up being exported to the wealthy. For example, according to Frances Moore Lappé, an authority on food and hunger, "two-thirds of the agriculturally productive land in Central America is devoted to livestock production, yet the poor majority cannot afford the meat, which is eaten by the well-to-do or exported."[6]

SOIL EROSION

Our desire for meat permits agribusiness to continue using technological agricultural methods that may yield them unprecedented profits, but are also causing unprecedented erosion of our topsoil. An Iowa state conservation official, William Brune, explains that "it can take 100 to 500 years to create an inch of topsoil," but due to current agricultural practices, this small amount "can wash away in a single heavy rainstorm."[7] Further statistics about soil erosion are staggering:

- The harvest of one bushel of corn in Iowa results in the loss of two bushels of topsoil.[8]
- Only six inches of topsoil remains on some Iowa farmlands.[9]
- Our present erosive conditions have been compared to those experienced during the Dust Bowl.[10]
- One-third of our topsoil is gone in the major farming states.[11]
- Corn is responsible for one-fourth of our national soil erosion problem.[12]
- Water erosion is accountable for annual monetary losses of up to $8 million; this is further aggravated by wind erosion.[13]

- Indirect costs of soil erosion, such as chemical fertilizers and water purification, amount to nearly $1 billion
  a year. Overall costs due to continual erosion of the
  soil are estimated to be nearly $2 billion a year.[14]
- In the U.S. alone, 1.7 billion tons of topsoil permanently
  erode every year.[15]
- Worldwide, over 25 billion tons of topsoil from farmlands are being lost annually.[16]
- The global loss of topsoil is nearly that of our depleted
  oil supplies.[17]
- For every inch of topsoil lost, we produce 6 percent
  fewer crops.[18]

Most of us do not experience the effects of soil erosion directly.
You can't see or hear it, and nobody taxes or bills you for it. But
that makes the problem even more insidious. If oil or utility prices
go up, first you know about it, then you demand to know why; and
meanwhile you do what you can to reduce your personal usage and
eliminate any possible waste. When is the last time you heard someone complain about the rapid rate of erosion? Yet, it constitutes "a
quiet crisis that could lead to famines in some parts of the world."[19]
There exist some thirty high-risk regions in the United States alone,
mostly in areas of extensive soybean and corn production. While
chemical fertilizers may somewhat compensate for depleted or eroded
soil, they are quite expensive. And guess who pays for them: the
consumer, who else?

THE DEPLETION OF OUR WATER SUPPLY

Water is an essential natural resource that, like topsoil, has been
taken for granted for a long time. Only recently has there been public
outrage over its pollution by toxic wastes, offshore dumping, and
other mindless activities. People are finally realizing how important
it is to protect and conserve our water supply. We are all concerned
about its pollution, and hopefully try to conserve it by cutting down
on showers, car washing, and lawn sprinkling. Still, there seems to
be little awareness of how much water is being used by agribusiness,
which uses a full third of our entire supply, particularly in animal
production.

Long ago, farmers were dependent on nature to water their fields, either by rain or, in some cases, by annual flooding. To increase the amount of arable farmland, irrigation came into use. By siphoning off water from rivers, and channeling it to where it was needed, farmers could grow crops even in arid regions or during dry seasons. While this has helped us increase crop production significantly, over the past two decades agribusiness has been irrigating land almost exclusively for the purpose of growing food for livestock. American agribusiness uses up to 85 percent of all irrigated water, with 50 percent being consumed for livestock[20]—not just used, but actually "consumed" in the way suggested by the dictionary: "destroy, to spend wastefully, to eat up, devour."[21]

If you are concerned about conserving water, you could begin to help by eating more vegetarian casseroles and fresh green salads, and less meat. If you prefer steak, keep in mind that it took 2,500 gallons of water to produce beef to get a 16-ounce T-bone[22]—fifteen times more than a vegetarian alternative with the same protein content. You need not compromise quality or nutrients, only make a decision to take responsibility for the gross waste of our precious water supply. Anyone who enjoys fast-food burgers or filet mignons should be aware that "the water that goes into a 1,000 pound steer would float a small boat."[23] If we passively allow the meat and dairy industries to continue using our limited water supply for livestock, we may not be able to find a glass of pure water in the near future.

You may have thought that rainfall replenishes our water supply. Under normal usage, this may be true. But is it normal usage when in just one day, the average American's food intake represents over a thousand gallons of water, of which nearly two-thirds went into the animal products being consumed?[24] In California, where nearly 50 percent of the irrigated water is used for animal production, land is drying out and actually starting to sink. Texas may soon follow, as 25 percent of its underground water has been used in a scant twenty years. There is no way rainfall can keep up.

OUR DWINDLING ENERGY SUPPLY

It may not take much energy to make any single food item, but the creation of animal products as a whole uses nearly 15 percent of our country's annual energy budget. That is equal to the energy needed to run all our cars. It almost equals the amount of oil we import. And it is more than double what our nuclear power plants generate. Watts wrong?!

As we have seen, meat and dairy products cost us much more than the shelf price alone, which is already about as high as one can imagine. The true cost is much higher. Every calorie of protein eaten, for example, required 78 calories of fuel to produce. Wheat and corn, by comparison, require only 3.5 calories of energy per calorie of protein; soybeans need forty times less than beef.[25]

Why should meat require such a vast depletion of our energy supply? To answer this we need to review briefly the economic implications of eating meat and dairy products.

When we consume a product that requires many stages of processing, energy expenditure must far exceed that for simple products that can be used in their natural state. The fewer the number of processing stages, the less energy is required to get the item into the hands of the consumer. Energy costs are one reason why, if you buy all the individual ingredients needed for a cake—a cup of flour, two eggs, and so forth—you spend far less than if you go to the bakery and buy an already prepared cake. And if you bought raw wheat straight from the harvest, you would spend far less than you would for the cup of flour.

Meat and dairy foods must go through many more stages of processing than vegetables and grains, therefore much more energy is used in their production. To begin with, animals must be fed, while plants need only water and fertilizer. A Department of Interior and Commerce study indicates that the livestock industry uses one-third of the value of all raw materials consumed in the U.S. just for feed. Plastic wrap, aluminum foil, styrofoam and cardboard containers, paper labels, ink, preservatives, artificial flavors and color additives—all used by the meat-packing industry—further deplete our raw-material supplies. These raw materials include aluminum, copper, iron, steel, tin, zinc, rubber, wood, and petroleum products.

Because animal products are so wasteful and destructive of our land, water, energy, and raw materials, it is imperative that we find better ways to feed our population. If we do not attend to this critical issue, and soon, the earth may suffer irreversible damage that could threaten the very survival of mankind. Water, soil, and energy are finite resources. They cannot be reproduced. When we destroy and waste them we threaten ourselves and our children.

Fortunately, there is an alternative to self-destruction. The vegetarian life-style is far more efficient than the outdated tradition of meat and dairy consumption. We have only to begin to enjoy it.

TWELVE

Food Resources

HOW BIG A PROBLEM IS WORLD HUNGER?

We hear so much about world hunger: people starving to death in underdeveloped countries, while Americans struggle to stay on diets. Although being overweight and obesity are major concerns for our overall national health, a significant proportion—about one quarter—of the world's population has been condemned to a life of hunger and eventual starvation. An estimated one-half to one billion people are suffering from malnutrition, receiving such inadequate amounts of nutrients that even their basic physiological functions are impaired.[1]

This is hard to believe since here in the United States we have so much wealth and food that we hardly know what to do with it all. Isn't it strange that children in the U.S. routinely throw away food that children in Ethiopia, the Sudan, Somalia, India, or Southeast Asia pray for, but seldom ever obtain? Children in drought-ridden northeastern Brazil, where some 350,000 *flagellados* or "tormented ones" have starved to death,[2] children suffer severe growth abnormalities and irreversible brain damage for want of the kind of nutrients that collect in our garbage pails. Infant brain damage is a serious problem in this region of Brazil because of chronic dietary protein deficiencies. "There seems to be little disagreement among scientists," according to an *American Scientist* article, "that a continuous protein-deficient diet produces irreversible damage to the brain."[3]

We have difficulty imagining the horrors of world hunger because in all our wealth and comfort we are so far removed from it. Most of us have to badger our children to get them to eat even half of their dinner. It's hard to believe that other children are dying because they have absolutely no food. But even though we have trouble feeling the immediacy of the starvation crisis, we do hear about it and try to understand it on an intellectual level. One of the most common explanations for the phenomenon revolves around the notion that overpopulation places an undue strain on the already tenuous food supply of an underdeveloped nation. This theory includes many closely associated assumptions. For instance, it is often presumed that underdeveloped countries are "backward." That is, they have failed to obtain the updated machinery and technology needed to keep pace with modern population growth rates and subsequent food demands. It is also presumed that widespread ignorance among the peoples of these countries plays a major role. For one thing, the argument goes, there is little understanding of those modern agricultural techniques that could help farmers increase their product yield, and to make matters worse, a general distrust of modern science and society is responsible for the fact that these people ignore birth control and continue conceiving children with no measure of restraint.

While there is undoubtedly some truth in these observations they only explain the problem, they don't solve it. Moreover, they tend to be somewhat culturally prejudiced too, assuming that modern ways of doing things are superior to traditional ways that have existed for centuries in many of these societies. But the most basic oversight in this sort of explanation is that it presumes that world hunger can be overcome by increased agricultural production coupled with more stringent birth control measures.

It may be that if we continue our present rate of population growth, "700 years from now people would be standing shoulder to shoulder on every foot of the earth's land surface.... In 7,000 years, our population would be expanding outward into space at the speed of light."[4] Even in the United States, where the birth rate is double the death rate, there will come a day when we simply won't have enough food to feed so large a population. Reducing the rate of population growth will obviously ease the strain on our limited food supplies, yet that cannot be the only solution to world hunger. Increasing agricultural production may be an immediate solution, but that in turn may create a lethal drain on our natural resources, as we saw in the last chapter. Moreover, increasing output is not an easy task for countries that can ill afford modern farm machinery.

What must be understood here, is that starvation is essentially man-made. Population increases coupled with production decreases caused by droughts or floods or other natural and man-made causes have played their roles. But experience shows us that these problems can be dealt with much more fruitfully if we simply begin to make more economically sound use of our land by developing a more efficient food supply. Frances Moore Lappé has shown us that famine is not a necessary part of the human condition, even in notoriously poor countries. "Bangladesh," she points out, "is by no means a hopeless basket case."[5] Yes, this small country does have an extremely dense population and that does create a problem. But Taiwan has twice the number of people per cultivated acre that Bangladesh has, yet its people are not starving. Population density is not the sole variable indicating whether or not a country's available food supply is sufficient to support its people. Far more significant is how a country's land is used and how efficiently its food supply is utilized.

The demand for animal protein is the single most significant factor that condemns millions to a life of hunger and eventual starvation. It has pitted man against animal as they are forced to compete over grain supplies for their very existence. The animal industry is based on gross misuse of the land, land that would be better used to feed people rather than cattle. It is responsible for creating a food supply of meat and dairy products that are highly inefficient in terms of nutritional return to the consumer, considering the amount of food and other resources that were required for its production. We will discuss these things in more detail later in this chapter.

For now, we need only recognize that while world hunger is real and does pose a threat to human existence on this planet, the situation is not hopeless. It is true that if the current population explosion continues, the world will eventually reach a saturation point for its food resources. But estimates predict that our present world population of four billion must increase ten times before we actually face this situation. This does give us time to calmly investigate this problem and begin working constructively toward its solution. Yet, we must also keep in mind the fact that famine—needless though it be—is a day-to-day reality for millions throughout our world. Americans may not be actually facing food shortages, but by their insistence on maintaining meat and dairy diets they are creating and perpetuating the problems for others ... and eventually for themselves. Remember, hunger is a problem that has been created by man far more than by overpopulation and drought. Its solution is also up to man. The way is clear, but we need to begin now. Every time we eat a meal of meat and dairy products, we are supporting an industry that is literally taking food from the mouths of starving people.

RAISING FOOD WITHOUT FEEDING PEOPLE

Increasing agricultural output may sound like a reasonable solution to famine, but unfortunately the increase in grain production in recent years has gone more and more to animals and less and less to people. Livestock consumes our grain supplies in gross amounts and gives us very little in terms of our dietary requirements in return. So while agricultural output may be going up, our ability to feed people continues to decline. Just how much food do we waste when we eat meat and dairy products? Let's take beef for an example. Cattle must consume 16 pounds of feed to produce a single pound of flesh. That means that for every pound of beef we consume, we must waste 15 pounds of grain!

You might think that agribusiness would try to cut down on this tremendous grain drain, if for no other reason than to save the high cost of feed. They do try, but they are unwilling to take the most obvious and sensible step: to produce less meat, and advise consumers to balance their diets better by eating more vegetables and grains to replace part of this meat intake. Instead, they find methods for maintaining full weight on their cattle, while having them eat less. To accomplish this they severely restrict their physical movement, therefore cutting their feeding requirements. No longer do the cattle graze freely on the meadows, and drink from babbling brooks beneath shady trees. Instead they are lined up in crowded and squalid "feedlots." The whole face of the animal industry has been changed by this new technology. Livestock fed in these mechanized feedlots can now attain a target weight, and be delivered to the slaughterhouse in about one-third the normal time.[6] This has greatly increased the profits for the animal factories that insist on maintaining their hold on the food market, even if it means tolerating gross waste that ultimately leads to world hunger.

Despite the industry's attempt to cut down on feed allocation, though, cattle still require a high caloric intake and since meat production is rising steadily, so is the overall feed requirement. Use of livestock feed in the United States is now averaging about 200 million tons annually, compared to only 100 million tons on the eve of World War II. Although this figure accounts only for feed consumption in the United States, it is equivalent to all the grain that is currently imported by every nation in the world. The number of poultry as well as livestock that are fed grain has doubled over the last thirty years, with 75 percent of all livestock being currently grain fed. Pigs consume as much grain as do cattle, each animal requiring an average 5,000 pounds of grain, soy, and additional crops annually.[7] Not that all the protein being consumed helps us much when we eat the animal. A lot of it goes for the normal growth, maintenance, and repair of the animal itself; and a large amount is also absorbed by the livestock hair, skin, bones, and excrement, parts that we do not even eat.

While agribusiness has stepped up its livestock production, the United States has still been growing enough feed to export abroad. But still, the hungry are not being fed. Over 60 percent of our grain exports go to affluent, industrialized nations rather than to the Third World countries that have high rates of hunger and starvation. Much of the grain that does eventually filter into the Third World goes to feed the livestock rather than starving mothers and children.

Reducing meat production is clearly the best solution to the problem of world hunger. Yet, industrialized nations tried to circumvent the issue by inventing the so-called Green Revolution some thirty years ago. This program has intended to end world hunger by introducing new crops bred specifically for rapid growth and high-yield performance. There were several problems with this highly touted system. One was that the new strains of crops were very expensive to grow because of the uncommonly large amounts of fertilizer needed. This allowed the wealthiest farmers to outprice their competition, putting many small farmers out of business in countries where farming was the traditional binding socioeconomic force.

An overemphasis on grain production was another weakness of the system. Grains largely replaced many varieties of legumes, and frequently ended up being used as feed for livestock anyway. In the industrialized countries, high-yield crops created a surplus which needed a market, thereby encouraging even greater animal production, which in turn placed even greater pressure on farmers to produce yet more feed for the oversupply of livestock. It became a vicious cycle of overproduction, yet nutrition was seldom considered. Dr. R. S. Harris, professor of biochemistry and nutrition at M.I.T., found that the indigenous strains of crops being replaced by the new high-yield varieties were actually superior in nutrition.[8]

In *Food for Naught*, Ross Hume Hall talks about the shortsightedness of the project: " 'The Green Revolution' devised in Western countries as a solution to the nutritional problems of other cultures, is based on the fully mechanized technology of Western countries. It is not just a matter of planting new strains of rice or wheat, it is also a matter of applying fertilizer at the right time, irrigating at the right time, applying insecticides, herbicides and using new types of machines—the whole complex of business."[9] The use of this modern technology put even further stress on the local economic conditions of underdeveloped countries. It led to an increase in unemployment and subsequently to poverty and even greater hunger among the working class. It seems that from every perspective the Green Revolution only made matters worse. Most of the production increases that it generated led to further economic decline in already troubled lands, and most of the increased food supply went to livestock for the meat and dairy industries. It seems to have been responsible for just about everything except getting more food to more people.

EATING MEAT IS WASTING FOOD

It is quite sobering to learn how much food is wasted by the meat and dairy industries, especially since vegetarianism exists as a simple and healthful alternative. In a recent year, our livestock used up 145 million tons of grain and soy to produce a meager 21 million tons of animal products. Can we really afford to waste 124 million tons of food every time we net 21 million? This colossal waste is enough to provide one cup of grain daily for every person in the world for an entire year.[10] How would you like to buy 145 gallons of gasoline for your car and only be able to use 21 gallons? You would undoubtedly be outraged, and rightfully so. You wouldn't dream of wasting gasoline for your car, so does it make sense to tolerate wasting food in those proportions, a waste which has the effect of starving your fellow human beings with whom you share this planet? Some might argue that they really don't know what to do about solving hunger in distant lands. Or they might think that governments should give more money to the needy, and that the Peace Corps and the United Nations should send more trained technical assistance to underdeveloped countries to teach modern farming techniques. But now that we see how grossly inefficient and wasteful meat is, we know that the most direct and powerful and immediate solution to the problem is to adopt a vegetarian life-style.

We have spoken at length about the waste of grain perpetuated by the meat and dairy industries. We have not even mentioned the other nutritious ingredients like wheat germ and fish meal that are pumped into feed. If everyone adopted a low-meat or vegetarian diet, the combined surplus of both grain and legumes could be eaten by 800 million hungry people in the world today.[11] We mentioned before that cattle must be fed 16 pounds of grain to produce a single pound of flesh. Smaller animals are more efficient in this regard. To get that same single pound of flesh, pigs consume about 6 pounds of feed, and poultry only need 3 to 4 pounds. Milk requires the least amount of input, averaging less than 1 pound of grain for each pint we drink.[12] From each of these examples, although the amounts vary, we can see how wasteful meat, poultry, and dairy products are. If 16 pounds of grain were eaten directly by people, instead of fed to cattle to produce a single pound of flesh, we would net twenty times the amount of calories and ten times the amount of protein from it. And as an extra benefit, while getting twenty times the calories, we would get only three times the fat. And even the fat is a more usable unsaturated type instead of the heavy, difficult-to-digest, saturated type that we get from animal products.

Eating meat wastes calories at the same time that it cuts into the amount of land we have available to raise vegetables and grains. Of 100 calories consumed for its production, milk gives us back a scant 15 percent, eggs 7 percent, and beef only 4 percent. How would you like to get involved in an investment portfolio that offered you four, seven, or even fifteen dollars for every hundred that you put up? You would say it's ludicrous. But those are the numbers we play when we consume meat and dairy products. Shouldn't we be as concerned about our food supply as we are about our passbook savings? Most people eat animal foods because they want the protein. But even here there is tremendous waste and inefficiency. We get to use only 25, 12, and 10 percent of the protein that goes into producing milk, pork, and beef, respectively.[13]

In terms of land use, a single acre of farmland can yield 800,000 calories growing vegetable food. If we feed the same vegetables to animals first, though, the meat and dairy products that we then get for our food yield us only 200,000 calories. That adds up to a 75 percent loss in terms of nutrition. You can see why, as meat eaters, we have to start worrying about whether or not we have enough land to feed the world's population. If we were all vegetarians there would be an ample amount of acreage for our dietary needs. Eating meat is robbing us of millions of tons of calories and proteins, without even offering the health benefits of a vegetarian diet. To sustain the meat and dairy producers, we must compromise the use of our fertile land and accept a 75 percent loss on return. And then we wonder why nature has not provided us with ample resources to feed all of the earth's inhabitants.

LAND FOR FOOD

Many people assume that most of the underdeveloped countries in the world simply do not have enough arable land and other resources to support their population. Frances Moore Lappé and Joseph Collins have dispelled this theory in their book, *Food First: Beyond the Myth of Scarcity*.[14] The root of the hunger problem according to this study is the misuse of land resources. Small but powerful groups of wealthy landowners typically use the land in their countries to turn profits. So instead of growing grain and legumes and vegetables and fruits for people, many of whom are starving all around them, these landowners choose to raise cash crops. Cash crops are things grown for dollar profit rather than to fulfill local dietary need. These crops are typically exported to people who will pay dearly for them. Coffee beans, sugarcane, tobacco, and beef are cash crops. The poor farmers who toil the fields to grow them rarely can afford to buy them. The bulk of these luxury items are exported to the wealthier industrialized world. While beef production rose over 90 percent in some areas of Latin America, for example, local meat consumption dropped over 30 percent. Alan Berg, an authority in the field of nutrition, declares that the truth of the matter is that "the meat is ending up not in Latin American stomachs, but in franchised restaurant hamburgers in the U.S." [15]

Staple crops are also raised in the Third World, of course. But even these are used indirectly as cash crops, being used primarily to feed animals for the lucrative meat and dairy industries. Once these affordable crops have been used for production of animal foods, they become unaffordable to all but the affluent minority, and the balance is shipped out of the country for cash. In a study of hunger in Bangladesh—a tiny country with 80 million inhabitants —Lappé and Collins found that two-thirds of the people were protein- and vitamin-deficient, although the land yields enough grain to provide each person with 2,600 calories daily! How can masses of people be starving where there is an abundant food supply?

Lappé and Collins found that the problem was not one of raising food, but one of redistributing the land wealth and political power. A very tiny minority owns the majority of the land in Bangladesh. This landlord group continually bleeds the poor tenant farmer for the bulk of his produce by constantly raising his rent. Many are not content simply to monopolize the market. They go on to become "moneylender-merchants," hoarding grain. As grain is held back from the populace in this way, food shortages ensue. By now, people are desperate and hungry and will pay almost anything for the release of some of this hoarded grain. The landowner, now the merchant, is finally ready to sell . . . at insanely inflated prices!

Lappé and Collins explain, "Landless laborers, dependent on meager wages, are particularly vulnerable. Precisely when floods and droughts deprive them of work altogether, speculative food prices due to hoarding shoot up 200 to 500 percent. Once we became aware of these realities, we were not surprised to learn that, while many starved after the 1974 floods, hoarders stocked up an estimated 4 million tons of rice because the vast majority . . . were too poor to buy it."[16]

A special committee was created by the U.S. Congress in 1976 to report on the Bangladesh situation. It found that "the country is rich enough in fertile land, water, manpower and natural gas for fertilizer not only to be self-sufficient in food, but a food exporter, even with its rapidly increased population size."[17]

The people are not the only ones suffering in this sad example of social abuse and political malaise. The land too is neglected and abused. Sharecroppers—tenant farmers—are reluctant to make any substantial improvement on their plots because it would only raise the value of the land, and therefore its rental value. Eventually, the reward for improving the land would be that the poor sharecropper would have to move on, not being able to keep up with rising rents. Small landowners could very well utilize conserved monsoon waters to irrigate their fields during droughts and dry seasons. They are afraid to take such initiatives, though, because the resulting increased value of their lands may only invite a takeover by the wealthy farmers.[18] On the other side of the coin, landowners intent on maintaining their stranglehold on the laborer and the sharecropper deliberately destroyed technological improvements, such as irrigation systems, that the sharecroppers did make. After all, if the land became more fruitful and hence profitable, the laboring farmer might begin to gain some sense of independence from the landlord. This is not allowed to happen, given the socioeconomic situation.

In the semidesert of northeastern Brazil, where a serious drought has persisted since 1978, similar land abuse has caused tremendous suffering. The wealthy landlords have reserved the vast majority of the land for cash crops and for raising cattle for the beef industry. The cash crops and beef use up all the water and are then exported for big profits, leaving millions of local Brazilians dying of thirst and starvation. Jose Matias Filho of Caera State University's Department of Agriculture explains that "with our present water resources and technology, we could produce five times as much food."[19] But landowners prefer to monopolize their land and water to feed animals for slaughter rather than raise grain for the starving populace. And the reason is clear. Meat can be sold to the Americans and Europeans for far more money, at prices that the poor peasants and laborers could not even imagine. So in order to capitalize on beef and other cash crops, the fate of millions is sealed, leading one nutritional expert to note that "no other region in the world has such low living standards."[20]

KING CATTLE

In the early part of the nineteenth century, cotton had become the chief cash crop of the United States. "King Cotton," as it was called, was the source of tremendous profit for the Southern gentlemen who farmed it, and also for the Northern industrialists who used it to make finished products. Everyone was profiting except for the slaves who were worked mercilessly pulling it in from the plantation fields, and the land that was depleted for years to come because of the reluctance to rotate cotton production with other crops. Plantation owners were bound to get while the getting was good. Of course cotton was eventually dethroned, slavery ended, and the vast plantation fields layed to waste. The magnificent Southern Plantation has never recovered and the economy in general is just beginning to be re-established where King Cotton once reigned.

In the twentieth century, cattle has become king, bringing with it much of the same human, ecological, and economic abuse. As recently as 1950, each American was consuming an average of 60 pounds of beef, the same amount of pork, and 25 pounds of poultry per year.[21] By the 1970s, though, per capita beef and poultry consumption had doubled. The American Meat Institute, having seen meat consumption drop considerably since 1930, was waging an all-out war to regain prominence in the American diet. In a published sourcebook, it described how: "From 1938 to 1956, the A.M.I. worked successfully against a declining rate of meat consumption by sponsoring an educational and promotional program. The Institute invested more than $30 million in consumer advertising in the 17 year period to convince Americans that meat is a fine food."[22]

The A.M.I. carefully plotted its every move en route to totally duping the wide-eyed American public. It ran ads in the *American Dietetic Associations Journal* claiming "magical results" from eating meat. It was presented as a cure-all that reversed everything from pernicious anemia to pellegra. It was even held up as "a nutritional necessity for the steady drinker and smoker," as if these blatant drug abuses could be ameliorated with complementary portions of pork or beef. More bluntly, meat was advertised as a "health guardian for man, woman and child."[23] Eating meat seemed to be as important as avenging the attack on Pearl Harbor. "To argue, as some governmental economists and experts do," it was reasoned in *Meat Three Times a Day*, "that Americans should reduce their standard of living by 10 percent through substitution of grains for a portion of the meat, eggs and milk that they now consume, is to misunderstand the spirit of Americans and what lies back of our country's greatness and productivity. Instead of talking about how low our meat consumption can be cut and conditioning researchers to discover whether or not an ounce or two a day is sufficient, we should be working at increasing it to a pound a day or even more."[24]

The dairy industry was not to be outdone. Americans had shunned dairy products and milk was generally known to create too much bodily mucus and allergic reactions. Many mothers nursed their babies, or had them tended to by a professional wet nurse. Cow's milk had been much criticized for the health hazards it posed for infants. The National Dairy Council struck back. The largest provider of nutrition-education materials for our school systems, it boasted the merits of milk and cheese, sponsored self-serving research and ultimately won the hearts of Americans. Infants were pulled from their mothers' breasts and introduced to the milk bottle, while milk in the classroom is now as common as beer in a bar.

The American public was not to be taken lightly, and the meat and dairy industries were not newcomers to public education and mass-appeal techniques. Knowing full well that the public could be convinced with some supporting government reports and statistics, they enlisted the aid of the United States Drug Administration (the USDA). The USDA proposed the dietary concept of the "Four Basic Food Groups" supposedly to help simplify the complexities of nutrition for the public. Along with the American Dietetic Association, an avid meat and dairy industry supporter, it proceeded to grossly oversimplify the guidelines to proper nutrition. Close examination of the diet suggested by the four-basic-food-groups concept reveals a regimen that does nothing to assure proper nutrition, but does assure a healthy profit for agribusiness. The plan suggests that each person eat from the four basic food groups to be sure of receiving a "recommended daily allowance" of all nutrients. The four food groups are aimed almost exclusively, of course, at meat and dairy products.

The Four Basic Food Groups was preceded in the 1930s by the "Twelve Food Groups" which became the "Basic Seven" by the 1940s. The twelve food groups were: milk and milk products; potatoes and sweet potatoes; dry mature peas, beans, and nuts; tomatoes and citrus fruits; leafy green and yellow vegetables; other fruits and vegetables; eggs; lean meats; poultry and fish; flour and cereal; butter; other fats and sugars.[25] The Basic Seven had three fruit and vegetable groups along with a butter and fat group. Clearly, neither of these groups sufficiently supported the "public education" demands of the meat and dairy industries. With too many people eating from the Twelve Food Groups and the Basic Seven, not enough animal products were being consumed to satisfy their profit plans. Let's take a look at why agribusiness is very happy to offer not twelve or even seven, but only four food groups.

THE "BASIC FOUR"

The "Basic Four" are well known to most consumers in the United States. The "milk group" contains dairy products like butter, cream, cheese, and milk. USDA recommendations are three to four servings a day for children, two for adults, three for pregnant women, and four for lactating women. A cup of milk is considered a single serving. In the Dairy Council's "Milk's the One" commercials, the word glassful was substituted for cups, so that four to six ounces above even USDA recommendations were actually being recommended.[26]

The "meat group" includes besides the beef and pork that we would expect, fish, poultry, eggs, and interesting to note, dried beans and legumes. Two daily servings are recommended. By the very name of the group, though, and because they are listed as secondary sources, the nonmeat items are easily overlooked by the casual consumer. Vegetarians and meat eaters alike are likely to be misled into presuming that the meats contain a better quality and greater quantity of protein. In actuality, the vegetarian items are just as good and frequently better in this regard. Still, the public is left with the impression that protein deficiency may result from a vegetarian diet.

The "vegetable-fruit groups" is the third category. It includes all fruits and vegetables—a wide variety of foods that certainly deserve subgroupings, but instead are lumped into one. Four servings is the daily recommendation, but there is no mention of how many should be fruits or how many should be vegetables . . . or how many yellow vegetables versus leafy greens. Is four servings of spinach equivalent to four servings of watermelon? Judging from the USDA recommendations you cannot tell. One must wonder if it is helpful at all to simply suggest four servings.

The last group is the "breads-cereals group." While four servings are again recommended we must repeat the same question about distinguishing the relative merits of various foods in this group. Is a serving of white bleached bread equal in quality to a serving of oatmeal? The answer is no, of course, since white bread is so processed and denatured that it has virtually no nutritional value at all, while the oatmeal, not having been processed or only minimally so, yields far greater value in nutrients and roughage. Again, these categories are so general and nondescript that they prove to be of little value in their application to daily diet planning.

Since Americans have been force-fed the propaganda of the "Basic Four," they have taken a beating in more ways than one. While the profits of the meat and dairy industries have increased greatly, the average consumer has had to big deeper and deeper into his pocket to pay the rising costs of their products. He is also paying more for medical bills and health insurance because of sharp increases in disease and sickness. The Senate Select Committee on Nutrition and Human Needs has found an increase in the rate of malnutrition and obesity alongside a decrease in the quality—not quantity—of food consumed.[27] At the same time there has been a direct increase in the rate of heart disease, cancer, hypertension, arthritis, and other degenerative diseases. The animal producers have successfully brainwashed Americans into believing that without meat and dairy products there is danger of malnutrition. But with the public health and nutritional well-being dramatically declining while meat and dairy consumption greatly increases, their scare tactics are wearing pretty thin.

THE VEGETARIAN ALTERNATIVE

A workable alternative to the "Basic Four" would be a five-group division that could be utilized not just by the affluent consumer of industrialized society, but also by the average citizens of the Third World. This transcultural food-grouping would comprise three principal dietary staples—grains, legumes, and vegetables—while the two smaller groups would be raw foods and foods containing vitamin B[12].[28] This categorization includes all the foods needed by people in any socio-economic or cultural group in order to maintain a healthy, normal, active life. The five-group division is not a new concept. The Canadians have separated fruits and vegetables into two separate categories, and together with the meat, cereal, and milk groups end up with five. The Puerto Ricans, who stress vegetables and fresh fruits, also work with a five-group plan.[29]

Adopting a vegetarian diet would make us healthier by doing away with the animal products that agribusiness has worked so hard to sell us on. This brainwashing has blinded us from seeing the health benefits of the vegetarian alternatives. The time has come, though, when the public begins to comprehend the enormous waste and health dangers involved in eating meat. We are starting to see through the thinly veiled "public education messages" of the meat and dairy industries that for years have fabricated our need for animal products. Agricultural expert Lester R. Brown informs us that if Americans cut their meat consumption by just 10 percent, it would save us about 12 million tons of grain. This savings alone could negate an entire year's nutritional deficit in India, where nutritional deficit is among the highest in the world. In *By Bread Alone*, Brown reasons that "if some of us consume more, others of necessity must consume less. The moral issue is raised by the fact that those who are consuming less are not so much the overweight affluent but the already undernourished poor."[30]

Continuing to eat animal products amid starving people the world over is not just thoughtless, it is also selfish. While the average person in the United States consumes some 2,000 pounds of grain annually—all but 150 pounds is in the form of animal food. As senseless as this seems, our gluttonous demand for meat has prompted us to waste 170 million tons of grain a year in this way. We could eat the grain directly instead of pumping it into livestock, thereby enabling us to feast on a greasy steak or fatty hamburger. If we did, we would alleviate the present caloric deficiency of the world four times over.[31] Instead of donating to world hunger organizations, try eliminating beef from your diet. It is the most effective and concrete thing you can do to help end human suffering and starvation.

Food experts agree that we should eat much more of a vegetarian diet in order to create more nutritional parity in the world. They note that a simple diet would free up our grain exports and thereby increase global food resources. By decreasing our demand for meat, we are releasing millions of tons of food that can be used to nourish our starving and malnourished brethren in underdeveloped parts of the world. And we are even becoming healthier for it!

On the other hand, if we refuse to change our wasteful food production and selfish food consumption amid the starving millions, the devastation will continue and no one—not even us—will be spared. Sickness and disease, hunger and famine, economic chaos and violent struggles for dwindling food supplies, will ensue and augment steadily. The time has come to reallocate our food resources while the problem can still be solved.

THIRTEEN

Personal Taste

M any things that we do and buy are a matter of personal taste. We buy a car that appeals to us for some reason. We choose certain styles of music and art that gratify or move us in some way, and we may even vote for a political candidate simply because there is something that we like about the person. Diet, too, is largely a matter of personal taste. We choose to eat foods that we like, but even more, foods and preparations that in some way say something about who we are. We can choose to express ourselves creatively by preparing meals that include a wide variety of natural flavors and textures, or we can express ourselves monotonously by limiting our preparations to only those flavors, spices, and textures that we have become accustomed to.

If we are intent on always eating the same few foods that we "like" without trying new and different ones in various forms and preparations, we are expressing our reluctance to take risks, to try new things, to have fun with the excitement and the adventure of traveling down untrodden roads and through unfamiliar territories. To this extent we are not allowing ourselves to enjoy the breadth of life.

We turn our backs on the many experiences that life makes available to us. We choose instead to be comfortable and sure of our every step. We certainly rob ourselves of the joys of cooking creatively, of developing new tastes, and of seeking out interesting ways of combining wholesome foods for the sake of optimizing their various nutritional aspects.

Gastronomy—the art of good eating—generally refers to eating for visual and taste gratification. Unfortunately, it rarely takes into account the basic reason for eating—nutrition. The professional chef and homemaker alike have frequently overlooked the nutritional aspects of food preparation in the name of gastronomy. The art and science of nutritious food preparation is something that ought to be cultivated whether one is a chef responsible for feeding hundreds a day, or the person who prepares meals for a family. As the popular vegetarian cookbook *Ten Talents* puts it, "the health of this generation lies with its cooks to a great degree. But alas, how little intelligent thought and study is put into this phase of human responsibility."[1] Too many people, for too long, have harbored the notion that preparing vegetarian cuisine is a limiting and unimaginative ordeal.

THE HEALTHY GOURMET

Anyone who attended Brother Ron Pikarski's "Pure Vegetarian Escoffier Dinner" at a classy Chicago club in October of 1979 knows how exciting vegetarianism can be. Pikarski, one of the finest chefs in the world, needed the professional assistance of an entire retinue of chefs and food preparers to present an eight-course masterpiece of French cuisine, vegetarian-style. Over a hundred guests were treated to nearly two dozen dishes of wholesome and primarily (about three-quarters) uncooked vegetables and soy-based items that were two weeks in the making. Total vegetarian guidelines were strictly adhered to, with no flesh, dairy, processed, or salted foods to be found. Of the many healthful and yet enticing dishes served, some of the favorites were canapés made from raw vegetable slices with carrot, lentil, or pea pâté; a Jell-O mold made from the sea vegetable agar-agar, garnished with cucumbers, carrots, parsley, and olives; a garlic tofu dip surrounded by raw vegetables; and tempeh Wellington; and, for dessert, carob cake, zucchini bread, and banana carob fudge.

Brother Pikarski first became interested in vegetarianism as a way to solve his own weight problem, which he has done. He then began to prepare healthful meals for his brethren in the Franciscan community where he lives and is principal chef. His nutritious meal planning over the last three years has helped put a halt to the high evidence of heart disease that had hit the community hard just before Pikarski's cooking began. Imagine, sixteen relatively young brothers and priests, mostly in their forties and fifties, had died of heart disease. There have been no such incidents since Brother Ron has become executive chef.[2]

Pikarski believes that "nutrition is almost ignored" by the professional chef. This is more than just unfortunate, it is an actual health hazard for the patrons of public dining places. Many illnesses are aggravated by thoughtless food preparation. The food preparers, as well as the consumer, must become more aware of why we eat in the first place; it is, as Pikarski notes, "to sustain life, not to sever it." In addition, he goes on to remind us that "if everyone understood the basics of nutrition, they would become vegetarians."[3]

In promoting vegetarianism on the professional level, he is helping to make nutrition as important a part of gastronomy as taste and visual appeal. Conversely, he has made taste and visual appeal an important part of cooking nutritious vegetarian meals, which have long suffered a reputation for being bland and boring. Brother Ron has proven that the vegetarian chef can artistically create dishes that are not only healthy and whole—salads, breads, soups, entrees, and even desserts—but that also taste delightful and enticing. There really is no need for the standard escoffier preparations of lamb and beef, or veal and stuffed poultry.[4]

Personal taste is frequently conditioned by misconceptions. The notion of vegetarians eating nothing but dried crusts of pumpernickel bread with unseasoned broths, or iceberg lettuce leaves topped with tasteless heapings of soybeans or sprouts, is obviously an outmoded one born of ignorance or prejudice. Some people cling stubbornly to such images. It may not be so much that they are either ignorant or malicious, but rather simply resistant to change. Perhaps they fear the risk of altering their time-honored life-style handed down to them by their parents and even grandparents. Dietary habits form a strong link in one's connection with his self-image and social role. To change a long-held pattern of eating may be too unsettling a change for some people to undertake all at once. But if they are willing to explore new associations and not be shackled by static self-images and traditions, they might become more rational and less emotional and defensive when it comes to re-examining the way they eat. After all, they may be rattling their psycho-social underpinnings some, but they have good health and a long, active life to look forward to.

For the person who is ready to venture into the land of broccoli and cauliflower, leaving behind the slum of sautéed kidneys, broiled chops, and chopped liver, there are many fine vegetarian cookbooks to lead the way. Vegetarian foods should be whole and natural. They must be prepared in such a way that their unique and subtle taste is allowed to gently present itself. Unlike meat, poultry, or processed foods, vegetarian dishes should not be heavy, strong, or overbearing. Vegetables, grains, beans, and fruits issue from the earth, and so should be grown in harmony with the environment. Therefore, as fine cuisine, they must be prepared and presented in a smooth, subtle, balanced manner. They should be eaten to both enhance and perpetuate life. This will undoubtedly be a very new (and rewarding) experience for the person accustomed to preparing animal products which came forth not through the gentle giving earth, but through the painful experience endured by living creatures being raised in cold, sterile animal factories only to be brutally slaughtered and butchered to satisfy our eager palates and enrich modern industry.

Food is life. Everything that one ingests becomes a part of his being through the process of digestion and assimilation. If we are what we eat, then it only makes sense to be sure that we eat foods that are natural, unaltered, and alive. It is important that they be tasty and appealing, but they must also possess integrity and substance. Vegetarian foods are those foods that meet all these criteria, because as a vegetarian you want to be alive and integral and substantial as well as attractive in both body and character.

Not everyone chooses a vegetarian life-style for the same reasons. Some seek the subtle strength and energy of mind, body, and spirit that may be obtained through this diet. Others suffer from long, debilitating illnesses and are trying to tap into the healing, rebalancing nature of the foods from the earth. Still others understand the horrors of world hunger and animal slaughter and wish to play their part in lessening the pain of others. They do this by refusing to support the wasteful, inefficient, and violent animal-food industries. There are many other reasons, and most vegetarians could be placed in several of these categories. For the most part, vegetarians are generally sensitive to the world around and within themselves. They seek the energy, balance, and healing of live foods, and are attuned to the needless suffering of their co-inhabitants, both man and beast.

Children in our society are so bombarded by the mass appeals of the meat and dairy and junk-food–convenience-food industries, that their visions of the profound role of food in their lives is frequently clouded. To make matters worse few have appropriate role models in the family to learn from. Still, some children do freely choose a vegetarian life-style. One such ten-year-old boy recently told an interviewer from *Vegetarian Times*, "You are what you eat. If you eat a chicken, it's dead and you're putting deadness inside you. If you eat fruit, it's alive. You're putting life inside you." He continued, "You know that McDonald's commercial? They show the meat being cut up, cooked and made into a hamburger. If they showed the first step, a beautiful cow and then a butcher chopping its head off, they'd go out of business."[5]

This boy was fortunate to have a positive role model. His father had turned to vegetarianism ten years before in an attempt to reverse a serious health problem. But most children and teenagers not only lack a close role model, but are not even aware that vegetarianism exists as an alternative life-style. Why should they question fast-food hamburgers when their whole lives are surrounded by McDonald's commercials and billboards, and their parents and friends all seem to enjoy them? If they are not directly exposed to vegetarianism, they probably don't even know what the word means. How many vegetarian commercials has your child seen while watching Saturday-morning cartoons?

Role models, you can see, are imperative if a child is to be given a choice. The young boy whose stories we have recounted here had the role model, and then went on to realize for himself that eating meat was making him sluggish, heavy, and unathletic. Now, as a vegetarian, he finds himself concentrating better on his studies, having more strength and energy to play sports, and his classmates say he's the healthiest kid in school.[6] Let's not underestimate the intelligence or resolve of a child, but simply introduce him or her to the available alternatives.

Many people turn to vegetarianism in their adult years to thwart sickness and disease. Magazines like *Prevention* (Rodale Press) and *Vegetarian Times* (Vegetarian Life and Times, Inc.), as well as many popular health books, list countless case histories of individuals who have reversed or stabilized life-threatening diseases and illnesses by omitting animal products from their diets. Most of these complications could be avoided by eating for health as well as taste, before the onset of debilitating sicknesses.

TASTE AS A HEALING MECHANISM

Eating right to prevent illness promotes health and is far more beneficial than waiting until we are already sick—perhaps hopelessly so. Our personal taste provides us with an innate mechanism to do just that if we are willing to work along with it. Western medicine recognizes four basic tastes: sweet, sour, salty, and bitter. The nasal and oral chemoreceptor cells allow us to recognize distinct taste qualities. The taste buds themselves are in the mucosa in our mouths and throats, and in the walls of our tongues.[7] Our perception of food is made possible by the interaction of all our senses: taste, smell, sight, and touch. The capacity to sense our food helps us not only to select and enjoy it, but also to avoid nonfoods or even dangerous foods like those that may be poisoned, rancid, or putrid. Each individual develops his own unique sense of taste that determines which flavors and foods he likes or dislikes.

An ancient healing system known as Ayurvedic medicine teaches us that flavors and tastes are not only useful for pleasure, they also have the ability to tune our bodies into the specific foods and nutrients, textures and qualities, that are appropriate for our internal balancing, wellness maintenance, and even cleansing and healing. In the Ayurvedic system, taste is not only useful to perceive pleasure, but it may also help us to integrate foods that benefit our well-being while eliminating those that block it. We should not think of taste as a static quality that, once established, can be stored in the archives of our personal preferences. Taste is a living, dynamic sense that is ever changing, adapting to the body's needs at any given moment.[8]

Choosing foods should not be as simple as, "I don't like peppers," or, "I'll only eat it if it's broiled," or, "I have to have a glass of orange juice every morning at 7:30." Taste allows us to determine what foods are appropriate for our specific needs at a given moment. Your body may really need a high-protein, high-fiber food at one moment, and reject those same qualities at another moment. You must learn to be aware of these subtle changes in your internal requirements and then feed your body what it needs when it needs it. If you are driving your car and the red warning light reading "hot" flashes on, you know a cooling agent is needed. So perhaps you put water in the radiator. You certainly wouldn't change your tires! And just because the radiator needed water at that moment doesn't mean that every day after that, at the same time, you should add water to your radiator. You maintain your car by attuning yourself to precisely what it needs—and how much and what quality—and then seeing that it gets precisely that. Doesn't it make sense to do the same thing for your body? You may not have squeaky brakes at your feet or red warning signals on your forehead, but you do have your sense of taste to help you.

Ayurvedic medicine dates back to somewhere around 1000 B.C., when, in ancient India, a medical specialist named Charak and a famous surgeon named Susruta wrote two texts describing the system. Known as "life's knowledge," from its Sanskrit root words *ayu* and *veda*, the Ayurvedic system dealt with many aspects of medicine, including toxicology, pediatrics, and gynecology. Its healing principle—little studied or understood in the West—goes beyond simple diagnosis of disease and treatment of its symptoms. The dual focus is on uncovering and remedying the root causes through a total approach of mental, physical, and spiritual discipline.[9] If someone has a cold, this approach might include an investigation of the person's attitudes toward his work, a detailed review of his diet, and the uncovering of his feelings about his purpose in life and his relationship to nature. A Western approach might well be purely symptom-oriented: give the patient two aspirins and send him to bed; if the stuffy nose and runny eyes clear up, he is cured—end of case.

The Ayurvedic system contends that through our sense of taste we are capable of deciphering six different taste qualities. Four of them are the same ones that we recognize in the West—the other two are pungent and astringent. These two different tastes play a critical role in health and healing, because they are like the warning lights on our car. They advise us what we require or should avoid at any given time, but only if we pay attention to them.[10] If you are dining at a Mexican restaurant and unwittingly bite into a seemingly harmless jalapeño pepper, you may suddenly feel like smoke is about to pour out of your ears. You have just received the message that this little bit of food is extremely pungent. Anyone who has ever puckered when sampling pickled cucumbers has experienced astringency. While these cues may be hard to miss, most tastes are far subtler, challenging us to be ever more attentive to what they are telling us about our body's requirements for total health and balance.

Our body does not know if we have a Western or Eastern perception of the universe. It has its own intelligence. If we bite into a bean taco with tofu dressing in a blue-corn shell, for instance, we are stimulating many senses simultaneously. Sight, smell, and taste all cooperate to cue our body that digestion must commence. Specific enzymes are then secreted to help us assimilate the food we have ingested. The more wholesome and nutritionally balanced the food is, the more uncomplicated is the process of enzyme secretion. Rich foods, processed flours, heavy sweets, and fatty meats make digestion a real chore instead of a simple, normal biological activity.

Understanding what our body has to tell us begins where digestion begins—in the mouth. When we chew our food, enzymes are released to break down food particles which, in turn, release a variety of flavors. The more we chew, the more flavors we receive. So in order to best "understand" what our food is telling us through the stimulation of our taste buds, we must chew thoroughly and thoughtfully. Some experts say we should chew each bite fifty times. Of course the more we chew the better we digest our food, so we get double benefits by taking our time when we eat . . . chewing slowly . . . digesting properly . . . sensing the effects that the food is having on our bodies. On top of all this, chewing slowly even helps us to control our weight because we feel full faster and so we eat less.

While wholesome vegetarian foods offer us many interesting smells, flavors, and textures as we chew them, overprocessed and junk foods only confuse our bodies. They require very little chewing because they have already been ultra-refined, and our bodies try to dispose of all the strange chemical and artificial tastes as quickly as possible. We tend, therefore, to eat far more in far less time, taking in huge amounts of empty calories which get stored as fat. To confuse our bodies even further, we try to make these denatured, monotaste foods more interesting by heaping salt, sugar, ketchup, mayonnaise, butter, and other worthless or harmful additives on top of them. It is not difficult to see how the onslaught of fast, fried foods; artificially colored, sugary soft drinks; and chemically fabricated "milk" shakes lead us to the door of obesity and disease.

REPROGRAMMING YOUR TASTE

If you are a junk-food offender, as so many Americans are, you undoubtedly find it difficult to enjoy good, wholesome grains and vegetables. This is because your body has become conditioned by repeated use and overuse to prefer refined and chemically treated foods. You are probably not used to having to chew your food well because these refined foods have so little substance that they require virtually no effort to swallow, especially if we chase them down with liquids. Eating good and fibrous foods may annoy you as you search for familiar tastes. The more you try them, though, the more your body will adapt to the new tastes and textures. You will ultimately find it to be a surprisingly pleasant experience. Your body will be glad to be getting the nutrients it craves.

Ayurvedic medicine teaches us that food cravings are one way that our bodies do in fact "tell us something." We should learn to "listen" to our instincts. They should be warning us of imbalances that need to be corrected. For instance, if we are craving water-soluble foods, it may be because our body tissues, which are mostly water based, are in need of them in order to continue functioning properly and efficiently.[11]

So if our body is craving something alkaline, it may be to offset a high acidity. Don't make matters worse by sending out for pizza and a six-pack of beer. The tomato sauce will increase your level of acidity while the beer will interfere with your ability to digest the fatty, high-cholesterol cheese and meat (if you chose one for a topping). Try instead something light and easily assimilated like tofu, or something particularly alkaline like oatmeal. If you tune into the messages your body is sending out, you will instinctively eat foods that balance and enliven you, adding to your health, vigor, and enjoyment of life.

FOURTEEN
Religious Beliefs

D iet has always had a definite place in the teachings of the world's
great religions. Particular doctrines and guidelines vary, of course,
but within each discipline there are specific things that are taught
about food. Religion has always recognized the fact that one's spiritual awareness involves to some degree his physical state. It is
difficult to be pure of spirit while inhabiting a polluted body. Physical
purity has been equated with a vegetarian regimen for thousands
of years by many religious groups.

Christian and Jewish dietary guidelines date back to the earliest
times, when all foods except fruits, seeds, and nuts were forbidden
by God. After the Great Flood destroyed the local vegetation, it did
become permissible to kill, only the clean animals, for food.[1] Clearly,
vegetarianism was considered to be more godly.

SEVENTH-DAY ADVENTISTS

The Seventh-Day Adventists are one Christian sect that has preached the benefits of whole vegetarian foods since first being formed in the nineteenth century. Considered to be among the healthiest people in the United States, they still believe that a strong, pure body is essential to the spiritual aspirant. What one eats is as important as how one prays, since both are ways of communicating with the divine.

Ellen G. White, one of the founders of the Seventh-Day Adventist Church, advised her loyal followers to adopt a vegetarian diet. An eminent clairvoyant, her words of advice—taken to be divinely inspired by her disciples—on the subject of meat were resounding: "Among those who are waiting for the coming of the Lord, meat eating will eventually be done away. Vegetables, fruits and grains should compose our diet. . . . The eating of flesh is unnatural. Many die of disease caused wholly by meat-eating; yet, the world does not seem to be the wiser. The moral evils of a flesh diet are not less marked than are the physical ills. Flesh food is injurious to health and whatever affects the body has a corresponding effect on the mind and soul."[2]

It is difficult to weigh the spiritual effects of meat consumption in terms of scientific research, but White's warnings of its physical effects have been shown to be accurate. An estimated one-half of the current church membership is orthodox in living by the church's founding principles of both spiritual and physical health. Only vegetarian meals are served in the hospitals and colleges run by the Seventh-Day Adventists. Determined to see just how physically beneficial this life-style really is, researchers studied its long-term effects. They found overwhelming evidence indicating that this group is far healthier than the national norm. It has a substantially lower incidence of all-too-common degenerative ailments like heart and respiratory disease, while the occurrence of cancer was shown to be less than half that of the national rate. Whatever the immeasurable benefits are of following the church's spiritual guidelines, there is no question of the healthful benefits of adhering to its dietary regimen. In fact, the contemporary Seventh-Day Adventist would tell you, as White did many years ago, that the two are inseparable, with physical health feeding spiritual calm and insight.

HEBRAIC TRADITION

Jewish tradition holds the preparation, consumption, and even storage of food to be of utmost spiritual concern. Meat and dairy products must not be eaten or cooked together, demanding that cooking utensils be kept separate and special kitchen arrangements be made. Animals and poultry must be carefully inspected before slaughter, and if found imperfect they are rejected. Otherwise they are slaughtered according to strict guidelines. The blood, for instance, must be thoroughly drained since its impurity would impair one's spiritual clarity. Food selection and handling is treated as a serious religious issue here, and has introduced moral and ethical as well as dietary awareness into the culinary habits of all who follow the Judaic tradition.[3]

In the Talmudic writings, Jews are taught that "danger to life nullifies all religious obligations." Psychology professor Dr. Louis A. Berman notes that this principle is one of the cornerstones of a long-standing Jewish preference for vegetarianism. Anything that poses a threat to, or even fails to promote the balance and harmony of, physical well-being diminishes one's ability to fully participate in the religious experience. Coupled with a time-honored compassion for all living creatures, this attitude points the disciple clearly in the direction of vegetarianism.

The rabbinic literature is replete with recommendations on the treatment of animals. It admonishes us to never allow an animal to be thirsty for the sake of reducing its food intake, and to even refrain from shouting at it just to stop it from eating. Its deep empathy for humankind, also, leads to an awareness of the fact that starving people the world over benefit from vegetarianism. The person who does not eat meat or dairy products has found a practical, healthful way of demonstrating love for his fellow man and reducing the suffering of animals. Judaism treats the human body not merely as a machine, but as a vibrating, vital force in the scheme of things. Food is not merely its fuel but, in a very real way, part of its spiritual essence.[4]

EASTERN TRADITIONS

The usual division between human and animal life is an arbitrary and schematic one according to the teachings of many world religions. Eastern religions, especially, have taught us the essential unity of all living things. To separate life into categories—man, animal, fish, insect, and so forth—is to deal with the world at face value, as it appears to be. At a deeper level, though, runs a unifying cord known as the soul. All life is essentially one, each being (soul) taking on various attributes at different times and in different embodiments. That the soul does not die but simply leaves the body, only to be "reincarnated"—or re-embodied—is one of the basic axioms in Hinduism and Jainism.[5] This belief in what is known as the "transmigration of souls" makes the intentional killing of animals a grave transgression against the spiritual law that binds the universe. To slaughter animals is to disregard the one-ness of all beings, to be misled by their apparent and transitory separateness.

These ideas may seem foreign to the Western mind accustomed to dealing with things as they appear, and not as they are at some deeper level of essence. We may or may not believe that souls actually transmigrate. On a very practical level, though, what is being taught is not very different from the concerns of universal love and kindness to follow creatures preached by Judaism and Christianity. If all living creatures are one in essence, then to kill an animal is no different than to kill a man or even God. All are inseparably one. In *Vegetarianism and Occultism*, C.W. Leadbeater discusses the reverence for life that explains the preference for vegetarianism among Eastern religions: "The man who ranges himself on the side of evolution realizes the wickedness of destroying life; for he knows that, just as he is here in this physical body in order that he may learn the lessons of this plane, so is the animal occupying his body for the same reason, and through it he may gain experience at his lower stage. He knows that the life behind the animal is Divine Life, that all life in the world is Divine; the animals therefore are truly our brothers."[6]

BUDDHISM

Vegetarianism is commonplace in both China and Japan—Buddhist strongholds for nearly fifteen hundred years. Some observers feel that this is partly due to general food shortages in these countries due to extremely dense populations and limited acreage suitable for tilling. In fact, fish and pork are popular, especially with the middle class that can afford them. Buddhism itself, though, must be considered to be largely responsible for the fact that most of the people in China and Japan still live on what Americans would consider an austere diet of vegetables and grains and legumes. There is a basic reluctance to sustain life by killing fellow creatures. The average middle-class Japanese person, therefore, eats little more than half a pound of meat in a full month's time.[7]

MACROBIOTICS

Many people today have adapted the macrobiotic diet developed by Japanese George Ohsawa around the end of World War II. Ohsawa was severely ill when he discovered that the ancient Taoist doctrine of yin and yang dualism was pertinent to the selection and preparation of foods. His application of a diet based on those principles led to his remarkable recovery from a case of terminal tuberculosis and propelled him into a fruitful, healthful life. He want on to elaborate the diet and called it *macrobiotics*, meaning "long life."[8] Others, since, have taken up this vital diet based on the religious principles and traditional medical knowledge of Japan.

Dualism is a common aspect of pre-Socratic Greek as well as of ancient Chinese philosophy. But it is perhaps in Zen Buddhism that it is put to most practical use. It is proposed, in this system, that there exists a fine balance between the yin and yang opposition. It is through the understanding and attainment of this vital balance that one reaches a state of physical as well as spiritual harmony. Herein lies the vast healing power of macrobiotics. It should be noted that yin and yang are not strictly dietary principles, and that as a healing system, macrobiotics is not simply a dietary regimen. All things in the universe are governed by these two forces, and it is only through balancing one's total life-style that one reaches a state of dynamic balance and vital health. Yin is the passive, female element responsible for such qualities as silence, stillness, cold, and darkness. Food with yin qualities promote relaxation and expansion. Yang is the active, male element responsible for such qualities as sound, motion, heat, and light. Foods with yang qualities promote contraction and activity.[9]

Examples of extreme yang foods are eggs, meat, poultry, and salt. Examples of extreme yin foods are sugar, chocolate, honey, saccharin, alcohol, refined flour, tropical fruits, and chemicals such as most food additives and drugs.[10] These foods, which are at one or the other extreme end of the yin/yang spectrum, are not the foods that we should be eating on a regular basis, since they tend to cause imbalance, extremism, and disharmony. We should instead look for foods that are in the middle of the spectrum. Ohsawa feels that grains, especially rice, are the most balanced foods in this respect, and therefore the most health-promoting.

The macrobiotic diet is specifically outlined with the primary design of eliminating imbalances in the body, which lead to disease. While the potential always exists for rebalancing and regaining ease and health, it is far easier to avoid the trauma of disease to begin with, by eating foods that maintain a peaceful harmony and holism of body, mind, and spirit. Macrobiotics is discussed in further detail in chapter 16.

HINDUISM

Hinduism is well known in the West for its adherence to the doctrine of reincarnation. Yoga—an offshoot of orthodox Hinduism—combines meditative exercise and breathing techniques with a vegetarian regimen into a religious tradition based on the idea of reincarnation. Yoga first became known to the West only for its exercise program, but today many people in our part of the world embrace it as a religion. The yogi believes that all living beings go through a series of rebirths, taking on many forms. It is not surprising, then, that meat eating is thought to bring on negative karma, and is therefore strictly forbidden.[11] A vegetarian yogic diet may emphasize fruits or vegetables or fermented dairy products, whatever is believed to create the greatest life energy. Meat is thought to be toxic, on the other hand, because decomposing flesh comes from death.

The New Vrindaban International Society for Krishna Consciousness is another Indian sect that has developed a significant following in the West in recent years. While this group has ties to the teachings of Lord Chaitanya going back some five centuries, it was founded in just 1966 by his Divine Grace A.C. Bhaktivedanta Swami Prabhupada. Krishna devotees seek to experience profound religious revelation and ecstasy after sessions of chantings of the Maka mantra. But in order to be prepared for this divine occurrence, one must live a proper life by keeping four rules of conduct: no gambling, no intoxication, no extramarital sex, and no meat eating. The foods that are eaten are thought to possess purifying qualities especially when

ceremoniously blessed. The food—called *prasadam* or "mercy"—
is thought to possess special qualities that are not only nourishing,
but spiritually stimulating and awakening.[12]

The Rajneesh Foundation in Maharashtra, India, also embraces
vegetarianism. Its founder, Bhagwan Shree Rajneesh, believes that
physical purification must precede spiritual evolution. The first step
in this direction is to refrain from eating anything dead, because it
only deadens your character. To eat something that has been delivered to us through violence only instills in us a violent and aggressive nature. The vegetarian is more graceful and at ease with
his environment and with his fellow creatures because his diet con-
sists of foods that are whole and alive.

Rajneesh tells us that there is a clear choice to be made between
eating or rejecting meat, with clearly different results: "Vegetarianism is a form of purification. When you eat animals, you become
heavy and gravitate towards earth. A light vegetarian diet, in contrast, gives more grace and power. Rather than gravitate, you levitate
towards the sky. Like a person who is going to climb a mountain,
the lighter the load, the easier the ascent. Why carry more than you
have to?"[13]

THE SUFIS

In the land of Mohammed, the Islamic Sufi sect has been known
for centuries for its mystical qualities that have been borrowed
from Zoroastrianism. They once wore undyed wool garments called
"sufi": hence their name. The wool garments were worn because
they caused bodily discomfort—a discomfort that was believed to
be pleasing to the god Allah since it showed a total disregard for
the comforts of the flesh and the material things of the world.
Modern Western sufis are not the ascetics that their Eastern counterparts are, yet some do practice the famous whirling-type dancing
of the "dervishes"—an esoteric group of Sufis who seek to elevate
their level of consciousness beyond the physical realm through
ecstatic forms of dancing. The Sufis also practice austerity in the
form of vegetarianism, a life-style adopted because of its simplicity
and denial of gluttony and excess. Their diets are akin to those of
the yogi.[14]

THE VEGAN SOCIETY

The Vegan Society, founded in England in 1944, is not really a religious group, but its emphasis on nonviolence and a reverence for life gives it a fundamentally spiritual focus. Vegans will not eat any animal products and they work hard to include in the diet the most wholesome, alive, and energy-filled foods. Therefore, they emphasize unaltered, unprocessed, whole foods such as raw vegetables and fruits, nuts, seeds, and grains. Alcohol, tea, coffee, soda, processed foods, and tobacco are entirely shunned.[15]

The meat and dairy industries are largely responsible for a spiritual pollution that is recognized by many of the world's religions and many other groups and individuals who have a reverence for life. The mindless slaughter of innocent animals to fill a dietary need that does not exist deteriorates the spiritual bonding of the earth's living beings. The violence and bloodshed and suffering sets loose a negativity that echoes throughout the vaulted halls of what we like to call civilization. A negative psychic effect that begins in the animal factories and slaughterhouses can be felt rippling throughout the world.

Amid this spiritual malaise, religions and humanitarian groups have attempted to establish the vegetarian way of life as the healthful antidote required by individuals and society alike. We have all heard that the human body is a temple which shelters our spiritual core. That is why religious leaders and teachers and novitiates and devotees have recognized the importance of adopting a vegetarian lifestyle. Whole grains give us substance, sprouts and juices offer us energy, and vegetables provide the vitality and variety essential to good health. But even more, a wholesome vegetarian diet is the underpinning of the harmony and balance of body, mind, and spirit.

FIFTEEN

Reverence
for
Life

We have heard that we live in a violent world. Do you believe it? The incredible statistics of how many animals were killed around the world in a single recent year speak for themselves: over 214 million cattle and calves, 615 million hogs, 377 million lambs and sheep, 128 million goats, 9 million horses and almost 19 million metric tons of birds.[1] In the United States alone, 140 million cows, calves, sheep, lambs, and pigs and 3½ billion chickens and turkeys are slaughtered on an annual basis.[2] In a seventy-year lifetime, the average American eats 11 cows, 1 calf, 3 lambs and sheep, 23 hogs, 45 turkeys, 1,097 chickens and 861 pounds of fish.[3]

The wanton slaughter of animals in such large numbers gives us an idea of just how violent our world has become and just how little regard we have for life. Many people that eat meat probably profess to like animals, but believe that if we were all to become vegetarians the animal population would soon outstrip that of humans. Can they really like animals, though, knowing the suffering and pain inflicted on them by their chosen dietary habits? The horrible way in which animals are treated in society shows a total disregard and lack of reverence for life in general. And should animal overpopulation be a matter of concern to the vegetarian? It seems rather obvious that without the meat eaters' demand for beef and pork, it would no longer be necessary or profitable to breed livestock and pigs. If they are no longer bred, then how can they overpopulate?

If people were truly concerned about animals, they would never condone the hell they are put through while alive, to say nothing about their tortuous slaughter. Animals do not enjoy the sunshine or roam the fields or smell the fresh grass after a gentle springtime rain. They are isolated in dark cells, herded into tight quarters so that they can barely move, and there, are fed and maintained while they await their slaughter. Their life is like that of the unjustly condemned prisoner who lives out his days on death row, awaiting his ultimate death by decree.

Animals are not raised on farms any more, but in animal factories. They are seldom cared for by a small farmer running a family business, but by factory management constantly seeking ways to increase profit and decrease overhead. At this time virtually all poultry and better than half of the cows, pigs, and cattle live their days like inmates of a mechanized factory environment. Poultry, pigs, and calves live in total confinement, never to see the light of day until they head for the slaughterhouse. Hens are frequently crowded into tiny cages which they do not leave for a year or two. Pregnant sows are tightly housed to control their movement. They can barely squeeze their bodies into the minute stalls that are their homes for three months at a time. Cattle and pigs sometimes get to enjoy open-air feeding lots, but even there they are tended to strictly by machines which feed them, water them and remove their waste. This factory method of animal farming has greatly endangered the small traditional farmers. Today, about 95 percent of hens, chickens, and turkeys, and more than half of the beef cattle, dairy cows, and pigs are raised in this kind of impersonal, high-tech environment.[4]

Agribusiness has little interest in the natural instincts of animals. Confinement is so complete that chickens don't even have enough room to flap their wings. Mating is so controlled and normal sexual activity so hampered that male animals commonly become impotent and females cannot even menstruate regularly. If you lived shoulder to shoulder with other people, day after day in a city of walls with no escape, no natural light, controlled central air systems instead of fresh air, what do you think would happen? Predictably, animals living under those conditions become so highly aggressive and violent that normal interaction is rare. Subsequent depression lowers the will and the ability to fight off disease and infection, which can easily become epidemic.

Agribusiness may not be concerned about the natural instincts of animals per se, but they are when their repression cuts into capital gain. Disease resulting from the horrendous living conditions described can be very costly. If animals die, they cannot create profits but become only so much spoilage. Rather than improve the animals' living conditions, though, producers prefer to initiate "health programs." These programs are not designed to improve health, but to control sickness. Over half the cattle and nearly all pigs, calves, and poultry are fed a steady diet of antibiotics and related medications to keep infection and contagious disease at a controlled level.[5] One FDA official advises us that "antibiotics are most effective in the early growing period and in warding off diseases in animals that are crowded or improperly housed or malnourished."[6]

Antibiotics in animal feed actually stimulate quicker weight gain while improving the efficiency of livestock feed some 16 percent. This might seem to solve the economic problems of producing meat in animal factories, but it bypasses the question of the rights of animals to decent, natural, and even happy lives. Moreover, no one is sure what the long-term side effects may eventually prove to be for the people who eat these meat and dairy products—products that may very well be substantially altered by the heavy antibiotic use in animal "health" programs.

"Commercially extraneous behavior" is what meat and poultry producers call activities that may be natural to an animal but economically undesirable.[7] Methods are devised to inhibit natural —"extraneous"—behavior. Poultry are "debeaked" so they will not peck when under stress, and pigs have their tails cut off because they tend to bite them. Not only physical behavior is controlled, but so are biochemical processes. Hormones are given to intervene in reproductive system activity: to produce an exceptionally large number of ova in the female, and to keep the animals' labor contractions and delivery time on schedule—that is, on the animal factory schedule.[8]

There is a recent trend in the United States toward creating fewer and larger feedlots. *Feedstuffs* reports that this trend is expected to mean big overhead cuts for the animal industries, but even greater discomfort and inhumane treatment for the animals. Chickens are now given only one-sixth the space that laying hens had in 1954, for instance. Animals are being pushed closer and closer together to cut the cost of operations as well as fixed overhead. On top of these savings, as an animal's physical activity is restricted by lack of space, it eats less and gains weight faster.[9] But even though overhead and feed costs may dip, obese animals can also become burdensome and undesirable. Chickens frequently gain so much weight that they cannot even stand up without industrial intervention. Obese cattle may have fatty livers and abscesses that may make them more difficult to market and certainly less desirable.[10]

Stress, accompanied by low tolerance to infection, disease, and unusual situations, is a typical problem with the factory-produced animal. Pigs are known to suffer greatly while they are being transported to the slaughterhouse. Their respiration and heart rate increase. The blood vessels may constrict from muscular tension, causing insufficient circulation of blood and oxygen deficiency. A circulatory and respiratory collapse may ensue.[11] Many pigs cannot even stand during the trip to the slaughterhouse because of skeletal rigidity, while others are dead long before they ever reach their destination. More than $1 billion is lost because of livestock injuries, stress, and death resulting from their mishandling and transport.[12]

Not all money-saving steps taken by animal producers result in bigger profits. Animal rights activist Dr. Michael Fox contends that happier, less stressed, and more naturally raised animals would spell greater productivity while cutting deeply into the costly problems of infection, sickness, and untimely death. He insists that "husbandry conditions should also allow the animal some opportunity to develop, explore and experience its *telos* to some degree—its 'pigness,' 'chickness' or whatever."[13] He goes on to list typical basic needs that should be fulfilled instead of curtailed.

> Freedom to perform natural physical movement;
>
> Association with other animals, where appropriate, of their own kind;
>
> Facilities for comfort activities (rest, sleep, body care);
>
> Provision of food and water to maintain full health;

Ability to perform daily routines of natural activities;

Opportunity for the activities of exploration and play, especially for young animals;

Satisfaction of minimal spatial and territorial requirements including a visual field and "personal space."[14]

Most cattlemen are not too concerned about the comfort of animals being herded off to slaughter. They are very concerned, though, that the color and quality of the meat be suitable for the marketplace. Flesh is known to turn darker than desired in frightened cattle; the terror that they experience creates actual chemical and physiological changes in the animals' bodies.[15]

Roy Atkinson, president of the National Farmers' Union of Canada, is one person who has complained about the inhumane treatment of animals and its effects on the consumer of meat products: "We are living in the midst of a social system gone mad, we are paying vast sums of money to sabotage public health." To control animal growth rates and disease, he says, producers "confine animals close together, feed them scientifically calculated diets and shoot them full of drugs to speed their growth and protect them from epidemics which are a real threat in the crowded conditions of livestock factories."[16]

People should know what they are eating. Leo Tolstoy, a vegetarian, once, it is said, presented a woman with a live chicken. She was told to decapitate and prepare it for cooking since she had requested chicken for dinner. She turned down the opportunity.[17] If more people were aware of what is involved in producing meat, they would probably be much less enthusiastic about dining on ham and hot dogs. Children are taught early to recognize all of their "barnyard friends"—their different sounds and peculiar habits. Yet, they may think nothing of eating a juicy hamburger or chicken leg until and unless they make the actual association between the food and its source. That juicy hamburger is the friendly brown cow with the big, gentle eyes, and the chicken leg is the same one that was being used by a real chicken that might have been seen running in the yard the day before.

Unfortunately, most people do not see the raw cuts of beef hanging on hooks while the blood drips dry, or hear the screams of the pig as it is hauled off to the slaughterhouse. Living in apartments in the city, and shopping for prime cuts of meat neatly packaged and nicely colored, we have lost touch with the actual processes of food gathering and food processing. We are too removed from the origins of our food, too insulated from the sights, sounds, and smells of the animal factories and slaughterhouses that we silently support by eating meat in fine restaurants and at the family table. Dr. Fox explains that "what the eye doesn't see, the consumer doesn't grieve: a styrofoam carton of impeccable eggs, neatly trimmed meat in plastic wrappers or a delicate slice of veal cordon bleu served on a silver platter does not tell the story."[18]

What would tell the story is a trip to an animal factory or slaughterhouse. Author Richard Rhodes gives us some idea of what such an experience might be like, as he describes his impressions at the ID Packing Company, a meat producer for the Armour Meat Company:

> Down goes the tailgate and out come the pigs enthusiastically after their drive. Pigs are the most intelligent of all farm animals, by actual laboratory test.... They talk a lot to each other, to you if you care to listen.... They do talk: Low grunts, quick squeals, a kind of hum sometimes, angry shrieks, high screams of fear.... It was a frightening experience, seeing their fear, seeing so many of them go by. It had to remind me of things no one wants to be reminded of anymore, all mobs, all death marches, all mass murders and extinctions, the slaughter of the buffalo, the slaughter of the Indian, the Inferno, Judgement Day.... That we are the most expensive of races, able in our affluence to hire others of our kind to do this terrible work of killing another race.[19]

Even though meat eating is allowed in the revised Judeo-Christian tradition, the inhumane treatment of animals is strictly forbidden. Rabbis have taught kindness to animals for centuries, while even the slaughter was performed as mercifully as possible by the *shochtim* (clergymen).[20] Still, it is difficult to reconcile compassion for animals and reverence for life with permission to eat meat, especially given the brutal reality of modern meat production. One may buy Kosher meat, but does that ameliorate the suffering of animals?

Isaac Bashevis Singer, author of *Yentl* and *The Family Moskat*, became a vegetarian when faced with the moral dilemma created by eating meat. He relates accounts of the brutal and heartless treatment of animals in *Blood* and *The Slaughter* and other works. He raises the issue of animals having as much right to life as man has, all creatures being God's creatures. He challenges the very basis of our social order in a *New York Times* article titled "When Keeping Kosher Isn't Kosher Enough." He asks, "How can we speak of right and justice if we take an innocent creature and shed its blood?"[21] Singer was interested in being a vegetarian even as a child, but his parents discouraged it. Now, for the past two decades he has championed the cause of vegetarianism, and has even adopted it as his religion. He had experienced understandable reservations with adhering to any religion that could justify the abominable practice of slaughtering animals.

Nowhere is reverence for life expressed more profoundly than in the philosophy of the vegans. No only do vegans refrain from meat eating, but they also shun dairy products and eggs. After all, they reason, animals suffer unbelievably in the production of these foods also. Mark Braunstein writes in *Radical Vegetarianism: Diet, Ethics and Dialectics* about the hapless hen—forced into endless labor throughout its life, and confined to tight quarters without hardly ever contacting the real world. The hen, he says, "must forever count her chickens before they hatch." Cows too, he notes, are treated sinfully. They are grossly overworked and have only the most meager quarters. They are even forced to surrender their young calves to the meat producers who are trying to fill the demand for tender veal. Braunstein ponders over just how vegetarian a person can claim to be if he insists on eating eggs and dairy. After all, he reasons, "what about the veal floating invisibly inside every glass of milk? There can be no quart of milk where there is no cutlet of veal." The vegetarian might protest that eggs and cheese have nutrients and protein essential to proper health, but Braunstein sees little difference between the vegetarian and the meat eater in this argument. Both insist that animals must be allowed to suffer so that people can have good nutrition. Braunstein counters that "this is the vegetarian dialectic of diet and ethic: that not coincidentally, but absolutely essentially, those foods which are the products of the least deprivation of life from others will contribute to the longest life in ourselves."[22]

The vegans' reverence for life runs deep and wide. They will not use any products that have been made possible by any degree of animal suffering. The list of banned items goes far beyond food. It includes fur, leather, silk, pearls, and animal-based soaps and cosmetics. A survey done in England indicates that some 83 percent of all vegans have chosen their life-style primarily for ethical reasons. They hold closely a reverence for life, coupled with a disdain for the atrocities wrought on animals in the name of convenience and commercialism. The second reason for their preferred life-style is their own personal health, and the third is to conserve our dwindling food supplies.[23]

The sort of mistreatment of animals that gives vegans so much cause for concern is exemplified by the dairy cow. A Vegan Society booklet tells us how dairy cows are scheduled by producers for annual pregnancies. They are only allowed to suckle the young calf for a maximum of three days, although in most cases the calf is taken for slaughter just after birth, to be processed as meat or to utilize its stomach lining as rennet for cheese.[24] It is little wonder that vegans are left scratching their heads when a "vegetarian" refuses to eat veal, and instead has a cheese casserole! Both require the suffering of animals—atrocities that few would care to hear about at the dinner table.

A certain number of calves are reserved to be used for white veal—a fine delicacy in many circles. But the animal must have its physical activity virtually stopped cold if it is to be tender and white. The calf is squeezed into a small crate where it stays for over a quarter of a year. Its diet is mostly liquid, frequently leaving the animal to eat at the siding of the crate in order to satisfy its natural craving for substance and roughage. By the time this confused animal is ready for slaughter, it can barely stand up without support —it is so lacking in normal muscle tissue, skeletal support, stamina, and vigor. Meanwhile, even the poor old dairy cow is chopped up into convenience-size meat packages after her milk dries up. Her flesh is too old for prime cuts, though, so it is only suitable for export.[25]

We must wonder why this violence and abuse is allowed to continue. The Texas Cattle Feeders Association's leader gives us a pretty good idea why: "We the cattle industry are willing to produce any kind of animal the consumer wants."[26] In other words this situation persists because we the consumers support it with our dollars and our eating habits. If you think that the consumer is not really capable of setting the pace for so vast an industry, think of what would happen to the meat and dairy industries if everyone became vegetarian. They would, of course, cease functioning. Land now being used and abused to grow animal feed could then be used to grow vegetables and grain for people. The wanton destruction of life would be diminished, and energy spent on killing and violence might begin to be used to foster peace and goodwill. How can we even hope for peace among men until we have taken steps toward establishing harmony with animal life?

An organizer of a World Vegetarian Congress in India is convinced that vegetarianism must precede international peace.

> "The demand for vegetarian food will increase our production for the right kind of plant foods. We shall cease to breed pigs and other animals for food, thereby ceasing to be responsible for the horror of slaughterhouses where millions of creatures cry in agony and in vain because of man's selfishness," he said. "If such concentration camps for slaughtering continue, can peace ever come to earth? Can we escape the responsibility for misery when we are practicing killing every day of our lives by consciously or unconsciously supporting this trade of slaughter? Peace cannot come where Peace is not given."[27]

Peter Singer, co-author of *Animal Factories*, is likewise concerned about the animal carnage that we too readily defend as a trade-off for human survival.

> The root of the problem is in our blithely taking power over the lives and deaths of other creatures, whose suffering is in no way necessary for our survival. If we so easily take the lives of animals who are only a few evolutionary steps removed from us, what is to prevent us from doing the same to humans who are physically very different from us—of a different color, or speaking an unintelligible language, or "primitive" in their customs?[28]

The exploitation of animals is nothing new to civilization. Its roots can be traced back a good 10,000 years.[29] But it has become a particularly perilous problem in the twentieth century in the presence of mechanized technology, antibiotics and hormones, and horrendously artificial living conditions. Animal care is no longer a simple matter of man caring for animal—feeding, watering, cleaning, and doctoring it. Now machines tend to the basic animal care, hormones are used to make them grow, antibiotics help keep them from dying prematurely. Raised in horribly close quarters and unnatural environments, obese and unhealthy from lack of exercise and excessive drug use, and depressed from lack of warmth, affection, and normal social interaction—modern-day animals are exploited more completely than animals have ever been before. They are physically abused, mentally tortured, and spiritually castrated.

Mahatma Gandhi taught us that "the greatness of a nation and its moral progress can be judged by the way its animals are treated."[30] If that is true, then Michael Fox must think little of our moral progress as a nation. He tells us that "today, many animal rights and welfare concerns are flatly opposed by economic cost/benefit justifications to an extent and consistency that seem to indicate that we think only in terms of economics and this now takes precedence over ethics. Yet, in the final analysis, surely the greater concern is poverty, not of the pocket, but of the spirit."[31]

Fox believes that part of the problem lies in our feeling that man is very different than animal, and certainly far superior. This separation hinders us from holding a respect for the animal as an equal—an equal in terms of the basic rights that all living creatures share in common. He says, "Although it is an established biological and ecological fact that humans, other animals and nature are inseparable, it is clear that both culturally and philosophically humans are very separate, if not alienated, from the rest of creation." He goes on to reason that to deny animals basic rights simply because their intellectual level is beneath ours, is like denying the rights of "all idiots, pre-verbal children and others who cannot or do not respect others' rights."[32]

The abuse and exploitation of animals is just business as usual in the United States. The meat companies campaign for our dollars, the mass media supports their efforts, the consumer puts up the money, and the slaughterhouse keeps churning. It is all symptomatic of "an unbalanced, if not distorted state of mind and of a growing atrophy of the human spirit."[33]

Supporting animal rights is a matter of upholding a reverence for life. All living creatures share a spiritual bond that, when broken, endangers their survival. We should stop the killing and slaughter of animals because it violates their rights and defiles our own spirit. The only alternative is adopting a vegetarian life-style. This would spare the lives of innocent beasts, allow us to use our natural resources and food supplies more efficiently, and help to re-establish an ecological balance in our world. Once these steps have been taken, we may finally find ourselves in a position for establishing a realistic base for world peace.

SIXTEEN

The Macrobiotic Way to Health

M any people are beginning to utilize the principles of a macrobiotic diet in order to prevent or overcome illnesses. There
have been many claims that people have been able to help themselves with diseases as serious as cancer by eating the macrobiotic
way. Yet, we are frequently warned by friends and physicians that
to abandon traditional medical care of disease could be terribly
misleading and even dangerous. We are urged to not waste effort
on diets and risk losing the opportunity for timely traditional care.
By the time we have decided that macrobiotics is not helping our
condition, the argument goes, it may be too late to get help from
the medical treatment that may have saved us.

In light of these two opposing views of the healing efficacy of
macrobiotics, we need to examine more closely just what the macrobiotic way is, and whether or not it may really be of therapeutic
value and under what conditions. If indeed, this diet can be helpful,
we will need to know just what is involved in adapting it to our
current life-styles.

Macrobiotics is really more than just a diet. It is a philosophy and a way of living that seeks to establish balance and harmony, and foster optimal health and a long life. (The very word *macrobiotic* means "long life.") The entire universe, including the foods we eat, is understood in terms of the dualism between expansion (yin) and contraction (yang). As a dietary regimen it challenges us to eat foods that are neither extreme yin nor extreme yang, but which fall somewhere in between. Yin and yang could be viewed as a continuum, with the extreme ends standing in complete opposition to one another—like hot and cold. Yin is female, passive, and expanding; extreme yin foods include light dairy items, coffee, sugar and other stimulants, alcohol, and tropical fruits and vegetables. Yang is male, active, and contracting; extreme yang foods include the heavy dairy items, meat, eggs, and poultry. Those foods that best avoid these two extremes are grains, most vegetables, legumes, and sea vegetables. Most of the macrobiotic diet revolves around these foods in various combinations.

Followers of this dietary discipline are also encouraged to eat mostly locally grown foods in season. Michio Kushi, who was instrumental in bringing the macrobiotic way to the U.S., explains that different climates are responsible for varying food qualities including mineral, protein, and fat content. Climatic regions are characterized by their different weather and rainfall patterns. These factors lead to different soil types which in turn directly affect the chemical substance of the foods grown in them. The substances and food qualities that are most beneficial to a person's health, it is contended, are those that are derived in season and from the same area in which he lives. If desired or essential foods cannot be obtained locally, they may be obtained from a different region, providing that it is in the same general climate zone. The "temperate zone," for example, includes most of the U.S., Europe, the Soviet Union, China, and Japan. Only in extreme cases should one resort to foods that are from a totally different climatic zone.

People who have adopted a macrobiotic regimen are quick to attest to its benefits. They typically say they sleep better and for fewer hours than they did before, they feel more vital when awake, they have more energy and better health, and they are able to participate more fully in life than they had thought possible. Many adherents to this life-style believe it will increase in popularity in the next decade as the incidence of degenerative diseases becomes even more alarming. They believe that cancer is caused chiefly by our poor and still deteriorating dietary habits which routinely include heavy, greasy meats, refined oils, chemical additives, high-sugar treats, overprocessed and chemically altered simple carbo-hydrates, and dairy products high in cholesterol and saturated fats. The macrobiotic diet replaces these disease-causing foods with ones that are organic, wholesome, and more readily assimilated by the body. In this way, it helps one attain physical balance, mental clarity, and spiritual harmony—factors that are all critical in maintaining optimal health and overcoming disease.

There have been many cases reported of miraculous cancer re-missions effected by adopting the macrobiotic diet. Probably the most publicized of these is the story of Dr. Anthony Sattilaro, who wrote of his own experiences in *Recalled by Life*. While he was acting president of the Methodist Hospital in Philadelphia, in 1978, Dr. Sattilaro learned that he had prostate cancer. It soon spread into his lungs as he underwent traditional medical therapy. Finally, when he was given only six months left to live, he discovered the macro-biotic method of healthful living. Having met with Michio Kushi, he determined to follow the diet and life-style prescribed. Not only did he live beyond six months, but in eighteen months a CAT scan showed conclusively that his cancer had completely abated, and he was not simply in a period of remission but was rid of the cancer.

In *Macrobiotic Miracle*, a mother and nurse from Vermont, Virginia Brown, tells of her unusual recovery from fourth-stage melanoma cancer—a deadly disease that few survive. She was told that without surgery she would die in six months. She refused surgery and took up macrobiotics. Brown is not only alive now, but working, directing a support group in the Kushi Foundation. Elaine Nussbaum, following three long and painful years of chemotherapy, heard about macro-biotics from one of her children. She decided to give it a try and soon recovered completely from the advanced uterine cancer that had seemed out of control. She went on to study nutrition and earned her master's degree in the subject. Even Jesse Jones, a spokesperson for the Kushi Foundation, used the macrobiotic way to overcome throat cancer. These are but a few of the many testimonies to the therapeutic claims of macrobiotics teachers and students alike.

Everyone who claimed to have been healed or who maintains optimal health through macrobiotics has done so by accepting a discipline that represents a drastic break from the average U.S. life-style of the 1980s. The dietary aspects of that discipline are based on the principles of harmony with nature and balance between the extreme yin and the extreme yang foods, as we discussed earlier. Foods that fall in between these unsettling and disturbing extremes are recommended, moreover, in specific proportions on a daily basis. The system is simple in structure and easy to adhere to for the person who is willing to gently let go of the foods and habits that he has held dear for so many years, that are at the root of his debilitating disease or chronic pain or lethargy or mere inability to enjoy maximum health.

The standard macrobiotic dietary regimen, for those who wish to implement it, is, as we have said, really quite simple. In a meal, 50 to 60 percent of the food should be grains. Almost a third should be fresh vegetables; ten percent, soups; another ten percent, beans and bean products; and five percent, sea vegetables. Although fish, fruit, seeds, and nuts are not recommended as such, they may be used sparingly if one has a need to. The beverage of choice should be mellow, nonaromatic, and a nonstimulant. Most of the foods eaten are cooked gently, although a portion of the vegetables can be raw. Only organically grown, completely natural and unprocessed, unaltered foods should be used.

You may be willing to start a macrobiotic diet but are not sure where to get the right kinds of foods. Health food stores and Oriental food marts should have most of the things you need to get going. It's also now possible to find macrobiotic restaurants in many large cities—and some not so large—in the country. A word of caution is in order here, though.

The macrobiotic cooking in a restaurant may not really be in accordance with classic macrobiotic principles. Restaurants are, we need to remember, usually businesses first and foremost. They will serve macrobiotic dishes, but they may sometimes compromise purity and quality in order to appeal to the average consumer who may have little patience—or perhaps it is only believed he will have little patience—for true macrobiotic dishes. You may end up, in other words, eating foods like tempura—deep fried and thus high in saturated fats and free radicals—or various dairy preparations that would find no place in the kitchen of a pure macrobiotic cook or chef.

If you do find a restaurant that adheres strictly to macrobiotic guidelines, the dishes offered may be monotonous and unattractive. Although there are many fine grains that can be used, for example, you might find that every dish available has rice as its base. Amaranth, barley, buckwheat, millet, bulgur, kasha, and rye are nowhere to be found. The foods may be unattractively presented: heaps of beans, a bunch of salad, a plain brown miso broth, all with little color or artistry. People who have eaten at macrobiotic restaurants that have corrupted the basic dietary regimen, or who have suffered through a pure, but monotone and austere three-course meal, have received the wrong impression of macrobiotics.

But once you have found the foods you need for your macrobiotic preparations, or have landed a suitable restaurant that might give you a sample of what this dietary regimen holds in store, you will enjoy a delightful eating experience. As a small example, to whet your appetite, I have provided three macrobiotic recipes.

(BREAKFAST)

DREAMY BUCKWHEAT-MILLET

- ¼ cup buckwheat
- ¼ cup millet
- 2–4 cups spring water
- pinch of sea salt
- chopped mushrooms to taste
- chopped scallions to taste
- mochi chunks (optional)
- 2 tablespoons sesame oil

Wash the buckwheat and millet, separately. Drain. Combine buckwheat, spring water, and sea salt in a pot and boil for 1¼ to 1½ hours. During last 30 minutes of cooking time, add millet. Simmer gently. In separate frying pan, lightly sauté chopped mushrooms and scallions in sesame oil. During final 5 minutes add mochi chunks and sautéed mushrooms and scallions to pot. Stir well. Serve hot.

Serves 1

(LUNCH)

TEMPEH PASTA

- ¼ pound tempeh square
- 2 tablespoons roasted sesame seeds
- ⅛ teaspoon umeboshi paste or soy sauce
- ¼ teaspoon brown rice vinegar
- 1 teaspoon grated fresh ginger
- ¼ pound soba (buckwheat pasta)
- 2 cups broccoli flowerets and stems
- parsley for garnish

Put tempeh square in an inch of water in saucepan. Boil, then lower heat and simmer until soft (20-30 minutes). Drain and cool, then cube. Dry roast sesame seeds in pan until lightly browned. Combine in bowl, umeboshi paste and brown rice vinegar, plus grated ginger, and roasted sesame seeds and blend for a marinade. Boil pasta and broccoli separately until done. Broccoli should be crisp and bright green—do not overboil! Mix all ingredients in a serving bowl and serve hot or cold. Add parsley garnish.

Serves 3

(DINNER)

MISO SOUP WITH CARROTS AND TOFU

- ½ cup carrots, chopped
- ¼ cup onions, shredded
- 1 teaspoon soy oil
- 1 quart spring water
- 3 tablespoons rice flour
- 1½–2 tablespoons miso
- ½ pound tofu, cubed
- 1 sheet nori
- fresh shiitake for garnish

Sauté the carrots and onions in oil. Cover carrots and onions with water and boil. Add remaining water and cook until carrots are tender. Purée ¼ cup of the broth from the pot with the miso and rice flour. Put the purée in the pot and simmer. Rinse nori and cut into small strips and add to the soup, along with tofu. Cut off shiitake stems and discard. Parboil and use to garnish each serving.

Serves 2

Notice that the foods used in these recipes include the foods that we mentioned earlier as those prescribed by macrobiotic guidelines —the grains, fresh vegetables, soups, sea vegetables, and bean products. Obviously missing are those foods that gravitate toward one end or the other of the yin-yang continuum—meat and dairy products, processed foods, chemically altered foods, refined simple carbohydrates, sugar, tropical fruits.

There have been many claims of the great healing powers of following a macrobiotic regimen. Most of these are of the anecdotal sort that we have already illustrated. It is difficult to determine through such case histories exactly what factors or combination of factors were responsible for the reversal of the illness. Outside of carefully controlled studies or clinical experiments, the number of variables that could be having an effect on the results are often too numerous and complex to accurately isolate. As the macrobiotic diet has piqued increasing public interest though, there has been more of an effort to study its isolated effects in a more controlled, objective manner.

Harvard University and Michio Kushi collaborated on such a study in an attempt to discern the effects of macrobiotics on blood and cardiovascular strength and overall condition. Approximately two hundred people living in and around Boston who had been living on macrobiotic diets for some time already were the subject of this study. They were requested to abandon their strict eating habits for a period of several weeks, and to eat a more standard American diet, with meats and heavy sauces, sweets, processed foods, and the like. The results were that the people's cardiovascular systems and blood conditions suffered after switching to the standard American diet.

The main culprit of the meat and dairy diet is apparently cholesterol. Cholesterol tends to make the blood sluggish while it attaches to the inner arterial walls, causing a plaquelike buildup. This plaque can damage healthy blood platelets, diminish arterial elasticity (leading to "hardening" of the arteries), and eventually cause blood clotting. The layers of plaque buildup, coupled with the lost elasticity, leave arteries with a smaller available diameter—that is, with a smaller channel for blood to flow through. Anyone who has ever put his thumb over half the opening of a hose knows that a decrease in the diameter of the hose means an increase in the water pressure. In the same way, cholesterol causes high blood pressure.

The Harvard studies of the macrobiotic diet indicate that it leads to lower cholesterol levels and lower blood pressure, hence better circulatory and heart conditions. The average U.S. population, suffering from high rates of heart disease, high blood pressure, arteriosclerosis, and atherosclerosis, could certainly benefit by adopting a macrobiotic diet or at least by modifying their present diets through understanding and applying some of the more significant and pertinent principles of macrobiotics. How exactly should one go about altering his diet to prevent or reverse degenerative diseases?

The first thing to do is to eliminate or seriously cut down on the foods that are creating biochemical imbalance, mental distraction, and spiritual lethargy. These foods are meats and dairy products, refined oils, simple carbohydrates and sugared items, stimulants like coffee and colas, and processed, chemically treated foods. Replace these foods with the macrobiotic groups of foods that we have already mentioned, and better health will certainly begin. The change from the "all-American" way to macrobiotic cooking should be an evolutionary process, Kushi warns us. He suggests a month to three months, at least, before you have completely changed over to a purely macrobiotic diet. Remember, our old dietary habits took years and years to be formed. It may be too physiologically traumatic to alter that overnight.

Once you are cooking and eating the macrobiotic way, you will do well to reflect on Kushi's observation that, just because the macrobiotic diet is a *strict* discipline, does not mean that it is a *narrow* one. Macrobiotic food selection, food preparation, and dining should not be monotonous or austere. Vegetables, for instance, have many brilliant and stimulating colors. Use these to dress up your meals and make them visually appealing. Use a variety of foods. Don't get your 50 to 60 percent grains from the same pasta every day, or from brown rice. Remember to rotate: use rice one day; millet another; oats, wheat, bulgur, corn, and so on. Tempeh is a delicious way to fulfill your protein and fat requirements—but don't have tempeh entrees, tempeh soup, and tempeh salad. Use variety, and rotate that variety. Macrobiotic cooking need never be boring. There are so many foods to choose from. Study some cookbooks, maybe take a macrobiotic cooking class where you can meet with other people that support and enhance and enliven your own resolution to learn more about this rewarding life-style. Then go shopping. Take your time and browse. Ask questions and learn. Try new foods and experiment. Rework some basic recipes to meet your individual expectations and requirements. Have fun and keep it interesting, challenging, always different and ever-changing.

We have given a broad overview of the many benefits of adopting a macrobiotic diet and life-style. We should be aware, too, of some of its possible shortcomings. From a dietary standpoint, it tends to overuse tamari, miso, and other foods and preparations high in sodium. Sea salt or other salt tends to draw water out of the blood cells, creating a dehydration of tissues and at the same time, causing a problem with water retention in the body. Excessive sodium overburdens the kidneys and forces the heart to work double-time in response to dehydration, hypertension, and increased blood pressure levels. To complicate matters further, the inclusion of water and other beverages as well as fruits—which have high water content—tends to be understated, or even discouraged. So on the one hand, the high-sodium foods are creating cellular dehydration, hypertension, and bodily fluid retention, while on the other hand we may not be replenishing our body with adequate amounts of liquid to help counter this circumstance.

Among vegetables, it is the starchy ones and sea vegetables that are in the driver's seat in macrobiotic diets, while dark leafy greens take a backseat and frequently don't even get taken along for the ride. Dark leafy greens are important sources of: vitamin E, an antioxidant which tends to protect the integrity of your red blood cells and hold the aging process in check; carotene, or vitamin A, which strengthens your eyes and the epithelial tissues that line the passages in your respiratory and digestive systems; and calcium, essential for strong bones and teeth and the prevention of degenerative skeletal disease like osteoporosis. To eliminate or underuse these greens is not sound, nutritional planning.

Fruits provide good sources of potassium and calcium as well as vitamins C and A. They also have important enzymes that would be particularly helpful to include for digestion in a macrobiotic diet that affords substantial amounts of starch from vegetables and protein from beans, tofu, and tempeh. Yet, this important food group is pretty much left out of the diet, especially in the case of imported fruits like those from the tropics.

This brings us to the matter of restricting our diet to only locally grown foods. Michio Kushi asks you not to make too narrow an interpretation of what is or is not locally available. In other words, you can choose foods not just from our immediate locality, but from our entire region and even from different regions within the general climatic zone. He even tells you that you can include foods from totally dissimilar climates if it is absolutely necessary. Despite these allowances, though, the overwhelming emphasis is on the avoidance of the non-locally grown foods. While you can comprehend the philosophy behind this macrobiotic principle, it clashes with practical nutritional sense.

If you eat primarily to enhance your well-being, then you must include the full spectrum of foods and nutrients that will contribute to that goal. For example, there exists a "goiter belt" in the Appalachian Mountains where people suffer from chronic dietary iodine deficiencies. Iodine-rich foods are not grown locally and therefore must be imported from different regions in order to fill this void. Those that eat only local foods will have a much higher incidence of thyroid problems. While Kushi says that eating locally available foods is "safer and more adaptable," we see in the case of the American Eskimo one of the lowest average life spans in the world. This fact might be largely attributable to the fact that the Eskimo adheres to a diet which virtually excludes nonlocal food sources. Their high-fat, high-animal diet is often cited as the reason that there is so little heart disease. If that is the case it would be hard to determine in a population with an average life span of less than 49 years. The Eskimo's health problems begin with their high intake of saturated fats and cholesterol from their meat and fish diet, and continue with gross vitamin C deficiencies that could be ameliorated by the importation of vitamin C–rich foods. The whole principle of restricting one's diet to locally grown foods is highly suspect.

Finally, we need to ponder the efficacy of macrobiotics as a healing system. Certainly, there is a wealth of first-person accounts of the results it has had in helping people with cancer. This is significant since cancer poses an ever-increasing health threat in our society, even though we never seem to stop spending research dollars and developing new therapies to fight it. There is enough scientifically documented and anecdotal evidence available to conclude that it is now clear that we must directly examine and modify our way of eating in order to deal with cancer.

Science is just now beginning to understand the role of animal foods and saturated fats and simple sugars in the formation of tumor and cancer cells. The macrobiotic diet has emphasized this for over a quarter of a century. Its reliance on foods high in fiber, organically grown and whole, and inclusive of complex carbohydrates while eliminating processed foods, has contributed to its status as a healing regimen.

Still, we must recognize that just because the macrobiotic diet may be superior to the all-American diet does not make it necessarily the *only* alternative . . . it does not even necessarily make it the best one. As we learn more and more about nutritional balance, we may find that even a macrobiotic diet may be improved—even if it means questioning some of its basic principles. Moreover, it is presumptuous to speak of *the* macrobiotic way, as if there were one single way, one single diet, one single life-style that is best suited to all people in all cultures. We all have different needs—socially, spiritually, and biochemically. Any dietary regimen must be flexible enough to account for wide variations in its principles and applications. If you find macrobiotics or any other program unwilling to bend toward your individual needs, you may find it best to adopt only those principles that you can use to enhance your own health. These can be blended with other approaches for your specific needs, until you have derived your own nutritional program that suits you best. Keep in mind that even that program should be constantly reworked and modified in keeping with your own body's ever-changing requirements.

The macrobiotic way has given us great insight into ourselves as human beings and into our health through nutrition. It is not intended to displace medical therapies, but to complement them. Its emphasis on live, whole foods and rejection of meat and dairy products and processed foods makes it essential for us to understand. To attain health and happiness through avoidance of extremes and excess—by discovering the harmony and balance within ourselves as well as with our environment and society—is to learn the way of gentleness and calm, vitality and clarity . . . is to find the key to "long life."

IV

HEALTH
AND
NUTRITION

SEVENTEEN

Do We Need Meat to Be Healthy?

O ne of the strongest proponents of vegetarianism has been Dr. Mervyn G. Hardinge, a medical physician and researcher with degrees from Harvard and Stanford Universities. He has done extensive research on the subject, and has published numerous articles on the merits of a meat-free diet. In "Do Human Beings Need Meat?" he concludes, "That human beings do not have to eat meat ... is impressively evident to anyone familiar with even the rudiments of world nutrition. It is in countries and among peoples where diets are almost wholly of plant origin and meat eating is virtually absent that fertility is high and population explosion the most threatening. ... on what basis can one claim a need for meat in America with its large variety of available vegetarian foods?"[1]

If a group of health educators, home economists, and average individuals were asked, "What is the most important nutrient to people's diet?" the overwhelming response would be "protein." And the main "protein foods" would be meat, milk, cheese, and eggs.

Dr. Hardinge is concerned with the medical profession's lack of understanding of the original source of all protein. "Even though the protein turnover may go through several animal bodies before it appears on the table of the consumer, always the food chain, regardless of its length, begins in the leaf or green portion of a plant. It is evident, then, that somewhere down the line the essential amino acids that go to make any protein 'complete' must be obtained from plant sources."[2] Why not simply eat lower in the food chain? he suggests. In light of the ease with which plant proteins can be mixed and matched to insure completeness, and our relatively small protein needs, "there remains no valid reason for frightening people into eating meat for fear of protein deficiency on a nonflesh diet."[3] With careful planning to meet the requirements for calcium, iron, and B_{12}, a vegetarian diet can be perfectly safe and will confer health benefits by reducing obesity and cholesterol.

Dr. Hardinge substantiates his position with the research findings of numerous nutrition and health experts. Even back in 1959, he notes, *The Lancet* wrote: "Formerly, vegetable proteins were classified as second-class and regarded as inferior to first-class proteins of animal origin, but this distinction has now been generally discarded. Certainly some vegetable proteins can't stand alone as growth-promoters, but many field trials have shown that suitable mixtures of vegetable proteins give children the power to grow as well as children provided with milk and other animal proteins."[4]

Most Americans are aware of the "Basic Four" (meat, dairy, vegetable, cereal) food groups developed by the USDA (United States Department of Agriculture) as our nutritional guideline. There are major shortcomings in this program. While including most of the nutrients we need, it does not include all of them, and can permit serious nutritional errors and distortion. There is overwhelming evidence that after years of persuasion, repetition, and refinement, the food guides have not made much impact on the nation's eating habits. Instead, they seem to have confirmed our troublesome overemphasis on protein, as two of the four groups—dairy and meat—contain animal protein; the value of fruit and a wide variety of vegetables—including legumes, tubers, and leafy and yellow vegetables—is played down; while seeds and nuts are forgotten.

Protein expert Dr. Nevin Scrimshaw, of MIT, wrote nearly twenty years ago: "Fortunately, there is no fixed nutritional requirement for the relatively costly sources of protein—milk, meat and eggs. Legumes and oilseed meals are acceptable alternatives. . . . One-third of a properly processed oilseed meal mixed with two-thirds of a cereal grain gives a mixture of a quality and concentration of protein adequate for all human needs, even of the infant and young child."[5] Another of Dr. Hardinge's experts asserted that milk and egg protein are superior in biological value to meat and poultry. Nobel Prize winner Dr. Arturi Virtanen agrees, "Lacto-vegetarians can receive easily all the necessary nutrients from fruit, vegetables, potatoes, cereals and milk low in fat."[6] Dr. Hardinge adds that relying on dairy products is unnecessary. "Properly prepared plant foods provide adequate protein for every age group, including infants."[7]

VEGETARIANS AROUND THE WORLD

It's no coincidence that people around the world who follow vegetarian diets are remarkably healthy. The Hunza people of northern Pakistan are often cited for their excellent health. A 1963 *Lancet* article described the life-promoting regimen of "the people who live at altitudes of 2,000–8,000 feet, deep in the valley of Kaghan, Gilgit, Hunza and other mountainous areas of northwest Pakistan. Consuming the simplest possible diets of wheat, corn, potatoes, onions and fruits, they trudge up and down the rough mountain paths for anything up to fifty miles a day. They have existed thus for perhaps many thousands of years, free of obesity and cavities, and sure to enjoy long, healthy lives."[8]

While vegetarianism has become increasingly widespread among young adults, who adopt this diet out of philosophical and/or religious conviction, there is nothing new about it. For most of human existence, meat has usually been relatively unattainable in most parts of the world, so that people normally obtain their nutrients primarily from plant foods. In the early years of our country's history, food supplies consisted solely of what nature provided—fish, plants, and grains. However, with increasing industrialization and improved economic conditions, the availability of beef came to symbolize the "status" of our "rich" land. Increased beef consumption became synonymous with increased prosperity. Mass-marketing practices gave the beef and dairy industries effective methods to brainwash the U.S. public.

There is evidence that other cultures have a better understanding of nutrition. In 1938, "Vegetarian China," by William H. Adolph, a professor of biochemistry at Yenching University in Peking, China, appeared in *Scientific American* magazine. "For centuries," he wrote, "China has unconsciously been working out a vast food experiment from which the Western World can learn practical lessons." This experiment "involved not merely a few selected white rats, or even a few human subjects sheltered in the artificial comforts of the nutrition laboratory, but it boasted several millions of Chinese peasants as experimental subjects ... not over a few weeks but over a score or more of centuries."[9]

The Chinese peasants derive 95 percent of their protein from vegetable sources, and they—hundreds of millions of them—have maintained good health. They managed to survive for over forty centuries without a drop of milk. So much for industry claims that "you never outgrow your need for milk"! Not only is milk not a natural for the native Chinese, it is simply not a practical food staple economically in such a densely populated country. Both meat and dairy products, involving the "cow converter" process by which large quantities of grain or grass are converted to much smaller amounts of meat, are prohibitively expensive and wasteful of energy and natural resources.[10]

Ironically, the United States is considered among the nutritionally rich of the world. If the food-rich and the food-poor of the world could share their traditional meals, once starvation were ended, it is we in the rich countries who would benefit most! How well are we eating when we have slipped into a fast-food addiction to "Big Macs" and "Whoppers," with Roy Rogers and the Dairy Queen to feed us? Animal protein is available on every street and highway; gone are the small farms and home vegetable gardens. Home baking and other time-consuming methods of food preparation have been replaced by the eat-and-run breakfast, the fast-food lunch, and frozen-food dinner entrees.

THE NEW VEGETARIANS

As people become better educated, they are becoming more concerned about what goes into their bodies, its effects on health and appearance.

The switch to vegetarian eating in recent years has been prompted by realistic health concerns. Even so, much literature on the subject still treats vegetarianism as a "bizarre and unusual diet." Even some nutrition textbooks place the vegetarian diet under the section on food fads, and articles depict those who practice vegetarianism as "young people often living in communes."[11] The truth is there are now over seven million vegetarians in the U.S., most of whom have never seen a commune.

The new vegetarians understand that, as an article in the *American Journal of Nursing* put it, "meat isn't the only protein source."[12] And that the discerning use of whole grains, vegetables, sprouts, and fruit will cover the "Recommended Daily Allowance" (RDAs) for the nutrients found in meat, without the heavy cholesterol count.

But there are still professionals who won't admit that a vegetarian diet can be as nutritionally complete as a meat diet. In a recent study, for example, most nutritionists were found to encourage vegetarian clients to eat meat, "indicating they weren't willing to work within the clients' food-related belief system."[13] Most registered dieticians have limited knowledge of vegetarianism and may not feel comfortable counseling on this eating style. Also, personal attitudes about diet may influence counseling more than knowledge of nutrition[14]—certainly neither a moral nor ethical approach. As an article in the *Journal of the American Dietetic Association* admonishes, "Dieticians and nutritionists must learn about the nutrient needs of the vegetarian, as well as support of this diet choice," adding that the best approach to nutritional counseling "is to respect the patient's dietary individualism and freedom, and try not to disrupt existing eating habits and life-styles unless they are potentially harmful."[15]

Meanwhile, if you consult a nutritionist, make sure to find one who understands the benefits of vegetarianism. A good nutritionist will help dispel common myths about a vegetarian diet. Some people, for instance, fear that a vegetarian diet is fattening—only true when sweets or other high-calorie foods fill in for meat. Some think that starchy foods like potatoes or pasta are fattening. But the excess calories come from garnishes like butter, sour cream, cheddar cheese, and bacon—not from the potato; pasta, too, is fattening only if laden with cream or cheese sauces. A plain, medium—sized potato has only about 70 calories, plus essential amino acids and vitamin C.

Before hastily judging vegetarianism, people should examine how this eating style actually stacks up against the typical meat-based diet. When the British Medical Association and the World Health Organization compared regular diets with vegetarian diets, they found that the vegetarian diets fulfilled the recommended daily allowances for all nutrients, and in a healthier way.[16] Vegetarians took in fewer calories and fat, and more complex carbohydrates and fiber. Even though calcium and riboflavin tend to be lower, the vegetarian diet is closer to the dietary guidelines recently given by the U.S. Department of Agriculture than the average American diet.

But even vegetarians who eat no dairy products can get enough calcium in their diet with some planning. While one cup of whole milk contains 288 mg. of calcium and .1 mg. of iron, one-quarter cup of sesame seeds has 580 mgs. of calcium and 5.25 mgs. of iron—far more than the dairy source.[17] Sesame seed butter—known in Middle Eastern cuisine as tahini—can be used to make a delicious, rich-tasting, high-protein sauce to serve with salads, vegetables, or pasta.

In this light, it seems worthwhile to test the theories of those who shun carbohydrates against some of the realities of nutrition.

A 1954 study found no significant difference between the physical, blood, and biochemical tests of vegetarians and omnivores. However, the vegetarians had significantly lower levels of serum cholesterol than the other groups.[18] Later studies also showed that the levels of folic acid, often deficient in omnivore control groups, were usually higher in vegetarians,[19] as the best sources of this nutrient are fruits and vegetables. Many vegetarian mainstays are not only economical sources of protein but are replete with other nutrients, as well. A meal, for example, of whole grains, beans, potatoes, carrots, cabbage, spinach, and watercress provides a wide variety of nutrients.[20]

Vegetarian diets depend heavily on four groups of plant foods: grains and cereals, legumes (including beans and peas), fruits and vegetables, and nuts and seeds. Including something from each of these "four vegetarian food groups" at every meal guarantees maximum nutrition.

The health benefits of vegetarianism aren't solely products of meat shunning. Doing without animal products is only part of the total effort. When you eat fewer meat and dairy foods, you leave more room for health-promoting foods. When you cook plant foods from scratch, you can avoid the additives so often found in processed and packaged items.

Other aspects of the vegetarian life-style can also affect overall well-being. Exercise and stress-reduction methods like meditation are often part of the vegetarian routine. Also, studies show that on the average "vegetarians usually abstain or are moderate in their use of alcohol, caffeine and tobacco."[21] This reduces the chances of health problems such as alcoholism, emphysema, lung cancer, and heart disease. Because vegetarians often opt for natural healing methods over invasive ones, they also avoid the chance of getting hooked on medications.

Children, too, can benefit from an early start on vegetarian eating. It is important to make sure children eat a wide variety of foods and get all the vitamins, minerals, and protein they need. But a carefully monitored nonflesh diet can lower their risk of disease and raise their chances of maintaining good health. Dr. Scharffenberg of San Joaquin Hospital in California reports, "Seventeen percent of sixth to eighth graders have serum cholesterol levels greater than 180 mg/dl, an obvious result of the usual 'good' American meat diet." According to Dr. Scharffenberg, a low-fat, high-fiber vegetarian diet could be the best health insurance a kid could get.[22]

A major concern for vegetarian children is vitamin B_{12} deficiency, but B_{12} is readily available in fermented products like tempeh. Seaweed also contains B_{12}, and some packaged cereals are fortified with it. It is also found in the same vitamin supplements most parents give their children as health insurance.

FIBER, DISEASE, AND VEGETARIANISM

Among the virtues of vegetarian food is its high fiber content. Increased fiber, the undigestible part of food which helps move food along in the digestive tract, has been associated with a lowered incidence of degenerative diseases. Even so, its role has been widely misunderstood in the medical world. A foremost researcher in the field of dietary fiber and disease, Dr. Denis Burkitt, explains that fiber has been "neglected because it contributes little nutritionally despite its important role in maintaining normal gastrointestinal function. . . ."[23]

Dr. Burkitt's work substantiates the wisdom of the common vegetarian practice of including "whole foods" in the diet—whole grains, whole-wheat breads and pastas, skin left on fruits and vegetables. "Many diseases common in modern western civilization have been related to the amount of time it takes food to pass through the alimentary tract, as well as to the bulk and consistency of stools," he writes. "These factors are influenced by fiber in the diet, especially cereal fiber." On the flip side, his research shows that lack of fiber leads to "changes in gastrointestinal behavior" that is suspect in such ailments as appendicitis, diverticulitis, gall bladder disease, cardiovascular disease, diabetes, hemorrhoids, varicose veins, hiatus hernia, and certain forms of cancer.[24] Your good health depends on getting enough fiber in the diet!

Many observers have noted that these problems occur much less frequently among non-Western, nonurban peoples who consume traditional diets high in fiber materials; and conversely, their incidence increases among people consuming a Western-style diet, which is fiber-poor.

BOWEL PROBLEMS

Epidemiological studies have shown that the occurrence of non-infective large-bowel disease—such as diverticulitis—is due to lack of fiber in the diet. This deficiency results from the refining of carbohydrate foods. Benign and malignant tumors and ulcerative colitis are "more dependent on environmental than on genetic factors," reported Dr. Burkitt in the *Journal of the American Medical Association*.[25] The "environment" of the colon is predominantly determined by the food passing through it.

Although dietary fiber contains no usable nutrients, it serves a very important function in the regulation of the passage of fecal wastes. A diet low in fiber will not provide enough weight and bulk to fecal wastes to move it through the intestinal tract. On the contrary, such a diet will cause the wastes to become more concentrated and sluggish, and hence to remain in the body longer. Remember, fiber is a component of plant foods only; it is not found in foods of animal origins. If you get most of your protein from meat, chances are you're at least mildly constipated.

Prolonged bowel transit time is also suspect in appendicitis and in colon and rectal cancer. A diet low in fiber not only slows down digestion, but it may lead to a change in the type and number of fecal bacteria. The wrong proportions of the wrong kind of bacteria corresponds with the increased incidence and severity of bowel disease.

A high-fiber diet can help bring about a better bowel disposition.

"The consumption of suitable amounts of indigestible fiber can both prevent and cure constipation," Dr. Burkitt writes.

> A diet lacking it—that is, one made up chiefly of meat, peeled potato, white bread, and concentrated sweets—is a common cause of atonic constipation, because the food mass moves sluggishly through the digestive tract and the lack of moisture-holding bulk makes the stool dry and difficult to pass. Constipation is a factor in health problems because of the straining it causes; varicose veins, one of the results, affects 10 percent of the American adult population. In this, the intra-abdominal pressure is abnormally increased, which may lead to the damaging of the proximal valves in our legs. This mechanism seems to lead to the onset of hemorrhoids and hiatus hernia. Almost half of our over-50 age group suffers from this preventable and often extremely painful condition.
>
> Constipation is uncommon among people who live largely on unrefined plant foods from which the cellulose (as in the bran of grains) has not been removed....
>
> We digest the digestible parts of what we eat and the rest remains as bulk for bowel hygiene. Cellulose residue absorbs and holds moisture and so gives bulk to the bowel contents. This stimulated peristalsis prevents stagnation of materials in the colon, and keeps the fecal matter soft and easy to evacuate.[26]

Alas, this clear and informative message, written nearly fifteen years ago, remains hidden in a periodical stashed in a back shelf in most medical libraries. These findings are simply not popular with most of the medical profession.

A recent study of American eating habits conducted at the University of New Hampshire helps substantiate Americans' ignorance about the effect of their diet on the health of their intestines. The findings showed that there are five distinct eating groups in America today. The largest, the "meat and potatoes" crowd, tended to be lower middle-class, conservative, small-town residents—and overweight. Chronic constipation was rampant in this group; many believed a weekly bowel movement was normal.

On the other end of the spectrum was the "naturalist" group, representing 15 percent of those surveyed. These people tended to be more affluent, younger, interested in creative cooking, and more conscious about food additives and preservatives. Most notably, constipation was far less likely to be a problem among the naturalists.[27]

DIABETES

Lack of fiber in the diet has also been linked to diabetes. Diabetes is the third-leading killer in America today, following cancer. The diet condoned by the American Diabetic Association and the American Dietetic Association only adds insult to injury for the diabetic individual. It is high in saturated fat, cholesterol, and refined carbohydrates, and deficient in complex carbohydrates and dietary fiber. Dietary fats decrease the diabetic's utilization of what little insulin he may still be able to produce. Fiber is needed to regulate blood-sugar fluxes. And a low-fat, high complex carbohydrate diet has been shown actually to reverse both diabetes mellitus and hypoglycemia, even as the side effects of the drugs used to treat diabetes often cause more destruction than the diseases themselves. All the more reason to rely on diet for health.

Based on the nutritional findings and the evidence presented, it is recommended that the diabetic's total consumption of carbohydrates should be increased, with emphasis on complex carbohydrates (the consumption of refined sugars should be decreased or altogether eliminated). Those goals can best be accomplished by substituting grains, legumes, and fresh fruits for meat, dairy products, and refined and processed foods.

VEGETARIANISM AND THE HEART

Coronary heart disease is presently the number-one killer in the U.S. and other "affluent" countries, and there is no sign of it being dethroned in the foreseeable future. While the role of diet in this disease still remains a controversial issue, it is obviously advisable to eliminate or, at least, attempt to reduce as many risk factors as possible. As vegetarianism has become increasingly widespread, vegetarians have surprised the medical community with their general good health. The studies continue, but the fact remains: reduced animal-fat consumption and higher intake of vegetable protein, complex carbohydrates, and dietary fiber are all seen to be cholesterol-lowering factors.[28]

CHANGING EATING HABITS

The low-fiber diet habit in the United States began in 1870, when new milling techniques replaced stone mills. White bread suddenly became cheaply available to everyone, replacing the hearty brown and black breads previously eaten as a staple by the less-than-wealthy. Overall consumption of bread and cereals has decreased since the late 1800s. Between 1890 and 1960, the national intake of sugar more than doubled; fat intake also rose. Protein is now being consumed in amounts that triple the recommended daily allowance. Thus, in only three generations, by lowering our intake of whole grains, increasing our intake of refined flour and sweeteners, and increasing meat and fat consumption, Americans, in the pursuit of prosperity, have been heedlessly risking their health: a high-protein, fatty, sugary, low-fiber diet is not conducive to optimal functioning.

Fortunately, now many people are returning to wholesome, natural foods in place of animal and processed products.

The vegetarian population's pattern of eating is quite different from the average U.S. diet. Vegetarians eat less fat and more carbohydrates and manage to fit in more than 100 percent of the RDA of calcium every day. Their iron, and vitamins A, B, and C intake are higher as well. Vitamin B_1 is more plentiful in the vegetarian diet because it is found in wheat germ, buckwheat, and legumes.[29] In fact, the vegetarian diet closely resembles the Dietary Goals for the United States developed by the Senate Select Committee on Nutrition and Human Needs.

Nutritional benefits of the vegetarian diet aside, the fact that our bodies aren't suited for meat is reason enough to consider erasing it from the diet. For instance, our dental structures are those of herbivorous animals. "While designed to subsist on vegetarian foods, [modern man] has perverted his dietary habits to accept the food of the carnivore. . . . Herein may lie the basis for the high incidence of human atherosclerotic disease."[30]

We think of ourselves, perhaps, as carnivores. Not so, our flat teeth are not sharp enough to tear through hide, flesh, or bones. Furthermore, carnivores' digestive systems are constructed to quickly get rid of the meat they eat before it putrefies, by secreting an enzyme that breaks down the uric acid in meat. Ours aren't. The enzyme secreted in our mouths is designed to break down complex plant cells. (Carnivores don't have this enzyme.) Furthermore, in its length, our long digestive system is more like those of herbivores.

Uric acid can, in fact, be a strain to the human body. The kidneys, in an attempt to neutralize uric acid's toxic effects, may eventually form calcium urate crystals. These are the crystalline deposits responsible for many painful conditions like gout, bursitis, rheumatism, and lower-back pain. Carnivores don't usually suffer these side effects of meat consumption. But, surprisingly, these diseases are becoming more common among our carnivorous pets, as they, too, have become victims of the modern diet. Moist pellets and canned food are an unhealthy change from their natural diets.

More and more medical experts are recommending the vegetarian alternative as a way of improving health, though interestingly, the notion isn't new: articles espousing the medical benefits of vegetarianism go back hundreds of years. In the 1700s, a vegetarian diet was prescribed for dissolving kidney stones and curing gout. In the 1800s, medical publications described flesh-free diets for treating tumors and cancerous ulcers. And in 1945, Antone Cocchi gained attention for proclaiming the healing and preventive attributes of the vegetarian diet.

Many modern health professionals are trying to educate their colleagues and the public about the health benefits of vegetarianism. In their book *Human Nutrition and Dietetics*, Davidson, Meiklejohn, and Passmore state that, "in many tropical countries, it is impossible to overemphasize the improvement in health that is likely to arise from even a small increase in the vegetable supply. A poor anemic woman with insufficient iron, vitamin A and ascorbic acid in her diet may find immeasurable improvement in her health as a result of taking one helping of good garden vegetables a day."[31] They hope Americans will realize that these changes would help them as well.

Other health professionals are trying to learn more about the effects of vegetarian diets. "Vegetable foods may become increasingly important as a protein source throughout the world," explains Dr. Philip White, a director of the Department of Foods and Nutrition of the American Medical Association (AMA). "Also, several studies have shown that vegans have lower serum cholesterol levels than their non-vegan counterparts, undoubtedly due to the substitution of vegetable oils for animal fats.... There have also been studies suggesting that a diet high in fiber can bring about a decrease in serum cholesterol."[32]

It is the job of other health workers and researchers to spread the word about vegetarianism. Mark Hegsted, who was chief nutritionist for the Federal Government, wrote, for example, about the many negative health effects of the meat diet. "The risks associated with eating this diet are demonstrably large. The question to be asked, therefore, is not why we should change our diet, but why not?" he wrote. "What are the risks associated with eating less meat, less fat, less saturated fat, less cholesterol, less sugar, less salt, and more fruits, vegetables, unsaturated fat and cereal products, especially whole grain cereals? There are none that can be identified and important benefits can be expected."[33]

Dr. Hegsted and his Harvard co-workers have also done a lot to spread the word. They published a study in 1955 stating that "it is difficult to obtain a mixed vegetable diet which will produce an appreciable loss of body protein." A vegetarian diet is quite healthy, the study said, "a step in the right direction."[34] But this sound advice never made headlines, despite the reputation of Dr. Hegsted, who served as an editor of *Nutrition Review* and a member of the National Academy of Sciences, among other posts. But then, we have already discussed the effect of the meat and dairy industries on the media.

But the battle continues. The Nutrition Institute of Mexico, for instance, released a study that concluded that "the Western habit of eating meat is not necessarily healthy. It is a false assumption that only a diet based on animal products helps you stay in good health.... The Western diet, which is based primarily on animal products, is an abuse of the world's limited food-stuff supplies."[35] This report stated that the traditional diet eaten by many people in the Third World, largely based on grains and vegetables, is the ideal diet for everyone. Certainly, the incidences of diet-related diseases (except for those caused by sheer lack of food) are quite low in Asia, Africa, and South America, where natives eat a healthful, high-fiber diet.

Then there is the other side of the battle. The AMA itself went so far as to assert, "A strictly vegetarian diet may lead to deformities and even death."[36] Luckily, that attack received a swift reply. "The AMA has experienced a loss of credibility and the vegetarian community has been needlessly alarmed," wrote Alex Hershaft, president of the Vegetarian Information Service.

> The biggest losers are those who have deferred their turn to vegetarianism and a healthier, more ethical life, because they

believe in the competence and honesty of AMA news releases.
    Each year, nearly 800,000 people in this country die of heart
disease, 200,000 of stroke and over 80,000 of cancer of the colon
and breast ... an overwhelming fraction of these deaths are
linked to the consumption of animal fat and meat, cholesterol,
salt and sugar. Any individual or organization who deters the
American people from embracing a meatless diet through care-
less reporting must bear the responsibility for some of these
deaths.[37]

The *Vegetarian Times* agreed, stating that "the handling of this story
by the press and the AMA show that we still have a long way to go
in clearing up the misinformation and confusion which exists when
it comes to vegetarianism."[38]
    Clearly, although there is still much research that remains to be
done, the public and professional view of vegetarianism is becoming
more positive. It's rarely still condemned as a faddish way of eating
or as a starvation regimen. More and more authorities are concluding that vegetarianism can be the best way of achieving a healthy
diet, and that vegetarianism is simply nothing but eliminating animal
products from this diet. The health benefits that result are no secret
now. There is abundant scientific evidence that proves the adequacy
and, in fact, superiority of the vegetarian diet. Perhaps, as this information is spread and gains even more credibility, people will
start to act upon the words of an eighteenth-century French econ-
omist who said, "The destiny of a people depends on the nature of
its diet."[39]

DEFICIENCY CONCERNS IN
THE VEGETARIAN DIET

Protein is not the only food that people worry they won't get enough
of if they switch to a vegetarian diet. They often wonder, too, how
they will obtain enough vitamin B_{12} and iron, two nutrients plentiful
in red meat, if they stop eating their beefsteak and lamb chops. But
plant foods can also provide you with these nutrients if you plan
your diet properly.

VITAMIN B_{12}

Vitamin B_{12} is one nutrient vegetarians must be careful not to skimp on. While B_{12} is generously supplied in meats and dairy foods, most plants fall short in their contribution. B_{12} is essential for normal motor function, regulation of heartbeat, and mental functions like memory. A deficiency could show up as problems in these areas, along with symptoms like facial swelling, weakness, fatigue, weight loss, depression, or thinning hair. Deficiencies often don't show up for five or ten years, since B_{12} is a storable vitamin. The most disturbing thing about vitamin-B_{12} deficiencies is that they are often undetected until irreversible damage to the nervous system or spinal cord occurs. Fortunately, several body processes make deficiencies rare: recirculation of this water-soluble vitamin, intestinal manufacturing of B_{12} by bacteria, and the body's ability to recycle the vitamin when it is in short supply. In fact, a comprehensive study of vegans in England showed no signs of vitamin B_{12} deficiencies, and many of the subjects hadn't eaten meat in thirty years.

How can a vegetarian make sure he or she gets enough vitamin B_{12}? Tempeh and miso both are high in this vitamin, since it is produced by bacteria during fermentation. Miso contains about .17 micrograms of B_{12} per 100 grams (.03 mcgs. per tablespoon). Tempeh totes 3.9 mcgs. per 100 grams. Depending on the type of miso, protein quantity can range from 12 to 20 percent, a more usable protein than beef, as its net protein utilization is 72 percent compared to 67 for a hamburger. One hundred grams of miso boasts 9.7 grams of usable protein. Miso accounts for nearly 10 percent of the protein intake in modern Japan, and is relied upon as a primary food staple. (Miso was introduced to the Western world by Buddhist priests in the 1700s.)

There is much scientific data to back the claims made in favor of soy products. Their protein contributions parallel that of beef. Clearly, soy products—free of saturated fat, additives, hormones, antibiotics, and uric acid—are excellent alternatives to beef and other meats. They are nutritious, versatile, and delicious!

IRON

Second to protein, iron is probably the most prevalent concern of non-meat-eaters. But even though the iron found in plant sources is slightly different from meat iron, with some conscious juggling of nutrients, vegetarians can keep their bodies adequately supplied with iron.

Plant iron is *non-heme* iron, meaning its absorbability is influenced by other foods in the diet. (Meat iron is *heme* iron; its absorption is unaffected by outside factors.) The magic iron booster for vegetarians is vitamin C. Lacto-vegetarians (since dairy sources are low in iron) as well as strict vegetarians should include lots of vitamin C–rich foods in their diets—green leafy vegetables; dried fruits, like apricots, figs, and raisins; blackstrap molasses and yeast—to guarantee proper iron absorption.

As we have seen, on all counts a vegetarian diet proves far better in providing for proper health and maintenance than a meat diet. It can provide all the protein, minerals, and vitamins we need and help us steer clear of many ailments. And there are millions of people around the world who confirm the truth of this in their daily, vegetarian lives.

Can We Be Healthy Eating Meat?

There's a healthy case for relying on grains and vegetables for all your nutrients. But what about the antimeat side of the vegetarian argument? Meat can contain substances that are potentially harmful to the human body. For example, meat is strongly susceptible to bacteria, and antibiotics are often injected into it. The problem has long been recognized. In fact, *Science Newsletter* reported in 1948 that in 1947 "40 million pounds of unfit meat reached the unsuspecting American public."[1] In this case, the problem was mainly a matter of inadequate inspection of poultry, but of the poultry which was inspected, 20 percent was declared unfit for human consumption. Clearly this whole issue merits a close examination.

"NATURAL" TOXINS

Animals, like humans, continuously eliminate waste products from their tissues and cells to the surrounding blood. This natural process comes to an abrupt halt when the animal is slaughtered. All the waste material present at that time remains intact. Thus, when you eat any flesh food, you ingest all the unsavory substances that should have been excreted. And, by doing so, you add unnecessary stress to your organs of elimination. The human body already has plenty of waste to get rid of: worn-out cells and by-products of digestion. Polluting the system with additional animal wastes may cause wear and tear on this biological mechanism. And the five organs of elimination—lungs, bladder, kidneys, sweat glands, and liver—may bear the brunt of the waste overload by developing any of several degenerative diseases.[2]

To make matters worse, meat, unlike fruits and vegetables, starts to decay the moment the animal dies, and continues to degenerate during processing, packaging, and transportation to the market or butcher. After slaughter, a steer is sectioned and moved into cold storage. Depending on the cut, the meat is then aged for a designated period of time to make it more tender. It may be stored in a meat warehouse before being sent to a butcher or supermarket where it is packaged. And there it sits in the meat section of the market until the unsuspecting consumer picks it up and, *finally*, prepares, cooks, and eats it.

Whoever eats that meat ingests millions of pathogenic bacteria. Even if the meat looks fresh, it is still replete with bacteria. Each gram of sausage stored at room temperature for twenty hours increases its live bacteria count by 70 million, each gram of beef by 650 million, and each gram of smoked ham by a whopping 700 million.[3] *Consumer Reports* says that "50 percent of the government-inspected frankfurter samples had begun to spoil and contained at least 20 million bacteria per ounce."[4]

You may reason that you would never leave meat out to spoil at room temperature for such a long time. However, you really can't know how this perishable item was handled before you bought it. The recent "Mystery Meat" scandal in Denver, Colorado, led to the conviction of a man named Butch Stanko. Lengthy testimonies against the owner of the Cattle King Packaging Company exposed his methods of operation. He ordered his workers to "not throw away anything, to use every bit and piece, even the blood clots."[5] As a matter of practice, Cattle King added rotten meat in with the chopped beef, and brought dead animals into its slaughterhouse. Inspectors also cited the plant for unsanitary conditions, including rodent and cockroach infestation; paint chips; people urinating in the work area; repackaging of returned, tainted meat; and falsification of inspection dates. The plant's health inspectors apparently weren't watching. Many of the illegal happenings occurred while they were on breaks.

And if you're a hamburger lover, you should know that before its shutdown, Cattle King was a major supplier of meat for the Department of Defense, many supermarkets, and for the Roy Rogers and Wendy's fast-food chains. They also supplied nearly one-fourth of the hamburger meat designated for our national school lunch programs.[6] The breaking of this scandal prevented an estimated 20 million pounds of questionable meat from entering the food market. But we will never know how much tainted meat has already been consumed by the public and how much is presently being sold.

The Cattle King case is not an isolated one. Nebraska Beef Processors was recently charged with shipping rancid meat and changing USDA inspection stamps, and was cited in the late 1970s for violations. In 1984 alone, the USDA had had to provide additional inspectors for thirteen meat-packing plants experiencing "chronic problems." However, even the USDA admits there is only so much they can control. "We're set up to provide our regulatory functions. We're not there to look for these gross violations," says USDA's Marshall Marcus.[7]

That is a big problem, because these problems are happening everywhere. Admitting the health violations at Cattle King, its attorney commented that, "Those things happened. Like they do in every other meat packaging plant in the United States."[8] The whole inspection system appears to be inadequate. Many meat inspectors are poorly trained. And often, over the period of a single day, they are expected to check more than a thousand poultry and a hundred head of cattle. Without the use of a microscope, this procedure becomes a joke, as billions of bacteria go marching by.

The Centers for Disease Control elaborates on the subject: "Although commercial 'ready-to-eat' pork products are required by law to be cooked, frozen, or otherwise treated to kill T. Spiralis larvae, federal or state inspection procedures do not actually include examination of pork for the presence of larvae at the time of slaughter. The burden of responsibility lies with the consumer."[9] And while reductions in the frequency of trichinosis have come about with the widespread use of freezers and the discontinued practice of feeding garbage to hogs, without the development of a program to detect the parasite in slaughtered livestock, the disease will continue to occur.

The main culprit in trichinosis today is undercooked pork products that carry the larvae of the nematode worm. These first stop off in the intestinal tract, then later in active muscles—like the calf, diaphragm, and tongue—which they weaken until the victim can barely move.

Even nonpork eaters can suffer, as this organism can be spread to other meats by the intentional or inadvertent mixing of pork with chopped beef in supermarkets, butcher shops, and restaurants. Of nearly three hundred reported cases of trichinosis in 1975, nonpork products, including hamburger meat, were responsible for sixty-eight cases.[10]

Among other viruses present in slaughtered animals is an aphthovirus that causes foot-and-mouth disease. Depending on the stage of infection at the time of slaughter, this RNA virus can go undetected. Initial signs of infection may not appear until after a two-to-eight-day incubation period, and it's possible they may never become apparent.[11] This highly infectious virus is biochemically active during the decaying process. However, when the action of enzymes and acids are halted due to the quick freezing of meat, the virus can remain intact and dormant, to become active again when the meat is thawed. This disease organism continues to thrive in the bone marrow, lymph nodes, blood, and muscles of animals long after slaughter. Studies investigating this health issue demand serious consideration, especially by those suffering from chronic degenerative diseases, or using immuno-suppressant drugs for cancer or other conditions in which immunity is already low.

Besides what goes on in the slaughterhouses and meat-packing plants, you must consider how the meat is handled in restaurants and other institutions. Patrons have little control over the treatment of these highly perishable products. According to a report issued by the Centers for Disease Control, the major factor in outbreaks of botulism, a serious form of food poisoning, is the mishandling of food. This includes improper storage temperatures, inadequate cooking time, and poor personal hygiene of food handlers.[12] An outbreak of food poisoning in a psychiatric hospital in England recently killed twenty-six patients. The culprit was roast beef that had been cooked and refrigerated overnight. At 7:15 the next morning, it was placed on the kitchen counter at room temperature. Approximately ten hours later it was served to patients for supper. This caused nearly 350 patients and 50 staff members to become ill.[13]

Cooking does curb some bacterial growth in decaying meats, yet there is evidence that not all the germs are destroyed, especially if meat is served rare. Wherever there is meat, there is bacteria. Even under very sanitary conditions, bacteria can be rampant, spread by the utensils used to cut the meat, the cutting board, or the counter top, or in a million other ways. All too often, we have a nonchalant attitude about sterility in the kitchen because bacteria are invisible to the naked eye. But bacteria can be deadly, especially salmonella.

There is no realistic hope of wiping out this disease as long as we continue to eat animal foods. As the National Academy of Sciences says, "Reluctantly, we are forced to recognize the unfeasibility of eradicating salmonellosis at this time."[14]

Dr. Scott Holmberg of the Centers for Disease Control says that salmonella poisoning affects "two to four million humans each year, and one of every thousand will die,"[15] many of them elderly people or infants. Scary, too, is the fact that symptoms seem innocuous: nausea, vomiting, and diarrhea may not trigger the immediate attention they deserve.

CHEESE AND FISH

The problems are not only with meat, but with animal products in general. All animal products are potential breeding grounds for salmonella. In 1976, twenty-eight cases of food poisoning were reported at once in Colorado and New Mexico—the culprit was a shipment of Cheddar cheese that had made its way into a group of Mexican food restaurants. In fact, there have been nearly sixty reports of food poisoning caused by cheese in the last hundred years, in which more than 2,900 people became ill and 117 died. There was a major incident involving Camembert cheese in 1971, and one involving cheese with jalapeños in June 1985.[16] Epidemiologists believe that the incidence of food poisoning is much more common than is actually reported. Many people do not recognize that their illness is from food contamination or may not think they require medical attention.

Those following a pesco-vegetarian diet, i.e., eating fish in addition to vegetables, are susceptible to poisoning from infected fish. The most widespread toxic fish are mackerel, tuna, and bonito.[17]

When these fish are contaminated with certain bacteria, chemical reaction causes the accumulation of histamine, a compound involved in the allergic response. Once this compound settles in the fish's muscle tissue, it becomes unresistant to cooking, canning, or other treatments. Histamine in fish is usually detectable by a change in odor or physical appearance, but sometimes toxic fish may appear normal. The response to eating such contaminated fish appears to be an allergic reaction, but is actually due to the high level of bacteria-induced histamines. Symptoms include light-headedness, rash, itching, headache, cramps, diarrhea, vomiting, sometimes shock, and rarely, death.

Clearly, when it comes to toxic substances, cutting down—or completely eliminating—animal products in *all* forms could be a wise disease-preventive measure. Vegetarianism is undoubtedly the safest way to eat.

ANTIBIOTICS

Exacerbating the problem is the common practice of agribusiness of feeding antibiotics to livestock, usually penicillin and tetracycline. These drugs are added to feed as growth stimulants and to prevent widespread breakouts of infection. It is estimated that 80 percent of the pigs, 60 percent of the cattle, and 30 percent of the chickens in the United States receive fortified chow. Some of the breeders have been accused of using the drugs to counter unsanitary and overcrowded animal living conditions.[18] Ironically, this overuse has caused drug-resistant bacteria to crop up. A report in a recent *New England Journal of Medicine* linked eighteen cases of food poisoning, which claimed one life and hospitalized eleven people, to hamburger meat riddled with a drug-resistant form of salmonella.[19] This spoiled beef was traced to a cattle farm in South Dakota where the livestock was consuming grain treated with tetracycline.

In humans, antibiotics are ineffective against new strains of bacteria. This becomes a special problem when people consuming the tainted meat are taking antibiotic drugs for medical reasons. For example, if a person is taking penicillin for a throat infection, the drug will wipe out the bacteria causing the sore throat, while the resistant salmonella bacteria rapidly multiply. Dr. Holmberg estimated that in 1984 alone, 1,500 humans died from this toxic effect.[20] Further studies on food-borne diseases have shown that human death is more common in cases involving consumption of these resistant strains of bacteria.[21]

Studies have also shown that many strains of E. Coli bacteria found in commercially slaughtered or frozen chickens are resistant to various antibiotics commonly used in medical practice.[22] Again, this is due to the widespread use of these drugs in livestock for rapid weight gain. Poultry is especially widely contaminated with these resistant bacteria and therefore poses a particularly high health risk for humans. The tuberculosis bacteria, which is extremely resistant to heat, is another germ common in poultry. Meat containing these micro-organisms can never be thoroughly sterile, even when well cooked.[23]

One of the more serious results of the farm ritual of treating livestock with antibiotics is the decreasing effectiveness of the drugs in human disease. For this reason, the FDA tried to ban antibiotics in the animal industry in 1977, but their efforts were shot down by the successful lobbying of the powerful livestock and drug companies like American Cyanamid, the biggest producer of antibiotics for livestock.[24]

Other countries have been quicker to deal with the issue. In 1971, Great Britain outlawed this antibiotic usage in animals, after an outbreak of food poisoning in the late 1960s killed eleven people. Germany, the Netherlands, and Japan soon followed.[25] In light of these decisions by other countries, the FDA is once again trying to ban the use of antibiotics in animal feed. Dr. Holmberg warns that "if we don't curtail the inappropriate use of antibiotics in animal feed, it will lead to more outbreaks of human illness."[26]

But there are still those like John Datt, director of the American Farm Bureau Federation in Washington, D.C., who will argue that curtailing the widespread use of antibiotics will cause a jump in the cost of meat. "That's the other side of the coin," he says. "Is it worth the cost?"[27]

The health-conscious answer is yes. But until the FDA can improve meat safety, it's up to the consumer to protect him or herself by avoiding meat. Even when antibiotics are eliminated from the feed for growth-spurring reasons, they are still widely used for the treatment or prevention of diseases in animals. England, for one, is still experiencing health problems due to resistant bacteria, even though the use of antibiotics in animal feed there has been banned for ten years.

On an ABC News television broadcast in November 1984, the "hidden dangers of meat" were highlighted. One anchorperson commented after the report that she was now going to become a vegetarian. Wouldn't others feel this way if they had access to the facts? This report treated the facts about the overuse of antibiotics and resultant human contamination as if they were a new story. But the truth about the health effects of medicating livestock was exposed seven years earlier in *How To Get Rid of the Poisons in Your Body* by Gary and Steve Null. One chapter, "The Meat Factory—Drugged, Dirty and Deadly," went into specific detail about this misuse.

The time lag in this case between actual discovery of ill effects and its reporting in the major news media may be explained by the cautiousness of "safe" journalists who don't want to step on the toes of special-interest groups—such as the meat industry.

Some animal producers have switched to less commonly used antibiotics in hopes of curtailing the human health hazards. Bambermycin is now widely used in chicken feed. "They're less expensive, they do a better job and they're not used to treat human illness," asserts J. Stephen Pretanik, science director for the National Broiler Council.[28] However, no one knows the long-term health risks involved with their usage. A biochemist for the National Resources Defense Council in New York believes that "all antibiotics can cause resistance to occur eventually."[29] So we may be only setting ourselves up for different health problems. For example, a 1984 FDA report said that many breeders are now using an antibiotic called chloramphenicol, which is inexpensive and works on resistant strains of bacteria. At very low doses, however, this drug can induce aplastic anemia in humans, a deadly disease which prevents the production of red blood cells by the bone marrow.

The FDA perceives this to be as dangerous a health threat as the drug DES was until it was outlawed in the late 1970s. Only 32 mgs. of chloramphenicol have induced aplastic anemia in humans.[30] It strongly appears that eating the flesh of animals fed with this drug is like playing Russian roulette.

This is not to say that all livestock breeders have sloppy standards. There are some who continue to raise livestock organically, i.e., without antibiotics, hormones, synthetic vitamins, or any other chemical additives. Instead they feed their animals organic, home-grown feed such as corn and alfalfa. Unfortunately, economic realities make this a difficult approach. Darrell Wilkes, director of Technical Services for the National Cattlemen's Association, says that "an operator who fattens cattle without drugs would spend an extra $50 on feed to get a steer up to 1,150 pounds—a formidable price to pay."[31]

Drugs, on the other hand, make mass production possible in close quarters, so their use makes for savings in manpower and land usage. Add to that the sad fact that programs established to encourage organic breeding were cut by the Reagan administration, and it's clear that organic animal breeding is unlikely to become prevalent.

HORMONES

Hormones and tranquilizers are often used to fatten livestock and keep them calm, respectively. In people, however, these drugs can be quite harmful. It is known, for instance, that certain hormones can cause abnormalities such as increased menstrual flow in women and decreased sperm count and impotence in men.[32]

Take DES (diethylstilbestrol), which was given to animals to fatten and tenderize them. This synthetic hormone, initially synthesized in 1938, was originally administered to cattle and poultry in their feed. But it has proven so detrimental to human health that in 1958, when the Food Additive Amendment to the Food, Drug and Cosmetic Act outlawed the use of any carcinogenic chemical in food, the use of DES was prohibited in poultry management. Although DES residues were detectable in poultry at that time, the analysis techniques available were not yet sophisticated enough to detect traces of DES in beef.[33] But by 1971 new regulations required it not be fed cattle for at least one week before slaughter.

Because of the "time bomb" effect of some carcinogens, it is sometimes difficult to prove a cancer-link until it is too late. DES was one such case. Given to women during pregnancy to prevent miscarriages, it had a latency period in their offspring for as long as 15–20 years (and maybe even longer) after the initial administration.[34] In the sixties and seventies, an unusual occurrence of vaginal cancer was diagnosed in some teenage daughters of mothers who had taken DES. Other gynecological abnormalities were also reported. Male offspring also developed structural and functional urogenital and cardiovascular abnormalities. The severity of these effects were related to the time of DES administration during pregnancy. DES is absorbed rapidly and 20–100 percent of an orally administered dose of this drug can be absorbed by humans.[35]

After further investigations into its carcinogenic and reproductive effects, DES in animal feed was entirely banned in 1972. However, breeders were now allowed to use this synthetic estrogen in the form of ear implants. It was erroneously believed by the FDA that with this method, no residues were left behind in slaughtered livestock. However, after traces of the drug were still found in animals, this method too was banned, in 1973. Residues were still being detected in meat after two years of refrigeration.[36] Before science improved its technology and banned all uses of DES in animal feed, it was used legally for several years in three-quarters of the thirty million cattle being raised for human consumption in the United States.[37]

Even though DES is a known carcinogen, many chose to ignore its negative health effects, insisting that its ban was politically motivated. One FDA official stated that, "DES has been used for over 20 years as a growth promotant in animals without any indication of danger to humans."[38] Once again, this attitude clearly did not represent the scientific data incriminating this drug.

Current studies on DES are showing new evidence associating the drug with an increased risk of cancer for women.[39] A report in a recent issue of the *Journal of the American Medical Association* links DES with cervical cancer. A study in the *New England Journal of Medicine* found that women who took DES were at greater risk of developing breast cancer. Concerned public groups feel that the federal government should issue warnings to women who took DES and to their daughters, as many local health groups have done.

In other parts of the world, the continued use of hormones is creating abnormalities in children. An epidemic of breast enlargement in a group of Italian children aged three to seven was linked to poultry and beef that had been treated with hormones.[40] Medical researchers in Italy stated that because the meat of young animals is preferred, estrogens are used for rapid weight gain.

Likewise, in Puerto Rico an estrogen-like drug used to promote growth in cattle is suspect in nearly three thousand cases of abnormal sexual development in children under the age of nine.[41] The cases include early menstruation, abnormal breast development in boys as well as girls, and ovarian cysts. Dr. Carmen Sáenz, director of pediatrics at the Hospital de Diego in San Juan, holds that this animal-feed drug has contaminated the island's food chain. And, supporting her hypothesis, higher-than-normal estrogen levels were detected in some chicken samples sent to the University of Pennsylvania for analysis. At this writing, the problem has yet to be corrected: animal breeders deny they might be responsible for the children's problems.

ADDITIVES

To preserve and to "prettify" meat, the meat industry often uses chemical food additives. No consumer wants to buy slimy, brownish green, rotting meat. Like morticians, meat packers artificially treat this organic material so that it looks better than it would if left alone. Red and violet dyes are added to beef and pork, while yellow dyes are put into chicken feed to enhance the color of the chickens' flesh. Even pet food is cosmetically treated in this way.

The majority of synthetic colorings used by the food industry are coal-tar derivatives. A number of these dyes—like the infamous Red Dye #2—have been banned by the FDA, and with good reason. There is no justifiable use for these artificial additives. Even those labeled "U.S. Certified" (which merely means they meet minimum government standards and limitations), are not necessarily safe. Low levels of some artificial colorings have been correlated with increased incidence of cancer and reproductive damage leading to birth defects, stillbirths, and infertility in animals.

Preservatives like the two petroleum derivatives BHT (butylated hydroxytoluene) and BHA (butylated hydroxyanisole) are also frequently added to meat to help prevent its fat from becoming rancid, though they may have some adverse effects on humans. These chemicals are commonly added to lard, chicken fat, butter, cream, bacon, sausage, cold cuts, and milk, as well as to some nonmeat products, including vegetable oils, potato chips, peanut butter, shortening, raisins, breakfast cereals, and chewing gum. BHA and BHT are either added directly to these foods during processing or to the packaging. Toxicity of BHA and BHT can lead to skin blisters, fatigue, eye hemorrhaging, and respiratory problems. However, these symptoms are often difficult to diagnose, and an affected person may continue to eat the symptom-causing foods.

Sodium nitrates and nitrites, found most often in smoked and cured animal products (even fish!) are precursors to a powerful group of carcinogens called nitrosamines. Animal studies clearly determined that these toxic compounds can cause cancer throughout the entire body. Even though this has been common knowledge since the 1950s, nitrates and nitrites are still widely used today.

There are thousands of other meat additives—lesser known, but just as potentially problematic:

- Artificial flavorings (some which have proven carcinogenic)
- Benzoil peroxide: a chemical bleach used in flour that can destroy the natural anti-oxidant vitamin E
- EDTA: used to prevent the oxidation of fats and oils
- Monosodium glutamate: a flavor enhancer most often linked with the symptoms of "Chinese restaurant syndrome"—headache, tightness in the chest, prickling skin sensations, impaired concentration, and fatigue. (Curiously, vitamin B_6 has been shown to block the effects of MSG.)
- Propyl gallate: another anti-oxidant
- Salt: sodium chloride, a problem for those whose blood pressure is salt sensitive

Most of these chemicals are used in combinations. For example, propyl gallate is commonly paired with BHA and BHT to help prevent fat rancidity. These chemicals have been judged safe when tested alone. However, scientists still don't know the long-term health consequences of multiple chemical bombardment.

Some animal products are allowed to be extended with cornstarch, sugar, soybean, and dry milk by more than 3 percent of their volume. And some meats, like franks and sausages, may even include, as secret ingredients, rat hair, pest excreta, or dead insects —depending on slaughterhouse and packing conditions.

Perhaps one of the most bizarre chemical treatments is practiced by some poultry breeders who inject a flavoring solution in live birds to cover up the artificial flavors caused by overuse of chemicals in feed.

PESTICIDES

The frequent uncurtailed use of drugs—including antibiotics, hormones, and tranquilizers—has caused several European countries to boycott U.S. meat imports. But antibiotics, hormones, and tranquilizers aren't the only synthetic ingredients that pollute animal products. It is estimated that over 100,000 people in the United States are subjected to pesticide poisoning annually—not only farmers and farm workers, but countless others who unknowingly eat pesticides in their breakfast sausage or lunchtime burger. Among the common pesticides found in meat are DDT, cadmium, carbon tetrachloride, and hexachlorobenzene.

The average American, in fact, ingests approximately 40 mg. of pesticide residue every year. Of this, about 4 mg. are stored in fat tissue and can lead to toxicity symptoms like headache, fatigue, muscle aches, and fever. Humans have literally become walking, breathing test tubes—but few doctors are aware of the experiment in progress. Unless they have a reason to suspect pesticide contamination, most doctors have trouble pinning such general, common symptoms on the real culprit.

USDA tests show that over 60 percent of cattle, 80 percent of poultry, and nearly 40 percent of swine are contaminated with the pesticide DDT, yet these animals are usually found to be fit legally for human consumption.

A recent government report estimates that one-sixth of all meat and poultry eaten in the U.S. contains "potentially harmful residues of animal drugs, pesticides or environmental contaminants." It also stated that out of nearly 150 known drugs and pesticides found in meat and poultry products, "42 are known to cause or are suspected of causing cancer, 20 of causing birth defects, 6 are suspected of causing mutations, 6 are suspected of causing adverse effects on the fetus, and others are reported to cause other toxic effects."[42] Clearly, this is a serious and far-reaching problem.

Interestingly, pesticides are actually generally unnecessary. But as the business of farming has become more and more "sophisticated," farmers are increasingly relying on chemical fertilizers to help keep up with demand for farm products. Many of these chemical alternatives to "natural" farming cause rampant soil depletion and erosion. To make up for this depletion, farmers often utilize synthetic fertilizers. One side effect: the proliferation of insects and other farm pests. To control them, farmers usually go the pesticide route.

Pesticides are stored in human and animal fat tissue. The implications of this fact are frightening. Consider this: when a cow consumes soybeans containing pesticide residues, much of the pesticide poison settles in its fat tissue—it is never expelled. The person who comes along and wolfs down a T-bone from this cow is also getting concentrated amounts of toxic residues. Even if the pesticide-treated soybeans were eaten directly, the pesticide content would be much less concentrated. Thus, if you have a choice between eating plant food treated with pesticides or animals who have eaten pesticide-treated plant food, you're better off consuming the plant directly. Unfortunately, the federal government is doing little to ease the situation, although some efforts have been made.

Pesticides also pollute the water supply, floating into lakes, streams, and rivers through soil erosion and seepage into underground waters. This enormous pesticide leak has "63 percent of rural America— some 39 million people—drinking water that may be unsafe," according to *The New Farm* magazine.[43] Three-quarters of the rural Western population are drinking water that is excessively contaminated; 65 percent in the Southern and North-central states; and 45 percent in the Northeast. Known contaminants include:

- lindane: a toxic insecticide which affects the central nervous system
- mercury: known to cause kidney damage
- cadmium: a toxic metal associated with high blood pressure and kidney damage
- lead: known to damage the nervous system and kidneys
- nitrates: the chemical precursor of cancer-causing nitrosames

The results of a five-year study showed that the quality of our drinking water is much worse than previously suspected. Over 60 percent of all rural households are dependent on water that is seriously plagued with at least one contaminant. One proponent of the 1974 Safe Drinking Water Act commented, "Now we see that 'pure' rural water isn't automatically safe." Still, the EPA is acting very slowly to warn the public of this potential health hazard: three years after an EPA study exposed the contaminated-water problem, the public is still unaware of these alarming findings. Congressman Dennis Echart of Ohio accuses the agency of covering up these findings because "it's damaging to the image of rural water and underscores the EPA's failure to set and enforce rules."[44]

Underwater wildlife also suffers from water contamination. Although the toxic pesticide DDT has been outlawed for over twelve years, traces of this chemical were present in every fish tested from the southern California coastline recently. Willard Bascom, executive director of the Southern California Coastal Water Research Project, pessimistically reported that "DDT is going to be with us for a long time—twenty, fifty, perhaps one hundred years."[45]

Not only fish eaters are at risk. Fat-soluble substances like DDT tend to build up in fish liver. So if you take fish-liver oil as a source of vitamins A and D or for essential fatty-acid supplementation, you may be unwittingly ingesting unwanted pesticides as well.

Dr. Michael Fox, director of the Institute for Animal Problems, warns us to "get off the agribusiness treadmill of using herbicides and pesticides," and advocates that we move toward self-sufficiency. Instead of thinking about short-term profits for agribusiness, the government should be concerned with the future of the environment.[46]

NINETEEN

Vegetarianism and Health: What the Studies Show

T here's a line of reasoning we hear repeatedly these days, both in the media and among friends. It's about diet, and it goes something like this: *The experts are always changing their minds about what's good for us and what isn't. One week they say that Food A is great for us, and the next week it's Food B that's wonderful, and Food A is totally out. The experts are beginning to seem a bit unreliable, and what's more, we're getting real confused about what to eat. We might as well give up trying to adopt a healthy lifestyle. With all the disagreement, what's the use?*

Sound familiar? This reasoning is voiced so frequently that you could almost call it part of the conventional wisdom. Except for one thing—it isn't wisdom because it isn't based on truth. At least when it comes to the benefits of adopting a properly balanced vegetarian way of eating, there is no disagreement. In fact, on January 2, 1996, for the first time, the U.S. Secretary of Health and Human Services,

Donna E. Shalala, endorsed the healthfulness of a vegetarian diet. The data have been in for decades now and they demonstrate one thing: Vegetarianism offers incontrovertible health benefits. The studies are there—hundreds of them—in peer-reviewed scientific journals. I know because I've got a lot of the reprints in my office—cartons full, in fact.

I'd like to share some of their findings with you. Part of the reason for people's confusion about health and their resulting defeatist attitude is that most people, not being in the science field, don't have access to the technical literature. Yes, the mass media do use these research articles when they distill the news for us. However, those who mold the news into the form that we consume each day often bypass less flashy but ultimately more significant research findings in favor of the more dramatic or seemingly contradictory. After all, confusion and conflict are profitable for the news business. And dramatic reversals are even better. On the other hand, reaffirmations that, yes, vegetables and whole grains have been shown, yet again, to be healthful, are stodgy.

Yet such reaffirmations can be life-saving. That's why I think it's important to delve into the scientific literature and see what it's been telling us all along.

THE HEART-HEALTHY DIET

Cardiovascular disease is the number-one cause of death in America today, and a major risk factor in heart disease is hypertension, or high blood pressure. This condition is sometimes called "the silent killer" because people often don't realize that they have it until it's too late. The symptoms—such as fatigue and poor circulation in the extremities—are frequently ignored, because people consider them normal parts of aging. But they're not. What's actually happening when a person has high blood pressure is that a constant, increased burden is being placed on the heart as this organ has to pump harder to get blood through the generally ever-narrowing artery walls. Extra exertion, in the form of exercise or stress, can then put the body in jeopardy because there may be insufficient oxygen supply to the muscles and the brain. Heart attack and stroke are possible consequences.

The good news in all of this is that a vegetarian diet has a blood-pressure–lowering effect, and it's one that has been documented numerous times. In fact, as noted in one of the recent studies,[1] scientific interest in this salutary effect of a meat-free diet goes back to the early decades of this century. That's when it was shown that patients' hypertension was worsened by meat intake, and that when vegetarian college students added meat to their diets, their blood pressure increased significantly within two weeks.

The thinking on this diet–blood pressure connection continues to be the same to this day, with a recent article in *The American Journal of Clinical Nutrition* concluding that, ". . . there is now strong evidence for a blood-pressure–lowering effect of a lacto-ovo-vegetarian diet . . . ; the effect is independent of sodium and energy intake and of other aspects of lifestyle that tend to characterize vegetarian populations."[2] What's more, the researchers involved in this report point out that "Cardiovascular risk in general is low in people adhering to a lacto-ovo-vegetarian diet, not only because their blood pressures are lower and tend to rise less with age, but also because they carry less excess fat and tend to have healthier blood-lipid profiles than do meat eaters."[2]

Studies of the effects of vegetarianism often look at Seventh-Day Adventists, a conservative religious group that encourages abstinence from meat, as well as from alcohol, caffeine, and tobacco use. These people have a general interest in a wholesome lifestyle, and a deep religious commitment. A problem, though, in comparing members of this group with meat-eating members of society at large is that these other lifestyle factors — religiosity and abstinence from substances besides meat, may confound the results. To avoid this pitfall, researchers writing in the *Australian & New Zealand Journal of Medicine* paired a group of about a hundred Adventist vegetarians with a group of Mormons who were similar in strength of religious affiliation, as well as caffeine, alcohol, and tobacco avoidance, but differed only in that they ate meat. What the researchers found was that the vegetarian Adventists had significantly lower blood pressure, obesity, and cholesterol levels than the Mormons did.[3] Similar results have been found in many other studies, involving comparisons between vegetarian Seventh-Day Adventists and other groups,[4] and between groups of Adventists that differed only in that one experimental segment adhered to vegetarianism and one didn't. Here's an excerpt from this last type of study:[5]

The serum cholesterol levels and the dietary habits of a voluntary study group of 466 Seventh-Day Adventists . . . were compared to determine the influence of diet on serum cholesterol levels in an adult population whose only environmental differences related to dietary practices—adherence to vegetarianism. This study matched vegetarians with nonvegetarians from the same base population according to several physical and demographic variables—place of residence, age, sex, marital status, height, weight, and occupation—and examined the effects of various levels of meat, fish, and fowl consumption (degrees of nonvegetarianism) on serum cholesterol levels. With the exception of those under 25 years of age, the results showed that the nonvegetarians had higher serum cholesterol levels than the vegetarians.

In another study,[6] even those under 25 were shown to have cholesterol levels adversely affected by eating meat. Scientists writing in the *British Medical Journal* reported that at a Seventh-Day Adventist high school near Sydney, Australia, children aged 12 to 17 completed questionnaires about their dietary habits. The children were then divided into two groups according to their answers— those who occasionally or regularly ate meat, fish, or fowl, and those whose protein came entirely from dairy and vegetable sources. The vegetarian youngsters had significantly lower cholesterol levels than did their meat-eating peers. While adolescents don't generally have to worry about heart disease, patterns established early in life tend to get carried on in later years, when health risks increase.

In addition to blood pressure and cholesterol levels, triglyceride levels have been shown to be adversely affected—i.e., raised—by meat eating.[6, 7] But perhaps it's most significant to look at the coronary heart disease picture from the perspective of mortality. Researchers writing in *The American Journal of Clinical Nutrition*[8] compared vegetarian Seventh-Day Adventists with nonvegetarian members of the same group. What they found was that "the risk of fatal coronary heart disease among nonvegetarian Seventh-Day Adventist males, ages 35 to 64, is three times greater than [that for] vegetarian Seventh-Day Adventist males of comparable age." The report cites lower total or saturated fat intake, and higher intake of dietary fiber, as probable factors in the better statistics for the vegetarian group.

LOWERING CANCER RISK

There's a wealth of published information that points to a plant-based diet as a way of avoiding cancer. For instance, the *International Journal of Cancer* has reported that cancers of the colon, rectum, pancreas, breast, ovary, uterine corpus, and prostate are correlated with the amount of animal products used in various countries.[9] Returning to the vegetarian-oriented Seventh-Day Adventists, it's been reported[10] that "the risk of fatal cancer among Seventh-Day Adventist males is 53 percent of the risk among all U.S. white males of comparable age. For Seventh-Day Adventist females, the risk is 68 percent of that in all U.S. white females."

An article in the *Journal of Environmental Pathology and Toxicology*[11] elaborates on the Seventh-Day Adventists' lower cancer rates:

> Perhaps as a result of their vegetarian diet, Adventists have a lower intake of benzopyrene and nitrosamines and a higher intake of flavones, which are strong inducers of the enzyme systems responsible for detoxifying such carcinogens. In addition, they may have a higher intake of vitamins A and C, recently suggested as possible protective agents against certain chemical carcinogens. Thus, it seems reasonable to suggest that the typical Adventist diet may protect against many of the major sites of cancer.

A prime benefit of eating plant-derived foods is that they contain fiber. Indeed, fiber is, largely, what plants are made of. The importance of fiber in a healthy diet and as a preventive measure against disease cannot be overstressed. Fiber aids in the speedy digestion and elimination of our foods. It works like a scrub brush to scour away accumulating deposits from our intestinal walls. Left to accumulate, these particles would otherwise decay and putrefy, sending toxins throughout the entire body and acting as a local irritant within the intestines. Since foods of vegetable origin are naturally rich in high amounts of fiber, they are easily digested. Meat and other animal products, on the other hand, do not contain fiber. They are difficult to digest and can often remain in the intestines for three to four days.

Now consider what the literature reports about dietary links to colon cancer. This is from the journal *Annals of Surgery*[12]:

Current epidemiologic data have shown that there are striking differences in the incidence of colon cancer in various parts of the world. It has been demonstrated that the occurrence of cancer of the colon is much lower in East Africa, India and Japan than in Western Europe or North America. A series of studies of migrants have revealed that these differences are most likely environmental and not genetic. Investigations of various environmental influences have frequently linked dietary habits to the development of carcinoma of the colon. Nutritional substances such as fiber, refined carbohydrate, animal fat and protein have all been advanced as being the significant factor responsible for the variance in incidence rates of colonic cancer.

Epidemiologic data have also shown that the incidence of cancer of all types, including carcinoma of the colon, is 30 percent to 40 percent lower in American Seventh-Day Adventists, who are strict vegetarians, than in the meat-consuming general public. Further studies have shown that the levels of bile acids, as well as the degradation products and enzymes responsible for the degradation of bile acids in the colonic lumen, are decreased in this group of vegetarians.

The bile acids referred to in that journal article are substances associated with colon cancer risk, and they have indeed been shown to be lower in vegetarians.[13] It's noteworthy that the vegetarian-oriented Seventh-Day Adventists have a colon cancer mortality rate only 61 percent that of the general U.S. population, for males, and 70 percent for females.[14] A paper reporting these statistics, in *The American Journal of Clinical Nutrition,* goes on to note that "socioeconomic status and educational level are factors that influence mortality rates, and these are generally higher among Seventh-Day Adventists. However, the standardized mortality ratio for colon cancer is equally low among Seventh-Day Adventists with a low and high level of education. This implies that the higher educational level of Seventh-Day Adventists does not account for their lower colon cancer mortality rate."

Again and again diet comes up as an important factor in colon cancer. From *The American Journal of Clinical Nutrition*[15]:

Recent epidemiological studies associate colon cancer with specific types of diet. In general, highly developed countries have a high incidence of colon cancer, and less well developed countries have a low incidence. Japan represents an exception in that it is highly developed but has a low incidence of large bowel cancer. Japanese who adopt a Western diet, however, develop colon cancer with increased frequency; among Japanese immigrants, the frequency approaches that of native Americans.

From another report[16]: "Cholesterol and its metabolites, together with bile acids, are implicated as risk factors in the genesis and progression of colon cancer . . ." Again, a high-meat regimen will increase levels of these harmful substances.

Among men in the U.S., cancer of the prostate is the second most common malignancy, after lung cancer.[17] But it's been shown that Seventh-Day Adventist men between the ages of 45 and 70 have a mortality rate from this disease that's only 30 percent that of males in the general California population (California is where many Adventists live), suggesting that vegetarianism may be a protective factor here. Say researchers who have studied this, in *The American Journal of Clinical Nutrition,* "Implications include the possible modification of prostate cancer risk through dietary intervention."[18]

"Cancer incidence among California Seventh-Day Adventists, 1976–1982" was an important paper that appeared in *The American Journal of Clinical Nutrition* in 1994.[19] Some excerpts:

> For prostate cancer, a high consumption pattern of beans, lentils, peas, tomatoes, raisins, dates, and other dried fruits was associated with lower cancer risk in this analysis. . . .
> High consumption of fruits was significantly associated with lower lung cancer risk even after adjusting for smoking. Higher risk of colon cancer was associated with higher consumption of saturated fats. Lower risk of colon cancer was associated with higher fiber and legume consumption.
> Higher consumption of soy-based products was associated with markedly lower risk of pancreas cancer in this population. Consumption of dried fruits, beans, lentils, and peas was also significantly associated with lower risk. . . . Risk of bladder cancer increased twofold in association with high meat intake.

And this is from an article dealing solely with pancreatic cancer risk, which appeared in the journal *Cancer*[20]: "Increasing consumption of vegetarian protein products, beans, lentils, and peas, as well as dried fruit, was associated with highly significant protective relationships to pancreas cancer risk."

In the area of brain tumors, the journal *Neuroepidemiology* published research showing that "increasing use of meat, poultry or fish . . . was associated with increased risk estimates for gliomas. This increase in risk was especially apparent for consumption of pork products. . . ."[21] The report went on to explain that "since many pork products are cured with sodium nitrite, this may be consistent with the hypothesis that foods containing high concentrations of N-nitroso compounds may increase brain cancer risk."

WOMEN'S HEALTH CONCERNS

Compared to the general female population, Seventh-Day Adventist women have a lower mortality rate from breast and endometrial cancers, and the fact that 50 percent of the Adventists are vegetarians seems to bear on this. Dietary patterns affect hormonal ones, and these are crucial factors in women's disease risk.[22]

One contributor to increased breast cancer risk is early onset of menstruation, and, in fact, the age of menarche, or first menstruation, has been decreasing over the years in Western Europe and the U.S. Our changing diet, with increased amounts of fat, simple carbohydrates, and meat, has contributed to this trend. But researchers writing in the journal *Medical Hypotheses*[23] have proven experimentally that "the present trend toward early menarche can be reversed when a balanced vegetarian diet is selected in place of the ordinary American diet." Other researchers underscore the importance of this concept when they write in the *Journal of the American Dietetic Association* that the maturation delay of vegetarian Adventist teenage girls, compared with meat-eating schoolgirls, "may carry potential health benefits in adult life. A later age of menarche has been consistently associated with decreased risk for several cancers, particularly of the breast."[24]

An issue of interest to older women is the maintenance of mineral content in their bones, and once again, vegetable eaters have an advantage. Vegetarianism has been shown to contribute to strong bones in postmenopausal women. Researchers explain that "The primary dietary characteristics of a lacto-ovo-vegetarian diet that may be of benefit to bone tissue are the sources of protein and quantities of calcium and phosphorus in the diet. Investigators . . . suggest that vegetable protein produces a lower-acid ash than animal protein when metabolized and thus, helps to conserve calcium."[25] The statistics are there to back this up[26]: "Lacto-ovo-vegetarian women 50 to 59 years of age lost 18 percent bone mineral mass while omnivorous women lost 35 percent."

FROM DENTAL HEALTH TO DIABETES

The reports go on and on, and to fully document vegetarianism's health benefits would require volumes. But here are just a few more sample quotations from the literature to give you an idea of the scope and depth of the research that's been done—and replicated time and again:

". . . the dental and periodontal status of the Seventh-Day Adventist group was significantly better than that of the controls, suggesting that vegetarianism is beneficial to oral health."[27]

". . . when healthy elderly vegetarian women are compared with closely matched nonvegetarian peers, the vegetarian diet is associated with several benefits, primarily lower blood glucose and lipid levels . . ."[28]

". . . After controlling for height, boys and girls in the Seventh-Day Adventist schools were found to be leaner than their public school peers. . . . These results suggest that a health oriented lifestyle in childhood and adolescence, such as the one followed by Seventh-Day Adventists, is compatible with adequate growth and associated with a lower weight for height."[29]

"During 21 years [of study and follow-up], the rate of diabetes as an underlying cause of death in Adventists was only 45 percent of the rate for all U.S. whites."[30]

"All-cause mortality showed a significant negative association with green salad consumption and a significant positive association with consumption of eggs and meat. For green salad and eggs, the association was stronger for women; for meat, the association was stronger for men. All the observed associations were adjusted for age, sex, smoking history, history of major chronic disease, and age at initial exposure to the Adventist Church."[31]

"Systolic blood pressure in Adventists was lower in early adult life and rose less with aging than in the other two groups [from the general population]. This pattern also occurred with diastolic blood pressure. . . . The differences in plasma lipid levels between Adventists and other population groups can be explained by a vegetarian diet, and this may have contributed also to the blood pressure levels."[32]

"Vegetarian students consumed significantly higher amounts of calcium and phosphorus than did omnivore students, suggesting that . . . the vegetarian students were making superior food pattern selections."[33]

THE BOTTOM LINE—A LONGER, HEALTHIER LIFE

This last concept—that vegetarians tend to have superior nutritional status as shown by measures of important nutrients—has been borne out in multiple studies. In one, which was detailed in the *Journal of the American Dietetic Association,*[34] groups of vegetarian and nonvegetarian elderly women were matched for a variety of nondietary factors and then asked to keep records of what they ate over a week-long period. The analyzed results showed that the vegetarians consumed significantly less cholesterol, saturated fatty acids, and caffeine, but more carbohydrates, dietary fiber, magnesium, vitamins E and A, thiamin, pantothenic acid, copper, and manganese. "In summary," says this report, "when healthy elderly women were compared with closely matched nonvegetarian peers, the vegetarian diet was associated with improved nutrient intake and associated reductions in blood glucose and lipid levels."

Another study pairing vegetarian and omnivorous postmenopausal women[35] yielded similar results, with the vegetarians' diets providing higher nutrient density for folate, thiamin, vitamin C, and vitamin A; as well as lower total fat, saturated fatty acids, and cholesterol; and higher dietary fiber.

Other studies[36, 37, 38] further emphasize the nutrient- and fiber-rich nature of vegetarian eating. But of course, in the final analysis, what really matters is that we can affect the quality of our lives by our eating patterns. Once again, the scientific literature can guide us as we make our choices, if we will only read its findings:

"Compared to Adventists who heavily use meat, the vegetarian Adventists have a substantially lower risk of fatal coronary disease, fatal diabetes and death from any cause, especially among men. Among men who use few animal products . . . the risk of fatal prostate cancer is one third that of Adventist men who heavily use such products."[39]

"Recent studies at Loma Linda University revealed that Seventh-Day Adventists (aged 45–54) who eat meat six or more times per week are three times as likely to die of heart disease as vegetarian Seventh-Day Adventists. . . .

"Seventh-Day Adventist men and women who eat meat six or more times per week have twice the incidence of obesity (30 percent overweight or above) which is related to increased death rate from diabetes. This may be related to a higher caloric density, low fiber diet. . . .

"Vegetarians also have a lower mortality rate from several cancers. . . .

"Vegetarian Seventh-Day Adventist women aged 55 and above have significantly less osteoporosis than the meat-eating non-Seventh-Day Adventists."[40]

Finally, consider a study on lifestyle and the use of health services described in a 1994 issue of *The American Journal of Clinical Nutrition*.[41] In this research, a group of close to 30,000 Seventh-Day Adventists in California were given questionnaires on lifestyle and divided into four groups—vegetarian and nonvegetarian groups of men, and of women. These people were than tracked for a period of a year to see how much health care they required, and whether there were differences between the amount of medical attention needed by vegetarians versus meat-eaters.

There were. In a year's time, vegetarian females reported significantly fewer overnight hospitalizations and surgeries than did their nonvegetarian female counterparts in the study. Nonvegetarian males reported more overnight hospitalizations and X-rays than did their vegetarian cohorts. The average numbers of chronic diseases were 1.24 in nonvegetarian females, compared to 1.03 in vegetarian females, with nonvegetarian and vegetarian males averaging 0.93 and 0.79, respectively, in the chronic disease count. Medication use was higher by 70 to 115 percent for the nonvegetarian females compared to their vegetarian peers, and for males, the meat-eaters' medication use was double that of the abstainers. In short, the vegetarians were healthier.

"We conclude that a vegetarian diet may decrease the prevalence of chronic disease, medication use, and health services use, and thus, potentially, health care costs," said the study.[41] Of all these conclusions, I myself am convinced, and have been for a long time. One has only to examine the vast body of scientific literature to see why.

TWENTY

The Healthy
Vegetarian Today

I f you've read through the last chapter, on research studies, you've gotten a grounding in why we who advocate the vegetarian way of life are convinced of its health benefits. And if you've delved further into the subject, and actually gone to the primary source material yourself, you've gained more of an understanding of how years of study have proven the vegetarian lifestyle to be the healthiest. But how does all of this impact upon *you–today?* Let's update our look at the literature and concentrate on the very latest studies and their practical ramifications.

THE MESSAGE OF THE NINETIES

Do you want to be healthier? Go vegetarian. That, by and large, is the message that today's studies are telling us. And, significantly, that message has filtered down from the ivory towers of the research world to those working in the trenches to keep Americans healthy— our family physicians.

Consider, for example, the review of the health effects of vegetarian diets in the journal *American Family Physician* in November 1994. People eating vegetarian diets often have lower weight and blood pressure than the population at large, the article says. In addition, "the lower intakes of cholesterol and saturated fat decrease cholesterol and low-density lipoprotein fractions in vegetarians. They have lower mortality rates attributable primarily to lower death rates from ischemic heart disease and certain cancers. High fiber intake also may reduce risk of other diseases such as bowel cancers, gallstones and diabetes." Most important, the report concludes that "considering the improvement in health that may be derived from vegetarianism, patients (especially those at risk for cardiovascular disease and cancer) should be encouraged to consume increasingly vegetarian diets."

The American Dietetic Association is now on the vegetarian bandwagon too, as evidenced by a position paper of theirs that appeared in the November 1993 *Journal of the American Dietetic Association.* "It is the position of The American Dietetic Association that vegetarian diets are healthful and nutritionally adequate when appropriately planned," they state. But they go on to say substantially more, as they discuss the benefits of this way of eating:

> Studies of vegetarians indicate that they often have lower mortality rates from several chronic degenerative diseases that may be attributed to diet as well as to other lifestyle characteristics. . . . Mortality from coronary heart disease is lower in vegetarians than in nonvegetarians. . . . One study demonstrated reversal of even severe coronary artery disease without the use of lipid-lowering drugs by using a combination of a vegetarian diet deriving less than 10 percent of its energy from fat, smoking cessation, stress management, and moderate exercise. Vegetarians have low rates of hypertension and non-insulin-dependent diabetes mellitus than do nonvegetarians; lessening these risk factors may also decrease the risk of cardiovascular and coronary artery disease in the vegetarian population. . . .

In other words, the American Dietetic Association is now not only conceding that vegetarianism is an acceptable dietary choice, but also that it offers concrete health benefits. And there was more in this position paper:

Obesity, a major public health problem in the United States, exacerbates or complicates many diseases. Vegetarians, especially vegans, often have weights that are closer to desirable weights than do nonvegetarians. Vegetarians may be at low risk for non-insulin-independent diabetes because they are leaner than nonvegetarians. Also, vegetarians' high intake of complex carbohydrates, which are often relatively high in fiber content, improves carbohydrate metabolism and may lower basal blood glucose levels. . . .

Although most vegetarian diets meet or exceed the Recommended Dietary Allowances for protein, they often provide less protein than nonvegetarian diets. This lower protein intake may be associated with better calcium retention in vegetarians and improved kidney function in individuals with prior kidney damage. Further, lower protein intakes may result in lower fat intake with its inherent advantages, because foods high in protein are frequently high in fat also. . . .

Vegetarian diets that are low in animal products are typically lower than nonvegetarian diets in total fat, saturated fat, and cholesterol, factors associated with reduced risk of coronary artery disease and some forms of cancer.

While this information is vital, it's not new; it's all been reported before in studies published in a vast variety of journals. What's particularly noteworthy here, though, is that the influential American Dietetic Association has now assimilated all of this information into its own world view and policy. This is the group that's instrumental in molding the way America's dietitians are trained, and previous generations of dietitians were taught that a vegetarian diet was inadequate or, at best, difficult to implement. It used to be taught that, if you weren't eating meat, you had to consciously combine vegetable and sometimes dairy sources of protein in order to get the complete protein that your body needs. You had to do this within a given meal, and the strictures on protein-combining sometimes left would-be vegetarians puzzled or wondering if they were short-changing themselves nutritionally. That's all been changed, though. Look at this additional excerpt from the ADA article:

Plant sources of protein alone can provide adequate amounts of the essential and nonessential amino acids, assuming that dietary protein sources from plants are reasonably varied and that caloric intake is sufficient to meet energy needs. Whole

grains, legumes, vegetables, seeds, and nuts all contain essential and nonessential amino acids. Conscious combining of
these foods within a given meal, as the complementary protein
dictum suggests, is unnecessary. Additionally, soy protein has
been shown to be nutritionally equivalent in protein value to
proteins of animal orgin and, thus, can serve as the sole source
of protein intake if desired.

To their credit, this group has acknowledged studies, such as my
own, showing that vegetable foods provide everything that humans
need for healthy life.

THE MEDICAL PROFESSION IS CATCHING ON

An article in the May 1994 *Western Journal of Medicine* details a
number of points about the benefits of vegetarianism. Written by
doctors in the field of family and preventive medicine, it begins with
these words directed toward other clinicians: "Physicians often
evaluate and recommend changes in the diet of their patients. Just
as the role of dietary saturated fat in coronary artery disease led
physicians to recommend moderation in red meat consumption, the
data on the physiologic effects of vegetarianism should encourage
further reductions in meat consumption."

What are some of the physiologic effects discussed in the article?
One is that vegetarians have lower weight, on average, compared to
omnivores. Then there is the fact that they have lower total serum
cholesterol levels, and lower blood pressure as well. Also, vegetarians have lower mortality rates than the population at large, because
heart disease, and certain cancers, occur less frequently in this
group.

Vegetable eaters are, of necessity, fiber eaters; they generally
don't have to worry, the way omnivores do, whether they're ingesting enough of this healthful substance. The article mentions the
vital, health-promoting role fiber plays:

Dietary fibers—especially soluble fibers such as guar gum, pec-
tin, and oat gum—have been shown to lower total cholestrol
levels, primarily by lowering LDL-cholesterol and triglyceride
levels, without consistent effects on HDL-cholesterol levels. Be-

cause vegetarians (especially vegans) may have fiber intakes two to three times those of omnivores, fiber intake may contribute to vegetarians' favorable lipid profiles. Higher fiber intake may also help reduce risks of other diseases such as bowel cancers, gallstones, and diabetes.

The authors' conclusion couldn't be clearer:

> Many consider vegetarianism a matter of individual taste, an ethical choice, a political statement, or even a personal quirk. Yet, the balance of the data suggests that vegetarianism likely improves individual as well as societal health. . . . Our review of the data suggests that people, particularly those at high risk for cardiovascular disease and cancer, should be encouraged to consume increasingly vegetarian diets.

The *Mayo Clinic Health Letter,* in January 1995, ran an article entitled "Vegetarian Diets: They're No Longer Radical, Just Good for You." And that about sums up the change in attitude that's come about of late, as officialdom comes to accept the mountain of evidence showing that vegetarianism is the sensible dietary choice. This evidence comes from all over the world; this particular article talks about a study of 6500 families in China that showed that those who ate the least meat were the healthiest.

Going from China to another part of the world, people living in the Mediterranean have traditionally enjoyed health benefits stemming largely from their plant-product–centered diet. The June 1995 issue of the *American Journal of Clinical Nutrition* contains an article on the Mediterranean diet, referring to it as a dietary pattern that deserves to be preserved and promoted. The article discusses the researcher Ancel Keys, who, beginning in the 1950s, examined the Mediterranean diet and helped establish it as the original prototype for the way people in the United States and elsewhere should be eating. Here are some of Keys's reflections on the Mediterranean diet and public health today:

> My concern about diet as a public health problem began in the early 1950s in Naples, where we observed very low incidences of coronary heart disease associated with what we later came to call the good Mediterranean diet. The heart of this diet is mainly vegetarian, and differs from American and northern

European diets in that it is much lower in meat and dairy products and uses fruit for dessert. These observations led to our subsequent research in the Seven Countries Study, in which we demonstrated that saturated fat is the major dietary villain. Today, the healthy Mediterranean diet is changing and coronary heart disease is no longer confined to medical textbooks. Our challenge is to persuade children to tell their parents to eat as Mediterraneans do.

PRACTICAL SOLUTIONS FOR AMERICANS' MEDICAL PROBLEMS

It's always heartening to see that nutrition research findings are being put to practical, life-enhancing use, as opposed to just being academically rehashed. This does seem to be happening in our 1990s approach to nutrition; we're finally in the mode of actually doing something good for our health nutritionally, as we realize that the "magic-bullet" or wonder-drug approach to health has serious problems.

In 1994, researchers from the Howard University Medical Center published a review article on the dietary management of blood pressure. Here's some of what they had to say:

> Hypertension is a major cause of morbidity and mortality in the United States, particularly in the African-American population. Although there have been indications since the beginning of this century that blood pressure might be influenced by dietary factors, this has been generally ignored, and the mainstay of hypertension treatment has been the use of pharmacologic antihypertensives. Attention is now being focused, however, on dietary management of hypertension because of the high cost of drug therapy, the adverse reactions associated with some antihypertensives, and the fact that hypertensives treated only by pharmacologic means remain at risk for target-organ damage.
>
> The literature is replete with evidence that vegetarian and low-sodium dietary patterns are associated with lower blood pressure levels. This implies that if many people could adopt vegetarian and low-salt dietary habits, the prevalence of hypertension would be significantly reduced.

The article goes on to discuss the importance of developing palatable and socioculturally acceptable vegetarian menus for African-

Americans in particular and of course for everyone interested in lowering their blood pressure.

Another thing is that many people are interested in is lowering their risk of stroke. Information that's relevant here appeared in an April 1993 *Medical Tribune* study that highlighted the health-enhancing virtues of two vegetables in particular—carrots and spinach. Eighty-seven thousand nurses were questioned about their eating habits. Those who ate five or more servings of carrots weekly had a 67 percent lower stroke risk than those who ate one or fewer servings a month. And eating spinach daily was shown to have a protective effect against stroke as well.

More on this area appeared in the *Harvard Heart Letter* of September 1995, whose "Vegetable and Fruit Lowers Stroke Risk" article refers to a study, published in the April 12, 1995, issue of the *Journal of the American Medical Association* demonstrating a correlation between a vegetable- and fruit-rich diet and a reduced risk of stroke. Specifically, "men who ate the most vegetables and fruits had a 59 percent lower stroke rate than those who ate the least."

As to what in the fruits and vegetables was the protective factor, there were probably several. The Harvard article mentions some possibilities: the potassium content of the fruits and vegetables, their folate, and their antioxidant vitamins. Another factor mentioned is that "people who eat lots of vegetables and fruits may eat smaller amounts of potentially harmful foods that contain excessive calories, fat, and salt." The article concludes that "even though the mechanisms responsible for this protective effect are not definitely known, this study reinforces the belief that eating large amounts of fruits and vegetables may be a fundamental step in reducing the risk of vascular disease—in this case, stroke."

WHAT EXACTLY IS HAPPENING HERE?

As this last article indicates, it's not always easy to identify exactly what component of a food is responsible for the food's salutary effects. While the article mentioned some vitamin and mineral possibilities that might account for plant foods lowering stroke risk, plants are in fact composed of hundreds, and perhaps thousands, of naturally occurring chemicals. These are known as phytochemicals (i.e., chemicals found in plants) and they're not classified as vitamins, minerals, fiber, or complex carbohydrates. They're of nutritional value, though, in both understood and not-yet-understood ways that no doubt involve complicated synergisms. That's why you could take the most sophisticated "nutritionally complete" regimen of vitamin and mineral pills and still not be as well nourished as you would be if you ate the actual plant foods that the regimen was trying to duplicate.

Phytochemicals were the subject of a June 1994 *Medical Update* article entitled "Would You Eat Food Containing Saponins, Indoles, Or Phytic Acid? (Phytochemicals)." The idea was that you should, because "at least 150 studies around the world have shown that people who eat the most fruits and vegetables are half as likely to have cancer as those who eat the least. Whether this dietary differ-ence alone accounts for their lowered risk is not known, nor is it yet known how phytochemicals prevent cancer. Nonetheless, the evidence strongly suggests the importance of these chemicals—and the possible mechanisms involved."

The report goes on to explain that

> Limonene in citrus fruits, for example, is known to increase the production of enzymes that help the body dispose of potentially carcinogenic substances. Similarly, allyl sulfides in onions, chives, leeks, and garlic increases the production of glutathione 5-transferase, an enzyme that may make carcinogens easier to excrete. Dithiolthiones in broccoli trigger the formation of the same enzyme. Other phytochemicals in grapes, soybeans and dried beans, fruits, grains, and cruciferous vegetables (broccoli, Brussels sprouts, cabbage, etc.) may have other effects on car-cinogens.

Whatever the mechanisms involved, plant foods are health-pro-moting, and the documentation to this effect is virtually endless. Here are just a few more recent citations:

A May-June 1994 study in *Digestive Diseases* reported that vege-tarians in the United Kingdom had lower incidences of gallstones, diverticular disease, constipation, and gastrointestinal cancer than their meat-eating counterparts.

Concerning breast cancer, a July 1994 article in the *New Scientist* elaborates on the cancer-inhibiting effect of soy protein, which seems to mimic the anti-cancer drug tamoxifen in the way it alters women's hormones.

The Journal of the American Medical Association (February 5, 1992) published a study showing the effectiveness of fasting followed by one year of vegetarian eating in healing rheumatoid arthritis. A follow-up study in the September 1994 issue of *Clinical Rheumatology* indicates that improvements resulting from this approach can be sustained through a two-year period.

THE COST FACTOR

In addition to the health consequences of the way we eat, there are cost consequences. In these days of increased attention to the national costs of health care, an article in the November 1995 issue of *Preventive Medicine* approaches vegetarianism from this perspective. Specifically, the authors ask this question: How much does meat-eating cost our society in terms of increased medical bills? The results are staggering: The consumption of meat adds somewhere between 28 and 61 billion dollars annually to Americans' health care costs. Looked at another way, the figures mean that if we were all vegetarians, America would have 28 to 61 billion dollars extra, every year, to spend on other things.

Cost-of-illness studies have been done for tobacco use. But medical cost estimates related to meat consumption are relatively new. What the authors of the *Preventive Medicine* article did was research the differences in the prevalence of a variety of diet-related illnesses between omnivore and vegetarian populations, using studies that controlled for other lifestyle factors. The diseases considered were heart disease, hypertension, cancer, diabetes, gallstones, obesity-related problems, and food-borne illness; the final estimate is the sum of the costs of the increased incidences of all these.

And the final estimate is a conservative one, the authors point out. That's because many of the studies upon which their work is based were of Seventh-Day Adventist vegetarians. They were compared to Adventist omnivores in the studies, so that nondietary, lifestyle factors would remain the same for the two groups. But Adventists who eat meat don't eat all that much meat. Explain the authors: "Studies of Adventists may understate differences between omnivores and vegetarians, because Adventist omnivores tend to be modest in their meat consumption. The small dietary differences between omnivores and vegetarians in this group make it all the more remarkable that the prevalences of disease in these groups are so stikingly different." In other words, had the Adventist omnivores eaten as much meat as average American meat-eaters, they would have been even sicker.

REVOLUTION AT THE DINNER TABLE

Perhaps by dint of sheer numbers, the voices reporting on vegetarianism's health benefits do seem to be getting through. Many Americans' dinner tables look different than they did a few years ago. People are no longer automatically filling their plates with a hunk of meat in the center, potatoes on the side, and a token side dish of vegetables. Dinner may well be a meatless vegetable-and-grain dish paired with a large salad—and not just at home but in restaurants, on planes, in schools, and in other institutions. Consider summer camps for instance. While children at summer camps these days are still served meat at many meals, there are options offered for vegetarian youngsters, including well-stocked salad bars. Such alternatives were unheard of for the campers of yesteryear.

DO IT THE RIGHT WAY

If you are one of the many Americans who is making the transition to a plant-based diet, there are things to keep in mind as you make this lifestyle change that can help you stay on track and optimize your health along the way. Two important nutritional dicta to remember are that, whenever possible, you should use unrefined rather than refined foods, e.g., old-fashioned oats rather than cold cereal flakes, and whole-grain flour rather than white flour. Also, eat a wide variety of foods; don't stick to the same menu day after day, no matter how wholesome the foods are, because you won't be getting a wide enough spectrum of nutrients that way.

Additionally, consider the following seven ideas for making the vegetarian transition an easy, healthy, and long-lasting one.

1. Make it a true transition rather than a—pardon the expression—cold-turkey change. Here's how I recommend doing this: Take one unhealthy item out of your diet each week, or every two weeks if that's a more comfortable pace for you. The key is to take that item out of your diet *forever,* so that by the end of a year you'll have cleaned up your eating habits considerably.

Remember that the gradual approach is the one that works, so when you're eliminating meat, for instance, you might start with fatty, processed meat, and then later go on to red meat, and, still later, chicken. Other items to banish from your diet include sugar; artificial sweeteners; margarine; deep-fried foods; alcohol; caffeine; refined carbohydrates, such as cookies and pastries; artifically colored and flavored foods; and perhaps dairy products.

2. Go to a qualified nutritionist to get a complete nutritional evaluation. (Qualified here means board-certified by a recognized nutritional organization such as the American Society of Clinical Nutrition. This person will have at least a master's degree from a fully accredited college or university.) The nutritionist should do a simple SMA-24 blood chemistry evaluation to see if you're deficient in any nutrient, and he or she should devote a couple of hours to consulting with you on your nutritional habits and status, and how to improve both.

3. Along with an analysis of your blood chemistry, an impedance test to determine the percentage of lean muscle tissue, fat, and water in your body is quite helpful. Your weight doesn't give you the total picture concerning your fitness; in fact, it can be misleading because you can weigh the "right" amount according to the charts and still be overfat. If you are, lessening your fat percentage and increasing lean muscle tissue will help you feel your best.

4. The flip side of Idea 1—cutting unhealthful foods from your diet on a periodic basis—is adding new, wholesome foods into it. Each week, or every two, add a new-for-you grain, legume, or vegetable into your diet, or perhaps a new high-quality oil, or a soy product, such as tofu. Incorporate these foods into vegetarian recipes, and see which products are easiest for you to work with, and most tasty. By the end of one year, even if you don't keep every new item as part of your diet, you'll still be eating a much wider variety of healthful foods than the average nonadventurous meat-eater.

And since you'll have combined this add-in-the-good technique with the take-out-the-bad approach, you'll be feeling substantially better than you did at the beginning of the year. You'll probably have eliminated, or at least lessened, such symptoms as excess fatigue, artificial weight gain, mood swings, and body aches and pains.

5. Plug into the health network. Read some of the hundreds of books and magazines geared toward the vegetarian lifestyle. And, by all means, join a vegetarian support group. One great thing about America is that there are support groups for everything, and a group centered around healthy eating can be a tremendously positive force in your life. While there may be only a couple of million honest-to-goodness vegetarians in this country, there are probably 25 million Americans who are making healthful dietary changes, and many of them are in organizations. Joining a local group is a way of gaining emotional support, keeping informed on health issues, and keeping motivated.

   By the way, if you're single, you don't have to become part of the bar scene to socialize. There are "healthy singles" organizations where you can meet like-minded people without being subjected to cigarette smoke or surrounded by alcohol. The image of the closeted, lonely vegetarian is a thing of the past!

6. Incorporate a vigorous aerobic exercise program into your life. While a good, plant-based diet is vital to health, exercise is just as important. Note: Despite what media messages imply, you don't need to buy costly machines, join a health club, or hire a personal trainer to be fit. Be your own trainer with the aid of an inexpensive book or cassette tape.

7. There are over 90,000 holistic health practitioners or practitioners of alternative healing in the United States, and they can be found in every city and town. Use them to help with your health concerns and keep you motivated to eat right. The Internet and World Wide Web can help lead you to the right professional, as can more traditional reference sources. Today's healthy vegetarian does not have to go it alone.

TWENTY-ONE

Natural Food Recipes

BEANS AND GRAINS

Both beans and grains should be thoroughly sorted to remove any hulls, stones, and dirt. For the larger grains and beans, rinsing in a colander will dissolve dirt and remove at least the tinier stones, but you still should be careful to remove the larger stones by hand. This may seem tedious, but if you have ever cracked a tooth by biting into one of these stones, you know that it is well worth the effort. Smaller grains like rice, couscous, and millet are generally cleaner, but they too should still be rinsed in a strainer to remove any surface dusts, molds, and dirt.

All beans except for split peas and lentils must be soaked overnight or at least 12 hours before cooking. After soaking, drain the rinse water and rinse the beans thoroughly a couple of times. Beans may then simply be boiled, or you may want to sauté an onion in the pot first, then add beans, water, and other spices. The proportions for cooking beans are approximately 5 parts water to 1 part soaked beans.

With grains, the cooking proportions are about 2 parts water to

1 part grain. Bring the water to a boil, add grains, and reduce heat to a medium-low flame. You may add a pinch of salt. A tablespoon of oil will also keep the grains from becoming sticky. My favorite is toasted sesame oil, which imparts a nutty flavor to cooked grains. Cover and cook for about 45 minutes to 1 hour until all the liquid is absorbed. Softer grains like millet and couscous require less cooking time.

Millet and buckwheat kasha can also be dry roasted in a frying pan before cooking, which will give the grains a nutty flavor and reduce the cooking time to only 20 to 30 minutes.

You can experiment with your grains to enhance both their flavors and protein content. For instance, roasted sesame seeds or sunflower seeds can be added whole to your grains after you have cooked them. You can also grind the seeds in a coffee or nut grinder and add them to the grains.

Cubes of carrots or butternut squash, or raisins or other dried fruits, can be added for sweetness, especially tasty in curry dishes.

Leftover grains can be cooked for a sweet breakfast or dessert in apple juice and raisins until it is creamy in texture.

Also remember that certain grains make great companions from the point of view of flavor, texture, and nutrition. Some examples and rice and millet, barley and millet, rice and rye, rice and corn, and different combinations of rice (e.g., short grain and basmati, wild rice and long grain).

SOUPS

By now you should be getting the idea that the creative possibilities in a vegetarian kitchen are virtually endless.

While soups are particularly warming and satisfying in the winter, they should not be overlooked the rest of the year. Many soups can be delicious when served cold (a gazpacho-type or a vegetarian vichyssoise are but two examples). Many of the summer vegetables such as corn, peppers, and tomatoes also offer a variety of delicious soup possibilities, and if you are really industrious you may want to can these summer soups for the winter months.

Here are a few suggestions which you may want to consider in making your soups:

- A sautéed onion, either alone or with celery, bok choy, or nappa cabbage adds wonderful flavor to any soup.

- For those of you who love chicken soup, you will be pleasantly surprised to find that chick-peas, especially when combined with onion, make a soup that tastes and smells almost identically to chicken soup.
- Use a variety of vegetables to create texture and accentuate flavor. Carrots, squash, and yams will add sweet flavor and creamy texture. Potatoes thicken soups and when the soup is puréed, make it almost indistinguishable from a creamed soup make with heavy cream. Spinach added to a tomato-bean soup gives a Florentine flavor.
- Beans offer not only a variety of flavors and textures, they also give a protein boost to your soups. Eaten with whole-grain bread or a side dish of grain, bean soups offer a complete meal. Puréeing some or all of your cooked beans can be another way of making your soup thick and creamy.
- Experiment with a number of spices, which should be added about 10 minutes before serving. Cumin and chili powder can be added to tomato-based soup for a Mexican flavor. Curry added to carrot-based soups will provide an Indian touch. Different misos can be used with brothy soups made of escarole, kale, spinach, or cabbage for an oriental flavor. Oregano and basil will give an Italian accent.
- Tofu or tempeh cubes can replace beans for protein and add a nice variety of texture to many soups.
- Garnishes for your soups can include croutons, roasted sesame (or other) seeds, scallions, parsley, and watercress.

SWEETENERS AND BAKING

In the past few years, the alternatives to cane or beet sugars as sweeteners have been greatly expanded by many creative cooks.

Honey and maple syrup are among the sweetest. Others include rice syrup, barley malt, date syrup, and fruit juices. Pears and apple juices are especially good. You are encouraged to experiment with these as well as different whole-grain flours which can turn unhealthy desserts into nutritious and wholesome foods. For your baking you should use nonaluminum baking powder which is available at most health food stores. Also these stores should carry high-quality extracts, which by enhancing flavors, decrease the need for sweeteners. Especially good are almond, lemon, and vanilla extracts. The milder flavored oils—such as sesame, sunflower, and corn oils—in most cases can be substituted for butter and hydrogenated or saturated fats (e.g., lard and Crisco).

ROTATIONAL DIET PLAN

There is increasing evidence that frequent consumption of the same food can lead to a food allergy which may affect the way we feel and think. Foods like wheat, corn, dairy products, and beef, for example, have been so overconsumed by most Americans that we show a demonstrated intolerance to them. Since this is a book on vegetarianism, we have obviously excluded beef and other meat products from our recipes. In most cases, we have also excluded dairy products, wheat, and corn, because so many people are allergic to these foods.

In order to prevent the development of new allergies, we recommend a four-day rotational diet for most foods. For example, if you have oatmeal for breakfast, then you should avoid having oats for three days after that. You could for instance have a millet cereal the next day, a barley cereal the next, and a rice cereal on the next. Certain foods, most green leafy vegetables in particular, do not need to be rotated as conscientiously, since they are not as apt to cause allergies. Rice, too, seems to be safe for most people, but still you should try not to "abuse" it by eating it every day, especially since there are so many delicious alternatives.

BREAKFAST

BANANA BULGUR

- 6 ounces bulgur, cooked (room temperature)
- 1½ ounces banana, mashed
- 1 ounce carob chips (unsweetened and dairy-free)
- 1½ ounces cashews, chopped
- 1½ ounces raisins

Combine all ingredients. Mix well.

Serves 1

TROPICAL PARADISE RICE CEREAL

- 2 cups coconut milk
- 1 banana, sliced
- 1 cup pitted fresh or frozen cherries
- ½ cup chopped pineapple
- ¼ cup shredded unsweetened coconut

- 2 cups cooked sweet rice
- ½ cup chopped macadamia nuts, toasted (see note below)
- 2 tablespoons almond extract
- 1 tablespoon vanilla extract

In a medium-size saucepan, combine the coconut milk, banana, cherries, and pineapple. Cook over medium-low heat for 2 to 3 minutes. Add the remaining ingredients, mix well, and cook and additional 2 to 3 minutes. Serve hot.

Serves 2

Note: To toast nuts, preheat oven to 375 degrees and place nuts on an ungreased cookie sheet for 10 to 15 minutes or until light brown.

BANANA-COCONUT PECAN RICE CEREAL

- ⅓ cup uncooked cream of rice
- 2¾ cups water
- 1 cup mashed banana
- ¼ cup coconut flakes

- 5 tablespoons monnukia raisins
- 2 to 3 tablespoons pure maple syrup
- 3 tablespoons pecans

Combine the rice and water in a medium-size saucepan and bring to a boil over medium heat. Cook 3 to 7 minutes, then add the remaining ingredients and cook another 1 to 2 minutes. Serve with rice milk on top.

Serves 2

BLUEBERRY BUCKWHEAT-SOY-BANANA PANCAKES

- 2 tablespoons egg replacer
- 2 tablespoons vanilla extract
- 1 banana, mashed
- ¼ cup rice milk
- ¼ cup whole wheat flour
- ½ cup buckwheat flour
- ½ cup soy flour
- 1 teaspoon baking powder
- 1 teaspoon baking soda
- 4 tablespoons raisins
- ¼ cup blueberries
- 3 tablespoons shredded unsweetened coconut (optional)
- 4 tablespoons canola oil

In a medium-size mixing bowl, combine the egg replacer, vanilla, banana, and milk, mixing with a fork until well blended. In a separate bowl, combine the flours, baking powder, and baking soda, mixing well. Add the flour mixture to banana and milk mixture, blending well with a spoon. Stir in the raisins and coconut. Heat the oil in a large skillet over medium heat. Pour in 2 to 3 tablespoons of batter at a time and cook for 3 to 5 minutes on each side until light brown.

Yields 14 pancakes

ALMOND CINNAMON MILLET

- 6 ounces millet
- 1½ ounces almonds, blanched and chopped
- 1½ ounces brewer's yeast
- pinch of cinnamon

Cook millet in a saucepan in 13 ounces water. When water comes to boil, lower heat and cook until water is absorbed. Stir occasionally. Add remaining ingredients. Mix well.

Serves 1

OLD-FASHIONED WHEAT BREAKFAST

- 6 ounces cream of wheat
- 1 tablespoon maple syrup
- 1½ ounces brewer's yeast
- 1 banana, mashed

Cook cream of wheat in 12 ounces of water for 10 minutes. Stir occasionally over medium heat. Add remaining ingredients.

Serves 1

VERMONT MAPLE SQUASH

- 6 ounces spaghetti squash
- 1 tablespoon maple syrup
- 1½ ounces brewer's yeast
- pinch of cinnamon

Preheat oven to 400 degrees. Cut squash in half, remove the seeds and discard them. Place in baking dish cut side down, with ⅓ inch water. Bake for 40 minutes in oven. When cooled, spoon out squash and place in a bowl. Add remaining ingredients and mix well.

Serves 1

SWEET SPICE AMARANTH

- 6 ounces amaranth, cooked (room temperature)
- 3 ounces peaches, cut into bite-size pieces
- 1 tablespoon honey
- pinch of nutmeg
- pinch of allspice

Combine all ingredients. Mix well.

Serves 1

TROPICAL SUNRISE

- 6 ounces basmati rice, cooked (room temperature)
- 3 ounces pineapple, cut into bite-size pieces
- 1 tablespoon honey
- pinch of cinnamon

Combine all ingredients. Mix well.

Serves 1

NUTTY OATMEAL

- 6 ounces oatmeal, cooked (room temperature)
- 3 ounces pears, cut into bite-size pieces
- 1½ ounces pecans, chopped
- 1 tablespoon honey

Combine all ingredients. Mix well.

Serves 1

NUTTY BANANA BREAKFAST

- 6 ounces barley, cooked
- 3 ounces banana, mashed
- 1½ ounces walnuts, chopped
- 2 tablespoons barley malt

Combine all ingredients and mix well.

Serves 1

STRAWBERRY SUNSHINE

- 6 ounces brown rice, cooked (room temperature)
- 3 ounces strawberries, halved
- 1½ ounces sunflower seeds
- 1½ ounces figs, chopped
- sprinkle of coconut, shredded and unsweetened

Combine all ingredients. Mix well.

Serves 1

COCONUT NUT RICE

- 6 ounces brown rice, cooked (room temperature)
- 1½ ounces coconut, shredded (unsweetened)
- 1½ ounces cashews, chopped
- 1½ ounces dried apricots, chopped
- 1½ ounces sunflower seeds

Combine brown rice with coconut, cashews, and apricots. Purée half the mixture in blender with 2 ounces water until coarsely ground. Add back to the rest of the rice. Sprinkle with sunflower seeds.

Serves 1

SWEET CINNAMON OATMEAL

- 6 ounces oatmeal, cooked (room temperature)
- 1½ ounces dried apricots, chopped
- pinch of cinnamon

Combine all ingredients. Mix well.

Serves 1

FLUFFY RAISIN COUSCOUS

- 6 ounces couscous, cooked (room temperature)
- 3 ounces raisins
- 1 tablespoon honey
- pinch of cinnamon

Combine all ingredients. Mix well.

Serves 1

AMARANTH PEACH DELIGHT

- 6 ounces amaranth, cooked (room temperature)
- 3 ounces dried peaches, chopped
- 1½ ounces pecans, chopped
- pinch of clove
- pinch of allspice

Combine all ingredients. Mix well.

Serves 1

NUTRITIOUS DRINKS

FROZEN CHERRY SUPREME

- 3 cups orange or apple juice
- ½ cup ice cubes
- 1 cup frozen cherries
- 1 tablespoon vanilla extract
- ½ teaspoon ground cinnamon

Combine all the ingredients in a blender and blend until smooth.

Serves 2

CAROB-PECAN-BANANA SHAKE

- 2 cups rice or soy milk
- 2 bananas
- 1 tablespoon vanilla extract
- ¼ teaspoon ground nutmeg
- 3 tablespoons rice syrup (optional)
- 1 cup ice cubes
- 3 tablespoons toasted carob powder
- 4 tablespoons toasted or fresh pecans

Combine all the ingredients in a blender and blend until smooth.

Serves 2

CIDER SMOOTHIE

- 8 ounces coconut milk
- 5½ ounces apple cider
- 2 tablespoons granulated dates
- 1½ ounces sunflower seeds
- ¼ teaspoon vanilla
- pinch of cinnamon

Place all ingredients in blender. Blend until smooth and frothy.

Serves 1

RIO REFRESHER

- 4 ounces soy milk (unsweetened)
- 1½ ounces apple cider
- 1½ ounces Brazil nuts, chopped
- 1½ tablespoons almond syrup
- ½ tablespoon soy oil
- pinch of cinnamon

Combine all ingredients in a blender and blend for 2 to 3 minutes or until smooth.

Serves 1

EASY NUTRITIOUS SOY MILK

- 8 ounces soy milk (unsweetened)
- 2 tablespoons barley malt
- pinch of cinnamon

Blend all ingredients together in a blender until mixture is frothy.

Serves 1

TROPICAL BANANA SOY MILK

- 8 ounces soy milk (unsweetened)
- 3 ounces banana, mashed
- ¼ teaspoon vanilla
- pinch of nutmeg

Blend all ingredients together in a blender until mixture is frothy.

Serves 1

SALADS

SPICY BULGUR MARINADE

- 3 ounces bulgur, cooked (chilled)
- 3 ounces alfalfa sprouts
- 3 ounces spinach, coarsely chopped
- 3 ounces marinated artichoke hearts, chopped to bite-size pieces
- 2 tablespoons sunflower oil
- 2 teaspoons cider vinegar
- ½ teaspoon salt
- ½ teaspoon basil
- ¼ teaspoon curry powder
- pinch of cayenne

Combine all ingredients and mix well. Allow to set in refrigerator overnight for best taste. Serve chilled.

Serves 1

ARUGULA-ORANGE-PEPPER SALAD

- 1 cup sliced red, yellow and orange bell peppers
- 1 cup sunflower sprouts
- 1 cup torn arugula
- ¾ cup chopped fresh Italian parsley
- 1 cup shredded beets, steamed 15 minutes
- ⅔ cup shredded carrots
- 1 cup chopped fresh yellow tomatoes
- 2 seedless oranges sliced

Combine all the ingredients in a large salad bowl, adding the tomatoes last as a garnish. Serve with a vinaigrette or light lemon dressing.

Serves 2

PECAN, WALNUT, PINE NUT SALAD

- 1 cup sliced fennel root
- 3 cups mixed mesclun greens
- ½ cup diced fresh peaches
- 1 diced pear
- 2 peeled sliced fresh seedless oranges
- ¼ cup chopped pecans
- ¼ cup walnuts
- ¼ cup pine nuts

Combine the fennel, mesclun greens, oranges, pear and peaches in a large salad bowl. Toss with a light, sweet salad dressing, like Orange Vinaigrette, and top with the walnuts, pecans and pine nuts. Serve chilled.

Serves 3

INDONESIAN SPROUT SALAD

- 2 cups sunflower sprouts
- 2 cups bean sprouts
- 2 cups whole walnuts
- ½ cup honey
- 3 cups sliced red cabbage
- 1 cup diced raw carrots
- 1 cup sliced nori
- ½ cup toasted sesame seeds

Coat the walnuts with the honey and place on a lightly greased cookie sheet. Bake in a preheated 375 degrees Farenheit oven for 20 minutes. In a large bowl, toss the sprouts, red cabbage, carrots, nori, and sesame seeds. Then toss the salad with dressing, and top with the walnuts before serving.

Serves 2

CRUNCHY COUSCOUS SALAD

- 3 ounces yellow squash, cubed
- 3 ounces celery, chopped
- 3 ounces scallions, chopped
- 3 ounces safflower oil
- 1½ ounces miso
- ½ teaspoon cumin
- pinch of cayenne
- 3 ounces black-eyed peas, cooked (chilled)
- 3 ounces couscous, cooked

Combine squash, celery, and scallions in a bowl. Set aside. In a blender, combine oil, miso, and 2 ounces water. Blend until you reach a smooth consistency. Add vegetables to miso mixture and blend until coarsely ground. Add cumin and cayenne. Combine with black-eyed peas and couscous. Mix thoroughly.

Serves 2

RAISIN BASMATI SALAD

- 3 ounces basmati rice, cooked (chilled)
- 3 ounces celery, chopped
- 3 ounces raisins
- 3 ounces pineapple, cut into bite-size pieces
- 1 tablespoon safflower oil
- ¼ teaspoon cinnamon

Combine all ingredients and mix thoroughly. Serve when rice is cooled.

Serves 2

NICE RICE SALAD

- 3 ounces basmati rice, cooked (chilled)
- 3 ounces amaranth, cooked (chilled)
- 1½ ounces watercress, chopped
- 1½ ounces red pepper, diced
- 2 tablespoons safflower oil
- 1 teaspoon minced onion
- ½ teaspoon salt
- juice of 1 lemon

Combine all ingredients. Toss and serve.

Serves 2

CHOPPED VEGGIE BEAN SALAD

- 3 ounces black-eyed peas, cooked (chilled)
- 3 ounces couscous, cooked (chilled)
- 3 ounces celery, chopped
- 3 ounces carrot, chopped
- 1½ ounces pecans, chopped
- 1½ teaspoons safflower oil
- 1 teaspoon chopped fresh parsley
- ½ teaspoon marjoram

Combine all ingredients. Mix well. Place approximately ¼ of mixture in blender with 2 ounces water. Blend until completely puréed. Return to the rest of the mixture and mix well.

Serves 2

ORIENTAL SEAWEED SALAD

- 3 ounces hijiki (1 ounce dry)
- 3 ounces carrots, cut in long thin strips
- 3 ounces daikon, cut in long thin strips
- 3 ounces scallions, chopped
- 2 tablespoons safflower oil
- 1 teaspoon minced garlic
- ½ teaspoon caraway seeds
- ½ teaspoon salt
- 3 ounces amaranth, cooked (chilled)

Soak and rinse hijiki three times and place in bowl. Lightly sauté carrots, daikon, and scallions in skillet with safflower oil for about 5 minutes, then add to the hijiki. Add garlic, caraway seeds, and salt. Combine with amaranth. Mix well.

Serves 2

CALIFORNIA MARINADE

- 3 ounces cauliflower flowerets, in bite-size pieces
- 3 ounces bulgur, cooked (chilled)
- 3 ounces avocado, cut into ½-inch cubes
- 1½ ounces sunflower seeds
- 2 ounces shallots, chopped
- 1 ounce coconut, shredded (unsweetened)
- 2 tablespoons sunflower oil
- 1 teaspoon tarragon
- ½ teaspoon basil
- 1 teaspoon soy sauce
- ¼ teaspoon salt
- 2 teaspoons cider vinegar

Steam cauliflower for 8 minutes. Combine with the remaining ingredients and mix well. Serve chilled.

Serves 2

MELLOW RICE SALAD

- 3 ounces basmati rice, cooked (chilled)
- ½ ounces pecans, chopped
- 3 ounces fresh dill, chopped
- 3 ounces yellow pepper, chopped
- 1½ tablespoons safflower oil
- 2 tablespoons cider vinegar
- ½ teaspoon salt

Combine all ingredients.

Serves 1

SUPERIOR SPINACH SALAD

- 3 ounces spinach, coarsely chopped
- 3 ounces cauliflower flowerets, in bite-size pieces
- 3 ounces avocado, cut into bite-size pieces
- 3 ounces marinated artichoke hearts, cut into bite-size pieces

- 1½ ounces peanuts, chopped
- 1½ ounces shallots, chopped
- 1½ tablespoons sunflower oil
- ¼ teaspoon oregano
- ¼ teaspoon sage
- ½ teaspoon salt

Combine all ingredients and mix well.

Serves 1

COOL GARDEN NOODLES

- 3 ounces brown rice, cooked (chilled)
- 3 ounces buckwheat noodles, cooked (chilled)
- 3 ounces avocado, chopped into bite-size pieces
- 3 ounces marinated artichoke hearts, chopped into bite-size pieces

- 2 tablespoons sunflower oil
- 1 teaspoon chopped fresh parsley
- ½ teaspoon minced garlic
- ½ teaspoon basil
- ½ teaspoon salt
- pinch of ginger

Combine all ingredients and mix well.

Serves 2

ADUKI VEGETABLE SALAD

- 3 ounces aduki beans, cooked (chilled)
- 3 ounces onion, chopped
- 3 ounces tomato, chopped
- 3 ounces green pepper, chopped
- 1½ ounces almond, blanched and slivered

- 2 tablespoons sesame oil
- ½ teaspoon minced garlic
- ½ teaspoon tarragon
- ¼ teaspoon basil
- 1 teaspoon salt

Combine all ingredients. Serve at room temperature.

Serves 2

MYKONOS BEAN SALAD

- 3 ounces okra, cut into ½-inch pieces
- 3 ounces aduki beans, cooked (chilled)
- 3 ounces scallions, chopped
- 3 ounces green pepper, chopped

- 2 tablespoons olive oil
- ¼ teaspoon thyme
- ¼ teaspoon sage
- ¼ teaspoon chopped fresh dill
- ½ teaspoon salt

Steam the okra for 7 minutes. Combine with remaining ingredients and toss gently. Serve at room temperature.

Serves 1

ITALIAN MUSHROOM AND POTATO SALAD

- 3 ounces potato
- 3 ounces mushrooms, chopped medium fine
- 3 ounces okra, cut into ½-inch pieces
- 3 ounces onion, chopped
- 3 ounces tomato, chopped

- 1½ ounces scallions, chopped
- ¼ teaspoon basil
- ¼ teaspoon oregano
- ½ teaspoon salt
- 1½ tablespoons olive oil

Preheat oven to 400 degrees. Bake potato for 45 minutes. When cooled, cut into ½-inch cubes. Sauté vegetables, basil, oregano, and salt in olive oil over a low heat for about 5 minutes. Combine all ingredients and mix well. Serve hot.

Serves 2

TAHINI POTATO SALAD

- 3 ounces potato
- 1½ ounces sesame seeds
- 3 ounces scallions, chopped
- 3 ounces mushrooms, sliced
- 1½ ounces triticale flour

- ½ teaspoon cumin
- ½ teaspoon basil
- ½ teaspoon salt
- 1½ ounces tahini
- 2 tablespoons sesame oil

Preheat oven to 400 degrees. Bake potato for 40 minutes. When cooled, cut into ½-inch cubes. Toast sesame seeds in a skillet, without oil, for 3 minutes over a low heat. Set aside. In a separate bowl, combine vegetables with remaining ingredients, except oil, and 2 ounces water. Sauté all ingredients, including potato cubes, with sesame oil for 4 minutes over medium heat. Place in bowl, and add sesame seeds and salt. Mix well. Serve hot.

Serves 2

MILLET AND GREENS SALAD

- 3 ounces green pepper, chopped
- 3 ounces onion, chopped
- 3 ounces collard greens, coarsely chopped
- 3 ounces millet, cooked (chilled)

- 1½ ounces pumpkin seeds
- 2 tablespoons sesame oil
- ½ teaspoon thyme
- 1 teaspoon tarragon
- ½ teaspoon salt

Steam all vegetables for 3 minutes. Combine all ingredients. Mix well. Serve hot or cold.

Serves 2

CHICK-PEA AND LIMA BEAN SEAWEED SALAD

- 1 ounce dulse, dry
- 3 ounces snap beans, cut into 1-inch pieces
- 3 ounces chick-peas, cooked (chilled)
- 3 ounces lima beans, cooked (chilled)

- 2 tablespoons corn oil
- 1 teaspoon dill
- 1 teaspoon tarragon
- ½ teaspoon salt
- juice of ½ lemon

Soak and rinse dulse 2 or 3 times in cold water. Steam snap beans for 10 minutes. Mix all ingredients together. Serve chilled.

Serves 2

MALAYAN MILLET SALAD

- 3 ounces aduki beans, cooked (chilled)
- 3 ounces millet, cooked (chilled)
- 3 ounces green pepper, chopped

- 3 ounces onions, chopped
- ½ teaspoon tarragon
- ¼ teaspoon thyme
- ½ teaspoon salt
- pinch of celery seed
- 2 tablespoons sesame oil

Combine all ingredients and mix well. Serve hot or cold.

Serves 1

WALNUT AND BLACK BEAN SALAD

- 3 ounces black beans, cooked (chilled)
- 3 ounces soybean sprouts
- 1½ ounces walnuts, chopped

- 1 teaspoon tarragon
- ½ teaspoon thyme
- ½ teaspoon salt
- 1½ tablespoons soy oil

Combine all ingredients together and mix well. Sauté for about 5 minutes in soy oil. Serve at room temperature.

Serves 1

SPROUT AND VEGGIE SALAD

- 3 ounces brussels sprouts
- 3 ounces lima beans, cooked (chilled)
- 3 ounces barley, cooked (chilled)
- 3 ounces soybean sprouts
- 1½ ounces Brazil nuts, chopped

- 2 tablespoons soy oil
- 1 teaspoon soy sauce
- ½ teaspoon chopped parsley
- ½ teaspoon rosemary
- ½ teaspoon salt

Steam brussels sprouts for 10 minutes. Combine all ingredients and mix well. Serve cool.

Serves 2

SOUPS

HOT BEAN SOUP

- 3 ounces kidney beans
- 6 ounces cauliflower flowerets, in bite-size pieces
- 6 ounces spinach, coarsely chopped

- 1 teaspoon minced onion
- 3 tablespoons sunflower oil
- ½ teaspoon basil
- ½ teaspoon salt
- pinch of cayenne

Soak beans overnight in water. In the morning, rinse well and add 32 ounces of fresh water. Bring beans to a boil and lower to medium heat. Place the cover on the pot. The beans should cook for about 2 hours. After 1½ hours, add the remaining ingredients, and continue cooking for an additional 30 minutes. Purée half the amount in blender for about 15 seconds and return to the rest of the soup. Mix well. Cook for an additional 10 minutes.

Yields 4 to 5 cups

TOMATO POTATO SOUP

- 9 ounces potatoes, sliced
- 3 tablespoons sesame oil
- ¼ teaspoon cumin
- ¼ teaspoon basil

- 1 teaspoon salt
- 3 ounces tomato, chopped
- 6 ounces pepper, chopped
- 3 ounces scallions, chopped

Boil potatoes for approximately 15 minutes in 4 cups water. Transfer potatoes and cooking water to blender and add seasonings. Purée until smooth. Return mixture to saucepan and set on stove again over low heat. Add in the chopped vegetables. Cook for an additional 10 to 15 minutes.

Yields 4 to 5 cups

ITALIAN STYLE PINTO BEAN SOUP

- 3 ounces pinto beans
- 3 ounces carrots, sliced
- 2 ounces mushrooms, sliced
- 1 ounce arugula, chopped

- 3 tablespoons safflower oil
- ½ teaspoon cumin
- ½ teaspoon salt

Soak beans overnight in water. In the morning, rinse the beans, pour into medium saucepan, and add 32 ounces fresh water. Bring beans to a boil; then lower heat to medium. Cook with lid on. When the beans have cooked for about 1 hour, add the remaining ingredients. Purée half the mixture in blender and blend for 15 seconds or until coarsely ground. Return mixture to the rest of the soup. Cook for an additional 15 minutes over low heat.

Yields 4 to 5 cups

FAVORITE VEGETABLE SOUP

- 3 ounces mung beans
- 3 ounces onions, sliced
- 2 ounces celery, chopped
- 2 ounces red cabbage, sliced
- 1 teaspoon chopped fresh parsley

- 3 tablespoons safflower oil
- ½ teaspoon salt
- ½ teaspoon oregano
- ½ teaspoon basil
- 6 ounces basmati rice, cooked

Soak beans overnight in water. In the morning, rinse the beans, pour into saucepan, and add 32 ounces water. Bring beans to a boil and lower to medium heat. Place the cover on the pot. Allow to cook for about 1½ hours. When the beans have cooked for 1 hour, add the vegetables, oil, and seasonings. Purée half the mixture in blender for 15 seconds or until coarsely ground. Return to the soup along with the basmati rice. Mix well and allow to cook for an additional 10 minutes.

Yields 4 to 5 cups

CASHEWY BEAN SOUP

- 3 ounces kidney beans
- 6 ounces brown rice, cooked
- 1½ ounces cashews, chopped

- 3 tablespoons sunflower oil
- ½ teaspoon minced garlic
- ¼ teaspoon chili powder
- ½ teaspoon salt

Soak beans overnight in water. In the morning, rinse the beans and add 32 ounces of fresh water. Bring to a boil and lower to medium heat. Cook with lid on. The beans should cook for about 2 hours. After 1½ hours, add the remaining ingredients. Continue to cook for an additional 30 minutes. Purée half of this mixture in a blender for 15 seconds and add back to the rest of the soup. Cook for an additional 10 minutes.

Yields 4 to 5 cups

JAMAICAN SQUASH SOUP

- 6-ounce butternut squash
- 1½ ounces sunflower seeds, raw
- 2 teaspoons maple syrup
- ½ teaspoon curry
- pinch of cinnamon
- 3 ounces celery, chopped

Preheat oven to 400 degrees. Cut squash in half. Remove the seeds and discard them. Place in a baking pan cut side down, with ⅓ inch water. Bake for 40 minutes in the oven. When cooled, remove the skin and place the squash in a blender along with remaining ingredients, except for celery, and 2 cups water. Blend until smooth; add the celery. Mix well. Transfer to medium saucepan. Cook over low heat for about 20 minutes or until thoroughly heated.

Yields 3 cups

GARY'S NOODLE SOUP

- 6 ounces celery, chopped
- 6 ounces spinach, coarsely chopped
- 6 ounces asparagus, cut into 1-inch pieces
- 3 tablespoons sunflower oil
- ½ teaspoon cumin
- ½ teaspoon basil
- ½ teaspoon salt
- 6 ounces buckwheat noodles, cooked

Put vegetables in medium saucepan with 4 cups water. Bring to a boil and add remaining ingredients, except for noodles. Lower to medium heat and continue cooking for an additional 10 minutes. Purée half of this mixture in blender for about 15 seconds and then return to saucepan. Add noodles and cook for an additional 10 minutes.

Yields 4 to 5 cups

TURNIP BLACK BEAN SOUP

- 4½ ounces black beans
- 3 ounces turnips, chopped into ½-inch cubes
- 3 ounces corn (fresh or off the cob)
- 3 ounces tofu, cut into ½-inch cubes

- 3 ounces fresh chives, minced
- 3 tablespoons soy oil
- ½ teaspoon cumin
- 1 teaspoon salt

Soak beans overnight in 32 ounces water. In the morning, rinse well and add 40 ounces fresh water. Bring beans to a boil and lower to medium heat. Cover. Cook approximately 1½ hours. When the beans have cooked for 1 hour, add remaining ingredients. Purée half of this mixture in blender for 15 seconds and add back to the rest of the soup. Cook for additional 30 minutes over low heat.

Yields 4 cups

SUMMERTIME POTATO SOUP

- 9 ounces potatoes, sliced
- 1 teaspoon chopped fresh dill
- 1 teaspoon peppermint (fresh, if available)

- 2 tablespoons sesame oil
- 3 ounces scallions, chopped

Boil potatoes for 15 minutes in 4 cups water. Transfer potatoes, cooking water, seasonings, and oil to blender. Purée until smooth. Place back on low heat for 10 to 15 minutes. Add scallions.

Yields 2 cups

VENICE NOODLE SOUP

- 5 tablespoons extra virgin olive oil
- ½ cup sliced zucchini
- ½ cup sliced potatoes
- ½ cup sliced celery
- 1 cup diced onions
- ¼ cup sliced mushrooms
- ¼ cup chopped fresh parsley
- ½ cup broccoli florets
- 1 teaspoon salt
- ¼ teaspoon freshly ground black pepper
- 2 bay leaves
- ¼ cup chopped fresh dill
- 6 cups water
- 2 cups uncooked noodles
- 4 cloves crushed garlic

In a large saucepan, heat the oil over medium heat and saute the vegetables about 10 minutes. Add the remaining ingredients, except the noodles, and let simmer over medium-low heat for 25 to 35 minutes. Add the noodles 10 minutes before finishing.

Serves 2

YEAR ROUND SAVORY CREAMY POTATO SOUP

- 1 cup peeled, cubed potatoes
- ¼ cup sliced celery
- ½ cup diced onions
- 2 tablespoons canola oil
- ¼ teaspoon salt
- ¼ teaspoon cayenne
- Dash of freshly ground black pepper
- 1½ cups of water
- 1 vegetable bouillon cube (Morga)
- 1 to 2 cups soy milk

In a large saucepan, saute the potatoes, celery, and onions in the oil over medium heat for 10 minutes. Add the remaining ingredients and cook, covered, over medium to low heat for 25 to 30 minutes.

Serves 3

LUNCH AND DINNER ENTREES

POPEYE'S PICK-ME-UP

- 3 ounces spinach, chopped
- 3 ounces okra, sliced
- 3 ounces red pepper, chopped
- 3 ounces split peas, cooked
- 1½ tablespoons sunflower oil
- ½ teaspoon soy sauce
- ½ teaspoon tarragon
- ½ teaspoon salt
- 3 ounces brown rice, cooked

Steam spinach, okra, and pepper for 7 minutes or until tender. Purée split peas in blender along with oil, soy sauce, tarragon, salt, and 2 ounces water until mixture achieves sauce consistency. Pour split peas over vegetables and brown rice and serve warm.

Serves 2

NAVY BEAN MUSHROOM SAUTÉ

- 3 ounces mushrooms, sliced
- 3 ounces onions, sliced
- 2 tablespoons safflower oil
- ½ teaspoon salt
- ½ teaspoon minced garlic
- ½ teaspoon chopped fresh parsley
- 3 ounces navy beans, cooked
- 3 ounces amaranth, cooked

Sauté mushrooms and onions in skillet with safflower oil until onions are translucent. Add salt, garlic, and parsley. Combine with navy beans and amaranth. Mix well and serve warm.

Serves 2

PEANUTTY BUTTERNUT SQUASH

- 3 ounces butternut squash
- 1½ ounces shallots, chopped fine
- 1½ ounces peanuts
- 2 tablespoons sunflower oil
- 1 teaspoon chopped fresh dill
- ¼ teaspoon thyme
- ½ teaspoon basil
- ½ teaspoon salt
- 3 ounces avocado, sliced

Preheat oven to 400 degrees. Lightly oil 4 × 8 baking pan with sunflower oil. Cut squash in half, remove the seeds and discard them. Place squash halves in a baking pan cut side down, with ⅓ inch water. Bake for 40 minutes. Take squash out of oven, and lower heat to 350 degrees. When cool enough to handle, remove skin from squash and cut the squash into 1-inch cubes. Combine the shallots with the squash and transfer to baking pan. In a blender, place peanuts, oil, dill, thyme, basil, and salt. Purée until smooth. Pour over squash and shallots, and bake for 20 minutes. Top with avocado.

Serves 2

SWEET-AND-SOUR BEAN STEW

- 3 ounces navy beans, cooked
- 3 ounces basmati rice, cooked
- 1½ ounces butternut squash, cubed
- 1½ ounces onion, chopped
- 1½ ounces raisins
- 1 tablespoon safflower oil
- ½ teaspoon thyme
- ½ teaspoon minced garlic
- ½ teaspoon salt

Combine all ingredients in medium saucepan. Set on stove over medium heat for about 20 minutes or until thoroughly heated. Stir occasionally. Serve at room temperature.

Serves 1

SWEET POTATO PATCH

- 3-ounce sweet potato
- 3 ounces carrot, sliced
- 1½ ounces pine nuts
- 1 ounce crushed pineapple (unsweetened in its own juice, if canned)
- ½ teaspoon cinnamon
- 3 ounces mung beans, cooked

Preheat oven to 400 degrees. Pierce sweet potato with fork and place in oven for 45 minutes. When potato cools, cut into ½-inch cubes. Steam carrots for 8 minutes. Combine potato and carrots. Add remaining ingredients and mix well. Serve cool or at room temperature.

Serves 1

SQUASHED POTATO CASSEROLE

- 3-ounce sweet potato
- 3 ounces yellow squash, cubed
- 1 ounce green pepper, chopped
- 2 tablespoons safflower oil
- ½ teaspoon thyme
- ½ teaspoon basil
- ½ teaspoon salt
- 3 ounces basmati rice, cooked
- 3 ounces amaranth, cooked

Preheat oven to 400 degrees. Pierce sweet potato with fork and place in oven for 45 minutes. When potato cools, cut into ½-inch cubes. Lower heat to 375 degrees. Steam squash and pepper until slightly tender. Lightly grease 4 × 8 casserole pan with safflower oil. Combine all ingredients and mix well. Transfer to casserole pan and place in oven for 15 minutes.

Serves 2

MACRO RICE AND BEANS

- 3 ounces black-eyed peas
- 3 ounces hijiki (1 ounce dry)
- 1½ ounces kale, coarsely chopped
- 3 ounces daikon, cut into bite-size pieces
- 3 ounces parsnip, cut into bite-size pieces
- 1 teaspoon soy sauce
- 3 tablespoons safflower oil
- 1 teaspoon salt
- 3 ounces basmati rice, cooked

Soak peas overnight in water. In the morning, rinse them, pour into saucepan, and add 32 ounces of fresh water. Bring black-eyed peas to a boil and lower to medium heat. Cook for about 2 hours with the lid on. While peas are cooking, soak and rinse hijiki two or three times. When peas have cooked for 1½ hours, add remaining ingredients, except rice. Continue cooking for additional 30 minutes on low heat until beans are tender. Serve with rice.

Serves 3

SOBA NOODLE SUPREME

- 3 ounces asparagus, cut into 1-inch pieces
- 3-ounce butternut squash
- 3 ounces buckwheat noodles (soba), cooked
- 3 ounces spinach, cut into bite-size pieces
- 5 tablespoons sunflower oil
- 1 teaspoon dill
- 1 teaspoon salt

Preheat oven to 400 degrees. Steam the asparagus until tender, approximately 8 minutes. Cut squash in half, remove the seeds and discard. Place squash in a 4 × 8 baking pan cut side down, with ⅓ inch water, and bake for 40 minutes. When cooled, remove skin from squash and cut the squash into bite-size pieces. Combine all the ingredients together and mix well. Serve warm.

Serves 3

SASSY BEAN AND BULGUR

- 1½ tablespoons sunflower oil
- 3 ounces kidney beans, cooked
- 3 ounces bulgur, cooked
- 3 ounces brown rice, cooked
- 3 ounces mushrooms, sliced
- 3 ounces carrots, sliced
- 1 ounce scallions, chopped
- 1 ounce tomato sauce
- ½ teaspoon oregano
- ½ teaspoon salt
- 3 ounces spinach leaves

Preheat oven to 350 degrees. Lightly grease 4 × 8 baking pan with sunflower oil. Combine all ingredients together except spinach leaves. Mix well. Transfer to baking pan and place in oven for 20 minutes. Serve on bed of spinach leaves.

Serves 2

SPLIT PEA RATATOUILLE

- 3 ounces eggplant, sliced ¼-inch thick
- 3 ounces zucchini, sliced ¼-inch thick
- 3 ounces onion, sliced
- 2 tablespoons sunflower oil
- 3 ounces split peas, cooked
- 3 ounces cashews, chopped
- 1 teaspoon minced garlic
- 1 teaspoon salt
- ½ teaspoon rosemary

Preheat oven to 350 degrees. Steam eggplant, zucchini, and onion for about 8 minutes. Lightly grease 4 × 8 baking pan with oil. Place split peas in blender with 2 ounces water, half of cashews, and the remaining ingredients. Blend until mixture achieves sauce consistency. Place eggplant in baking pan and pour the split pea sauce on top. Sprinkle with remaining cashews. Put in oven and bake for 20 minutes.

Serves 2

HI-PROTEIN GREEN AND WHITE BULGUR

- 3 ounces bulgur, cooked
- 3 ounces split peas, cooked
- 3 ounces spinach, coarsely chopped
- 3 ounces celery, chopped into bite-size pieces
- 1½ ounces coconut, shredded (unsweetened)

- 3 tablespoons sunflower oil
- ¼ teaspoon basil
- ¼ teaspoon thyme
- ¼ teaspoon cumin
- ½ teaspoon salt

Combine all ingredients. Mix thoroughly and serve.

Serves 2

KIDNEY BEAN BONANZA

- 1½ ounces filberts, chopped
- 2 tablespoons sunflower oil
- 1 tablespoon tarragon
- ¾ teaspoon basil
- ½ teaspoon salt

- ⅓ teaspoon curry
- 3 ounces brown rice, cooked
- 3 ounces kidney beans, cooked
- 1½ ounces cashew pieces

Preheat oven to 375 degrees. Lightly grease 4 × 8 baking dish with sunflower oil. Place filberts in blender with 2 ounces water, oil, tarragon, basil, salt, and curry. Blend until mixture achieves sauce consistency. Combine brown rice and beans. Transfer to baking dish. Top with filbert sauce. Sprinkle on cashews. Bake with cover for 15 minutes.

Serves 2

SAUTÉ FLORENTINE

- 3 ounces sunflower flour
- 2 teaspoons minced onions
- ⅓ teaspoon thyme
- ⅓ teaspoon oregano
- ½ teaspoon salt
- ½ teaspoon soy sauce
- 2 tablespoons sunflower oil
- 3 ounces spinach, coarsely chopped
- 3 ounces marinated artichoke hearts, chopped into bite-size pieces
- 3 ounces celery, chopped into bite-size pieces
- 3 ounces brown rice, cooked

Combine flour with onion, thyme, oregano, salt, soy sauce, and oil. Mix well. Sauté flour mixture with vegetables and sunflower oil in skillet or wok. Add rice and sauté for 7 minutes.

Serves 2

ASPARAGUS AND BULGUR

- 3 ounces asparagus, cut into ½-inch pieces
- 3 ounces bulgur, cooked
- 1 tablespoon sunflower oil
- ¼ teaspoon thyme
- ¼ teaspoon basil
- ¼ teaspoon salt

Steam asparagus for about 10 minutes. Combine all ingredients and mix well. Serve at room temperature.

Serves 2

PETER PAN RICE CASSEROLE

- 1½ ounces peanut butter
- 1½ tablespoons sunflower oil
- ¼ teaspoon thyme
- ½ teaspoon tarragon
- ½ teaspoon salt
- 3 ounces brown rice, cooked
- 1½ ounces sunflower seeds
- 1½ ounces shallots, chopped medium fine

Preheat oven to 325 degrees. Lightly grease 4 × 8 baking dish with sunflower oil. In a blender, combine peanut butter, oil, thyme, tarragon, salt, and 2 ounces water. Blend until mixture achieves sauce consistency. Combine with rice, sunflower seeds, and shallots. Mix well. Transfer to baking dish and bake for 20 minutes in oven.

Serves 1

MEXICAN MEDLEY

- 3 ounces asparagus, cut in ½-inch pieces
- 3 ounces cauliflower flowerets, in bite-size pieces
- 3 ounces celery, chopped
- 3 ounces kidney beans, cooked
- 1½ ounces filberts, chopped medium fine
- 2 tablespoons sunflower oil
- ⅔ teaspoon chopped fresh dill
- ⅓ teaspoon chili powder
- ¼ teaspoon basil
- ¼ teaspoon celery seed
- ½ teaspoon minced garlic
- ½ teaspoon salt

Steam asparagus and cauliflower for approximately 10 minutes. Combine with celery. Set aside. In a blender, place the beans, filberts, and remaining ingredients. Purée until smooth. Pour this sauce over the asparagus mixture. Serve at room temperature.

Serves 2

ITALIAN RICE

- 3 ounces celery, chopped
- 1⅓ ounces shallots, chopped finely
- 3 ounces brown rice, cooked
- 2 tablespoons sunflower oil
- 1½ teaspoons tarragon
- ¼ teaspoon dill
- ¾ teaspoon salt
- ¼ teaspoon soy sauce
- 3 ounces alfalfa sprouts
- 1½ ounces cashews, chopped
- 3 teaspoons cider vinegar

Sauté celery and shallots with brown rice in a skillet with sunflower oil for 5 minutes. Add herbs, salt, and soy sauce. Transfer to bowl; add sprouts, cashews and cider vinegar. Mix well and serve at room temperature.

Serves 1

BULGUR COCO-CADO

- 3 ounces asparagus, cut into 1-inch pieces
- 1½ ounces peanut butter
- 3 ounces coconut, shredded (unsweetened)
- 1½ tablespoons sunflower oil
- ½ teaspoon chopped fresh dill
- ½ teaspoon minced garlic
- ½ teaspoon salt
- 3 ounces bulgur, cooked
- 3 ounces celery, chopped finely
- 3 ounces avocado, sliced

Steam asparagus until tender, approximately 10 minutes. In a bowl, mix peanut butter with coconut, oil, dill, garlic, and salt as well as 2 ounces water. Combine bulgur and celery. Top with peanut butter mixture. Place slices of avocado on top. Serve at room temperature.

Serves 2

THREE-GREEN CURRY CASSEROLE

- 3 ounces sunflower flour
- 3 ounces split peas, cooked
- 2½ tablespoons sunflower oil
- ⅓ teaspoon curry
- ¼ teaspoon minced garlic
- ¼ teaspoon salt
- ¼ teaspoon thyme

- 3 ounces spinach, coarsely chopped
- 3 ounces cauliflower, cut into bite-size pieces
- 3 ounces brown rice, cooked
- 3 ounces avocado, sliced

Preheat oven to 375 degrees. Lightly grease 4 × 8 baking pan with sunflower oil. In a blender, combine sunflower flour, split peas, oil, curry, garlic, salt, thyme, and 2 ounces water. Separately, combine spinach, cauliflower, and brown rice. Transfer to covered baking pan, add the flour and beans, and bake for 15 minutes. Place avocado slices on top for garnish.

Serves 2

SWISS SPAGHETTI CASSEROLE

- 3-ounce spaghetti squash
- 3 ounces swiss chard
- 3 ounces onion, chopped
- 3 ounces green pepper, chopped
- 1½ ounces almonds, blanched and chopped

- 1 teaspoon minced garlic
- 2 teaspoons thyme
- ½ teaspoon salt
- sesame oil

Preheat oven to 400 degrees. Lightly grease a 4 × 8 baking pan with sesame oil. Cut squash in half, remove the seeds and discard them. Place the squash in a baking pan cut side down, with ⅓ inch water. Bake for 40 minutes. Then lower oven to 375 degrees. When squash is cool enough to handle, cut into ½-inch cubes. Steam swiss chard for 6 minutes. Combine all ingredients in a baking dish and bake for 15 minutes.

Serves 1

BRAZILIAN RICE

- 3 ounces cauliflower flowerets, in bite-size pieces
- 2 tablespoons fresh chopped parsley
- 2 tablespoons sunflower oil
- ½ teaspoon soy sauce
- ½ teaspoon salt
- 3 ounces black beans, cooked
- 3 ounces brown rice, cooked
- 3 ounces avocado, sliced

Preheat the oven to 375 degrees. Lightly grease a 4 × 8 baking pan with sunflower oil. Steam the cauliflower for about 5 minutes. Combine all the ingredients except for the avocado. Mix well. Transfer to baking pan and bake for 15 minutes. After 15 minutes, garnish with avocado slices.

Serves 2

GREEN BARLEY SPLIT

- 6 ounces split peas, cooked
- 6 ounces spinach, chopped coarsely
- 6 ounces barley, cooked
- 6 ounces asparagus, cut into 1-inch pieces
- 3 tablespoons sunflower oil
- ½ teaspoon minced garlic
- ½ teaspoon salt

Preheat oven to 375 degrees. Lightly grease 4 × 8 baking pan with sunflower oil. Combine all ingredients together. Toss and mix well. Transfer to baking pan and bake for 15 minutes or until thoroughly heated.

Serves 3

VEGETABLE ALMONDINE BAKE

- 3 ounces wheat flakes
- 3 ounces onion, chopped
- 3 ounces tomato, chopped
- 3 ounces green pepper, chopped
- 1½ ounces scallions, chopped
- 1½ ounces almonds, blanched and slivered
- ¼ teaspoon thyme
- ¼ teaspoon sage
- ¼ teaspoon curry
- ½ teaspoon salt
- 2 tablespoons sesame oil

Preheat oven to 375 degrees. Lightly grease 4 × 8 baking dish with sesame oil. Cook wheat flakes in 12 ounces water for 10 to 12 minutes. Sauté vegetables, almonds, thyme, sage, curry, and salt in a skillet with sesame oil for 5 minutes. Combine with wheat flakes and transfer to baking dish and bake for 15 minutes.

Serves 2

MAMA'S MAKE-BELIEVE SPAGHETTI

- 3-ounces spaghetti squash
- 6 ounces tomato, chopped
- 3 ounces scallions, chopped
- 3 ounces green pepper, chopped
- 1½ ounces onion, chopped
- 2 tablespoons olive oil
- ¼ teaspoon basil
- 1 teaspoon salt

Preheat oven to 400 degrees. Cut squash in half; remove the seeds and discard them. Place the halves in a baking pan cut side down, with ⅓ inch water. Bake for 40 minutes. Sauté the tomato, scallions, green pepper, and onion in a skillet with olive oil for 5 minutes. Add the basil and salt. Remove the "spaghetti" from the squash and combine with the sautéed mixture. Toss gently. Serve hot.

Serves 1

HALLOWEEN SPAGHETTI

- 6 ounces tomato, finely chopped
- 1½ ounces scallions, finely chopped
- ½ teaspoon oregano
- ½ teaspoon basil
- ½ teaspoon salt
- 2 tablespoons olive oil
- 3 ounces spaghetti, cooked
- 1½ ounces pumpkin seeds, roasted

Sauté tomato and scallions in a skillet with oregano, basil, salt, and olive oil over low heat for 15 minutes. Combine with spaghetti and pumpkin seeds. Serve hot.

Serves 1

PYRAMID PEA CASSEROLE

- 3 ounces chick-peas, cooked
- 3 ounces barley, cooked
- 3 ounces turnip greens, chopped
- 1½ ounces Brazil nuts, chopped
- 2 tablespoons soy oil
- 2 teaspoons chopped fresh chives
- ¼ teaspoon thyme
- ½ teaspoon curry
- ½ teaspoon salt

Preheat oven to 375 degrees. Lightly grease a 4 × 8 baking pan with soy oil. Combine all the ingredients and mix well. Transfer to baking pan and bake for 15 minutes.

Serves 2

BAKED SPAGHETTI CASSEROLE

- 3 ounces potato
- 3 ounces spaghetti, cooked
- 3 ounces tomato, chopped medium fine
- 1½ ounces scallions, chopped medium fine
- 1½ ounces sesame seeds
- 1½ tablespoons sesame oil
- ¼ teaspoon thyme
- ¼ teaspoon minced garlic
- ½ teaspoon salt

Preheat oven to 400 degrees. Lightly grease 4 × 8 baking pan with sesame oil. Bake potato for 40 minutes. When cooled, cut into ½-inch cubes. Combine all ingredients together. Lower heat to 375 degrees. Transfer to a baking pan and bake for 15 minutes.

Serves 2

MUSHROOM AND ONION SPAGHETTI

- 3 ounces mushrooms, sliced
- 3 ounces onions, sliced
- 3 ounces tomato, chopped
- ½ teaspoon basil
- ¼ teaspoon oregano
- ½ teaspoon salt
- 2 tablespoons olive oil
- 6 ounces spaghetti, cooked

Sauté mushrooms, onions, and tomato with basil, oregano, and salt in olive oil for 5 minutes. Combine with spaghetti and toss gently. Serve warm.

Serves 2

FLAVORFUL BEANS WITH MUSHROOMS

- 3 ounces mushrooms, finely chopped
- 3 ounces scallions, finely chopped
- 3 ounces aduki beans cooked

- 2 tablespoons olive oil
- ½ teaspoon tarragon
- ¼ teaspoon dill
- ½ teaspoon salt

Preheat oven to 300 degrees. Lightly grease a 4 × 8 baking dish with sesame oil. Combine all ingredients and place in the baking dish. Bake for 25 minutes with a cover.

Serves 1

MUSHROOM PEPPER SAUTÉ

- 1½ ounces triticale flour
- ½ teaspoon basil
- ½ teaspoon thyme
- ¼ teaspoon salt
- ½ teaspoon soy sauce
- 1 tablespoon sesame oil

- 6 ounces mushrooms, sliced
- 1½ ounces green pepper, chopped
- 1½ ounces scallions, chopped

Preheat oven to 325 degrees. Lightly grease a 4 × 8 baking dish with sesame oil. Mix triticale flour with basil, thyme, salt, soy sauce, and 2 ounces water. Sauté the vegetables, adding the triticale sauce, for 4 minutes. Transfer ingredients to a covered baking dish and bake for 20 minutes.

Serves 2

LITTLE ITALY SPAGHETTI

- 3 ounces onion, chopped
- 1½ tablespoons olive oil
- ½ teaspoon minced garlic
- ¼ teaspoon basil
- ¼ teaspoon oregano
- ½ teaspoon salt
- 6 ounces tomato, finely chopped

- 3 ounces mushrooms, finely chopped
- 3 ounces green pepper, finely chopped
- 2 ounces tomato paste
- 6 ounces spaghetti, cooked

Sauté onion in a saucepan with olive oil until onions are translucent. Add garlic, basil, oregano, and salt. Stir. Add vegetables and tomato paste. Continue to cook over medium heat, covered, for 15 minutes. Add spaghetti and toss, Serve hot.

Serves 2

MUSHROOM MILLET MAGIC

- 3 ounces millet, cooked
- 3 ounces mushrooms, sliced
- 3 ounces green pepper, chopped
- 3 ounces onion, chopped
- 1½ ounces pumpkin seeds

- 2 tablespoons olive oil
- ½ teaspoon salt
- ¼ teaspoon cumin
- ¼ teaspoon basil
- 1½ ounces triticale flour
- sesame oil

Preheat oven to 350 degrees. Lightly grease a 4 × 8 baking dish with sesame oil. Combine all ingredients together gradually stirring in triticale flour. Transfer to covered baking dish and bake for 20 minutes.

Serves 1

TANTALIZING TEMPEH DINNER

- ½ ounce dulse, dry
- 3 ounces chick-peas, cooked
- 3 ounces soybean sprouts
- 3 ounces broccoli flowerets, in bite-size pieces
- 3 ounces tempeh, cut into ½-inch cubes

- 2 tablespoons soy oil
- 1 teaspoon minced onion
- 1 teaspoon chopped fresh chives
- ¼ teaspoon salt

Preheat oven to 350 degrees. Lightly grease a 4 × 8 baking pan with soy oil. Soak and rinse dulse 2 or 3 times in cold water. Combine with the remaining ingredients and mix well. Transfer to baking pan and bake for 20 minutes.

Serves 2

VEGETABLE MILLET DELIGHT

- 6 ounces millet, cooked
- ½ teaspoon coriander
- ½ teaspoon salt
- 3 tablespoons sesame oil
- 3 ounces mushrooms, chopped

- 3 ounces red and green pepper, chopped
- 3 ounces onion, chopped

Place cooked millet in blender with 16 ounces water, coriander, salt, and oil. Purée until smooth. Pour into saucepan over medium heat. Add chopped vegetables, and cook for 15 minutes or until vegetables are tender.

Serves 3

BRAZILIAN BROCCOLI BEANS

- 3 ounces broccoli flowerets, in bite-size pieces
- 3 ounces snap beans, cut into bite-size pieces
- 3 ounces kale, coarsely chopped
- 3 ounces soybeans, cooked
- 1½ ounces Brazil nuts, chopped
- 1½ tablespoons soy oil
- ½ teaspoon minced garlic
- 1½ ounces fresh chives, minced
- ¼ teaspoon tarragon
- ½ teaspoon salt

Steam broccoli, snap beans, and kale for 8 minutes or until tender. Combine with remaining ingredients and mix well. Serve hot or cold.

Serves 2

ISLAND LENTIL DISH

- 6 ounces lentils, cooked
- 6 ounces brown rice, cooked
- 6 ounces celery, chopped
- 6 ounces cauliflower flowerets, in bite-size pieces
- 3 tablespoons sunflower oil
- 1 teaspoon thyme
- ½ teaspoon salt

Preheat oven to 375 degrees. Lightly grease 4 × 8 baking pan with sunflower oil. Combine all ingredients. Toss and mix well. Transfer to baking dish and bake for 15 minutes.

Serves 3

CURRIED CHICK-PEAS WITH VEGGIES

- 3 ounces turnips, sliced ¼-inch thick
- 3 ounces broccoli flowerets, in bite-size pieces
- 3 ounces chick-peas, cooked
- 3 ounces barley, cooked
- 2 tablespoons minced fresh chives
- 2 tablespoons soy oil
- ½ teaspoon curry
- juice of ½ lemon

Steam turnips and broccoli for 8 minutes. Combine with remaining ingredients. Mix well. Serve warm.

Serves 2

CRUNCHY BEANS WITH TURNIPS

- 3 ounces turnips, sliced ¼-inch thick
- 3 ounces lima beans, cooked
- 2 tablespoons minced chives
- 1 teaspoon curry
- 1 teaspoon soy sauce
- ½ teaspoon salt
- 2 tablespoons soy oil
- 1½ ounces walnuts, chopped
- 3 ounces soybean sprouts

Preheat oven to 375 degrees. Lightly grease 4 × 8 baking pan with soy oil. Steam turnips. Combine lima beans, chives, curry, soy sauce, salt, and soy oil in a blender with 2 ounces water. Purée until smooth. Combine all ingredients together and mix well. Transfer to baking pan and cook for 15 minutes.

Serves 2

SNAPPY BEAN BAKE

- 3 ounces broccoli flowerets, in bite-size pieces
- 3 ounces snap beans, cut into bite-size pieces
- 3 ounces tofu, cut into ½-inch cubes
- 3 ounces lima beans, cooked
- 1½ ounces Brazil nuts, chopped
- 2 tablespoons soy oil
- 1 teaspoon mustard
- 2 teaspoons minced fresh chives
- 1 teaspoon chopped fresh parsley
- ½ teaspoon tarragon
- ½ teaspoon salt

Preheat oven to 350 degrees. Lightly grease 4 × 8 baking pan with soy oil. Combine all ingredients and bake for 20 minutes with a cover.

Serves 2

AROMATIC GREEN CASSEROLE

- 3 ounces snap beans, cut into bite-size pieces
- 3 ounces brussels sprouts, cut into bite-size pieces
- 3 ounces broccoli, cut into bite-size pieces
- 1½ ounces walnuts, chopped
- 2 tablespoons soy oil
- ½ teaspoon chopped fresh dill
- ¼ teaspoon sage
- ½ teaspoon salt
- juice of ½ lemon
- pinch cayenne

Steam beans, brussels sprouts, and broccoli for 8 minutes. Combine beans and walnuts with remaining ingredients and 2 ounces water. Transfer to blender and purée until smooth. Pour sauce over vegetables. Serve hot or cold.

Serves 2

TANTALIZING TOFU

- 3 ounces tofu, cut into bite-size pieces
- 3 ounces broccoli, cut into bite-size pices
- 3 ounces turnip greens, coarsely chopped
- 1½ ounces walnuts, chopped
- ½ teaspoon basil
- ½ teaspoon salt
- 2 tablespoons soy oil
- 3 ounces romaine lettuce

Sauté all ingredients except for lettuce in soy oil for 3 to 4 minutes. Arrange on a bed of lettuce.

Serves 2

TARRAGON TEMPEH

- 3 ounces tempeh, cut into ½-inch pieces
- 1½ ounces Brazil nuts, chopped
- 2 teaspoons fresh chives, minced
- 1 teaspoon tarragon
- ½ teaspoon salt
- corn oil

Preheat oven to 350 degrees. Lightly grease baking sheet with corn oil. Sauté tempeh in corn oil for 3 minutes. Blend Brazil nuts in blender until finely ground. Mix nut meal with chives, tarragon, and salt, as well as 1 ounce water. Dip tempeh in this batter and place on baking sheet. Place in oven for 15 minutes.

Serves 1

STUFFED POTATOES WITH KIDNEY BEANS AND SOY CHEESE

- 3 Idaho potatoes, baked, halved, with center taken out and skins set aside
- 2 tablespoons chopped sweet onion
- 2 tablespoons chopped fresh parsley
- 1 cup mashed kidney beans
- ¼ teaspoon cayenne pepper
- ½ teaspoon paprika
- ½ teaspoon salt
- ½ teaspoon freshly ground black pepper
- 1 cup shredded soy cheese (optional)
- 2 to 3 tablespoons extra virgin olive oil

In a large bowl, combine all the ingredients in the order in which they are listed. Stuff the mixture back into the skins and bake in a preheated 425 degrees F oven for 10 minutes.

Serves 2

EXOTIC TOFU DIP

- 2 cups silken tofu
- 2 tablespoons chopped fresh chives
- 4 tablespoons prepared mustard
- ½ cup soy mayonnaise
- 3 tablespoons balsamic vinegar
- 1 teaspoon freshly ground black pepper
- 2 tablespoons chopped fresh dill paprika for garnish

Process all the ingredients, except the paprika, in a food processor or blender until smooth. Sprinkle with paprika. Serve chilled with raw carrot and celery sticks and broccoli and cauliflower florets.

Yields 2½ to 3 cups

THAI AROMATIC RICE

- 5 teaspoons peanut oil
- ¼ cup chopped zucchini
- 1 cup chopped yellow onions
- ½ teaspoon chopped shallots
- ¼ cup chopped unsalted roasted peanuts
- ½ cup roasted macadamia nuts
- 3 cups cooked long grain brown rice
- 5 artichoke hearts
- ¼ cup canned waterchestnuts
- 3 teaspoons chopped garlic
- 4½ teaspoons chopped fresh mint for garnish

Heat the peanut oil in a skillet or wok over high heat until hot but not smoking. Add the zucchini, onions and shallots, and sauté over medium heat for 5 minutes. Add the remaining ingredients one at a time, stirring after each addition, and cook until hot. Garnish with chopped mint.

Serves 4

CARMEN MIRANDA BRAZILIAN RICE

- 1 cup chopped onions
- 1 fresh tomato, chopped or ½ cup prepared tomato sauce
- 1½ teaspoons drained, crushed capers
- ½ cup large pitted black olives
- ½ cup hearts of palm
- 1 bay leaf
- 4 tablespoons extra virgin olive oil
- 2 cups cooked basmati rice
- 2 tablespoons roasted sunflower seeds
- 2 tablespoons pumpkin seeds
- ¼ teaspoon cayenne
- ¼ teaspoon dried thyme
- ½ teaspoon freshly ground black pepper
- ¼ teaspoon chile pepper
- 4 cloves crushed garlic
- 1 teaspoon sea salt

In a large sauce pan, sauté the onions, tomatoes, capers, olives, and bay leaf in oil over medium heat until the onions are clear. Add the remaining ingredients and sauté another 4 minutes until hot. Serve with black beans.

Serves 4

STEWED VEGETABLE MEDLEY

- 2 cups chopped red cabbage
- 2 cups chopped green cabbage
- 4 cups water
- 1½ cups sliced onions
- 2 tablespoons caraway seeds
- 1 tablespoon turmeric
- 4 tablespoons curry powder
- 4 tablespoons extra virgin olive oil
- ¼ teaspoon freshly ground black pepper
- 1½ teaspoons sea salt
- 1 cup peeled chopped potatoes
- ½ cup frozen peas
- ¼ cup frozen corn
- 1 tablespoon curry powder

In a large saucepan, combine all the ingredients and bring to a boil. Reduce heat to medium-low and cook for 30–35 minutes. Serve hot or cold.

Serves 4 to 6

SAVORY STUFFED ARTICHOKES

- 2 artichokes
- 4 tablespoons orange juice
- 4 tablespoons plus 1 teaspoon lemon juice
- 2 cups water
- ½ cup chopped avocado
- ¼ cup chopped fresh tomatoes
- ¼ cup chopped black pitted olives
- ¼ cup chopped onions
- 2 tablespoons extra virgin olive oil
- ½ cup chopped fresh basil
- 3 tablespoons toasted sesame seeds
- ½ cup roasted macadamia nuts
- 1 teaspoon salt
- 1 sliced lemon (for garnish)

Trim the thorns from the artichoke leaves with a pair of scissors and trim the bottoms so they will stand upright. In a medium-size saucepan, simmer the artichokes in the water and lemon juice over medium heat for about 50–60 minutes, until the leaves pull out easily. Remove the artichokes from the water and let them cool. Gently pull out the center leaves and scoop out the fuzzy choke with a spoon. Combine the remaining ingredients in a small mixing bowl and stir well. Spoon the stuffing mixture into the centers of the artichokes and garnish with lemon slices.

Serves 4

SOUTHERN SOUL DISH

- 1 cup finely chopped kale, steamed 5 minutes
- 1 cup diced apples
- 4½ teaspoons apple juice
- 1 cup sliced mushrooms
- ½ cup sliced fennel root
- 1 cup black-eyed peas, steamed 15 minutes
- ½ teaspoon cayenne
- 1 teaspoon sea salt
- 1 teaspoon freshly ground black pepper
- 2 tablespoons extra virgin olive oil
- 3 tablespoons chopped fresh parsley
- 3 teaspoons ground cinammon
- 1 teaspoon ground nutmeg
- ½ cup toasted almonds

In a large saucepan, sauté the kale, apples, mushrooms, fennel, salt, pepper and cayenne in the oil over medium-high heat for 7 minutes. Add the remaining ingredients and cook an additional 10 minutes. Serve hot.

Serves 3 to 4

SWEET BASIL SPAGHETTI

- 2 cups chopped fresh tomatoes
- 1 cup sweet peas
- 1 cup chopped green beans
- 1 cup chopped yellow onions
- 4 tablespoons capers
- 1 cup diced yellow and red sweet peppers

- 2½ cups chopped fresh basil
- ⅓ teaspoon sliced garlic
- ¼ teaspoon dried oregano
- ¼ cup extra virgin olive oil
- 4 cups cooked spaghetti

In a large saucepan, sauté all the ingredients, except the spaghetti, in the oil for 10 to 15 minutes. Serve hot as a sauce over the cooked spaghetti.

Serves 3 to 4

THAI SOBA PEANUT NOODLES

- 1 cup diced yellow onions
- ½ cup sliced scallions
- ¼ cup diced celery
- 7 tablespoons toasted sesame oil
- 1 cup stemmed and sliced shitake mushrooms
- 1 clove garlic
- ¼ cup smooth peanut butter

- 1 teaspoon pure maple syrup
- 1 teaspoon fresh lime juice
- ⅓ cup plus 1 tablespoon water
- 2 drops hot chili oil or Tabasco sauce Gomasio to taste
- ¼ pound cooked soba noodles

Combine 1 tablespoon oil, garlic, peanut butter, maple syrup, lime juice, water, and hot chili oil in a blender and mix until smooth, 2 to 3 minutes, and set aside. In a large saucepan, heat the oil over medium heat, then saute the scallions and mushrooms for 8 to 10 minutes. Remove from the heat and stir in the gomasio and peanut sauce. Toss the soba noodles with the sauce in a large bowl until all the noodles are covered. Chill for an hour and a half and serve cold.

Serves 2 to 4

JAPANESE RICE THREADS

- 4 cups stemmed and sliced shitake mushrooms
- 1 cup diced yellow onions
- 1 cup sliced scallions
- ¼ cup toasted sesame oil
- 2 teaspoons grated fresh ginger
- ½ cup plus 1 tablespoon tamari
- 3 cups thinly sliced carrot matchsticks, steamed 10 minutes
- 2 cloves crushed garlic
- 2 tablespoons lemon juice
- 2 tablespoons orange juice
- 6 cups water
- 2 cups dry rice noodles

In a large saucepan, heat the oil over medium heat and sauté the mushrooms, scallions, onions, ginger, and carrot sticks for 3 minutes. Add the tamari, noodles, and water and cook for another 4–6 minutes.

Serves 3 to 4

ANGEL HAIR WITH RADICCHIO

- 1 cup sliced mushrooms
- 1 cup sliced radicchio
- 1 cup fresh or frozen peas
- 1 tablespoon salt
- ½ cup soy milk
- 4 tablespoons capers
- 1 cup sliced black pitted olives
- 1 tablespoon sea salt
- ¾ teaspoon freshly ground black pepper
- 1 cup soy parmesan cheese (non-dairy)
- 4 cups cooked angel hair pasta

In a large saucepan, heat the oil over medium heat and sauté the mushrooms and peas for 6 minutes or until tender. Add the capers, basil, fennel, salt, pepper, and milk, cover and cook for another 2 minutes. Add the radicchio and cook for 1 additional minute. Remove from heat and toss with the cheese and pasta.

Serves 3 to 4

SWEET AND SOUR TEMPEH

- 2 cups cubed tempeh
- 1 cup cubed pineapple
- ½ cup chopped peanuts
- 1 cup broccoli florets
- 2 tablespoons sliced scallions
- 2 tablespoons hot sesame oil
- 2 teaspoons crushed garlic
- 3 tablespoons tamari
- 1 cup chopped roasted macadamia nuts
- 1 cup sweet basil leaves
- ¼ cup toasted sesame seeds

In a large saucepan, sauté all the ingredients in the oil over medium heat for 5 to 10 minutes, stirring constantly. Serve with brown rice.

Serves 2

VIETNAMESE CABBAGE ROLLS WITH PEARS

- 1½ cups chopped shitake mushrooms
- ½ cup diced carrots
- ¼ cup chopped scallions
- ½ cup chopped zucchini
- ¼ cup chopped fresh parsley
- 2 teaspoons tamari
- 1 cup cooked white beans
- Dash of freshly ground black pepper
- 5 tablespoons toasted sesame oil
- 1½ cups brown rice
- ¼ cup sesame seeds
- 2 cups sliced pears
- 1 cup apple juice
- ½ head or 10 leaves red cabbage, steamed 4 minutes
- 1 cup roasted cashews
- ½ cup chopped nuts

In a large saucepan, sauté the mushrooms, carrots, scallions, zucchini, parsley, tamari and pepper in the oil for 6–8 minutes over medium heat. Stir in the beans, rice and sesame seeds, and set aside. In a separate saucepan, cook the pears and juice over medium heat for 2 to 4 minutes or until tender, and set aside. Place one to two tablespoons of the vegetable stuffing on each cabbage leaf where the thick stem is. Fold the right side of the leaf over it, then the left, and roll it up. Place the stuffed leaves in a greased pan and top with the pear mixture and nuts. Cover and bake in a preheated oven at 375 degrees F for 30 minutes.

Serves 2

TEMPEH WITH ORANGE AND GINGER

- 1 cup red and yellow sweet peppers
- 3 tablespoons toasted sesame oil
- 1 cup cubed tempeh
- 2 tablespoons sliced scallions
- 1 cup peeled diced seedless oranges
- ½ teaspoon grated fresh ginger
- 2 tablespoons soy sauce
- ¼ teaspoon freshly ground black pepper
- ¼ cup gomasio for garnish

In a large saucepan, saute all the ingredients, except for gomasio, over medium heat for 10 minutes. Add garnish and serve hot with brown rice.

Serves 3

MEDITERRANEAN STRING BEANS

- 4 cups string beans, strings removed
- 1½ cup chopped or sliced onions
- 6 cloves garlic, sliced
- 5 cups sliced mushrooms
- 1 cup chopped fresh basil
- 3 tablespoons chopped fresh parsley
- 1 teaspoon chopped fresh oregano
- 2 tablespoons peppercorns
- ½ teaspoon red pepper
- 1 teaspoon dill
- 3 cups chopped fresh tomatoes
- ¼ cup extra virgin olive oil
- 1 cup grated soy parmesan cheese (non-dairy)

In a large saucepan, sauté the string beans, onions, garlic, mushrooms, basil, parsley, oregano, peppercorns, red pepper, and dill in the oil over medium-high heat for 5–7 minutes. Add the tomatoes, and cook another 15–20 minutes. Garnish with the cheese and serve with brown rice.

Yields 6 to 7 cups

SPICY BROCCOLI STIR-FRY

- 2 tablespoons hot sesame oil
- 2 cups cubed baked tofu
- 2 cups broccoli florets
- 1 teaspoon cornstarch, dissolved in ½ cup water
- 2 tablespoons grated orange peel
- 2 tablespoons grated lemon peel
- 1 tablespoon chili pepper
- 2 tablespoons tamari
- 2 tablespoons fennel
- ¼ teaspoon hot red pepper flakes (optional)
- 2 cloves garlic, minced
- 1 teaspoon grated fresh ginger

In a medium saucepan, sauté the tofu and broccoli in oil over medium heat for 3 minutes. Remove from the pan and place the mixture in a bowl. Combine the remaining ingredients in the pan. Cook on low-medium heat until simmering for one minute. Add the broccoli mixture, cover, and cook for 2 minutes. Stir well and serve with short-grain brown rice.

Serves 3 to 4

STIR-FRY GARLIC AND KOMBU

- 1 cup sweet peas
- 1 cup diced yellow and red sweet peppers
- 2 cups chopped bok choy
- 2 tablespoons mustard powder
- 5 cloves garlic, crushed
- 4 tablespoons toasted hot sesame oil
- 1 cup cubed firm tofu
- 4 tablespoons tamari
- ¼ cup sun dried tomatoes
- 1 cup kombu, soaked and drained (see below)

In a large saucepan, sauté the peas, peppers, bok choy, mustard powder, and garlic in the oil over medium heat for 15 minutes. Add the tofu and cook an additional 2–3 minutes. Add the tamari and kombu, mix in lightly, and serve with brown rice.

Serves 2

Note: Kombu leaves will disintegrate if stirred vigorously. Soak for 10–20 seconds, drain and use.

DESSERTS

COCONUT MANGO PUDDING

- 6 ounces mango
- 3 ounces brown rice, cooked
- 1½ ounces coconut, shredded (unsweetened)
- 1½ ounces dates
- 10 ounces coconut milk
- 2 heaping teaspoons Ener-G Egg Replacer
- pinch of cinnamon

Combine all ingredients in blender and purée until smooth. Transfer to saucepan and cook over medium heat for 5 minutes, stirring frequently. Chill in refrigerator for 45 minutes.

Serves 2

SUNNY RICE PUDDING

- 3 ounces mango
- 3 ounces brown rice, cooked
- 5 teaspoons carob powder
- 1½ ounces sunflower seeds
- 1 ounce date sugar
- 1 teaspoon vanilla
- 1½ ounces dates
- 2 heaping teaspoons Ener-G Egg Replacer

Combine all ingredients in blender and purée until smooth. Transfer to saucepan and cook over medium heat for 5 minutes, stirring frequently. Chill in refrigerator for 45 minutes.

Serves 2

CINNAMON PAPAYA PUDDING

- 3 ounces papaya
- 3 ounces oatmeal, cooked
- 6 ounces apple juice
- 3 tablespoons honey
- 2 heaping teaspoons Ener-G Egg Replacer
- pinch of cinnamon
- 3 ounces apples, cut into ½-inch cubes

Combine all ingredients in blender except apples. Purée until smooth. Transfer to saucepan and cook over medium heat for about 5 minutes. Add apples and stir. Chill in refrigerator for 45 minutes or until set.

Serves 2

APPLE-PAPAYA HONEY PUDDING

- 6 ounces pineapple
- 6 ounces papaya juice
- 3 tablespoons honey
- 2 tablespoons Ener-G Egg Replacer
- pinch of cinnamon
- 4½ ounces apples, chopped
- 1½ ounces pecans, chopped

Combine all ingredients in blender except apples and pecans. Purée until smooth. Transfer to saucepan and cook over medium heat for 5 minutes. Add apples and nuts. Stir. Chill for 45 minutes in refrigerator.

Serves 2

KIWI PUDDING

- 5 ounces strawberries
- 2 ounces kiwi
- 3 ounces millet, cooked
- 4 ounces maple syrup
- 6 ounces coconut milk
- 2 heaping teaspoons Ener-G Egg Replacer
- 1 teaspoon vanilla
- 1 teaspoon fresh mint
- 1 teaspoon lemon juice
- pinch of cinnamon
- 1½ ounces slivered almonds

Place all ingredients in blender, except almonds. Purée until smooth. Transfer to saucepan and set over medium heat for 5 minutes, stirring constantly. Chill for 45 minutes in the refrigerator. Top with almonds when chilled.

Serves 3

STRAWBERRY ORANGE PUDDING

- 4 ounces strawberries
- 3 ounces orange sections
- 1½ ounces plums
- 3 ounces maple syrup
- 6 ounces coconut milk
- 1½ ounces slivered almonds

Combine all ingredients in blender, except for almonds. Purée until smooth. Transfer to saucepan and set over medium heat for 5 minutes, stirring constantly. Chill for 45 minutes in refrigerator. Top with almonds when chilled.

Serves 2

CAROB BANANA TOFU PUDDING

- 6 ounces banana, mashed
- 3 ounces peaches, sliced
- 3 ounces tofu, cut into bite-size pieces
- 4 ounces barley malt
- 6 ounces peach juice
- ½ ounce carob powder
- 1 teaspoon vanilla
- 3 heaping teaspoons Ener-G Egg Replacer
- pinch of cinnamon

Combine all ingredients in blender. Purée until smooth. Transfer to saucepan and set over medium heat for 5 minutes, stirring frequently. Chill for 45 minutes in refrigerator.

Serves 2

PEACH JULEP PUDDING

- 6 ounces peaches, sliced
- 3 ounces barley, cooked
- 8 ounces peach juice
- 4 ounces barley malt

- 1½ ounces walnuts
- 1 teaspoon vanilla
- 2 teaspoons fresh mint
- 1 teaspoon lemon juice

Place all ingredients in blender. Purée until smooth. Transfer to saucepan and set over medium heat for 5 minutes, stirring frequently. Chill for 45 minutes in refrigerator.

Serves 2

PEAR-APPLE-HAZELNUT CRISP

- 2 pears, cored and sliced
- 2 apples, cored and diced
- 2 oranges, peeled and puréed
- 4 plums, peeled, pitted, and sliced

- ¾ teaspoon grated orange rind
- 2 tablespoons fresh lemon juice
- 2 tablespoons almond extract
- 1 tablespoon vanilla extract

TOPPING

- ¼ cup coarsely chopped roasted hazelnuts
- ¼ cup coarsely chopped roasted pecans
- ½ cup coarsely chopped macadamia nuts

- ¼ cup canola oil
- ¾ cup maple syrup
- ¼ cup oat or barley flour
- 1 tablespoon brown cinnamon

In a large bowl, combine the pears, apples, oranges, plums, rind, and extract. Pour into a square 9-inch baking dish. Combine the topping ingredients and sprinkle on top of the fruit mixture. Bake in a preheated 375 degrees Farenheit oven for 25 to 35 minutes.

Serves 6 to 8

BANANA HEAVENLY DELIGHT·

- 1 cup rice or soy milk
- 4 tablespoons egg replacer
- 4 teaspoons vanilla extract
- 2 teaspoons almond extract
- ¼ cup pure maple syrup
- ½ teaspoon ground nutmeg
- 1 cup sliced bananas
- ½ teaspoon cinnamon
- ¼ cup agar flakes
- ¼ cup roasted pecans

In a medium saucepan, bring the milk, egg replacer, extracts, syrup, and nutmeg to a simmer. Stir constantly with a whisk and use a tapered spoon to make sure the bottom doesn't burn. Once thickened, remove from the heat and stir in the banana slices, and chill for 2 to 4 hours. To serve, gently loosen the pudding from the sides of the dish by running a butter or small knife around the inside of the glass. Next, place a plate on top of the dish and invert the plate and dish.

Serves 4

PECAN-MAPLE CUSTARD

- 4 tablespoons apple juice
- 3 cups silken tofu
- 4 tablespoons vanilla extract
- 4½ teaspoons almond extract
- 1 cup chopped roasted pecans
- 3 tablespoons chia seeds
- ¼ cup agar flakes

In the blender or food processor, combine all the ingredients except the pecans, until smooth. Chill, top with pecans, and serve.

Serves 4

POACHED PEARS

- 4 pears peeled and quartered
- 2 cups apple juice
- 4 tablespoons orange rind and juice
- 1 tablespoon lemon extract
- 2 cups fresh or frozen raspberries
- ¾ cup maple syrup
- ¼ cup toasted macadamia nuts for garnish
- 4 fresh mint leaves for garnish

In a large saucepan, bring the pears, juices, and extract to a boil, reduce the heat to low, and cook for 5 minutes, covered. In a separate saucepan, combine the raspberries and maple syrup. Bring to a simmer and let cook for 2 minutes. Remove from the heat and serve over the drained pears. Add the garnish and serve with non-dairy ice cream.

Serves 4

APPENDIX

THE
PROTEIN
COMBINATION
LIST

LEGUMES

Snap Bean (raw)
Cowpeas (Black-eyed Pea)
Green Pea
Mung Bean
Soybean
Black Bean
Red Miso (Rice)
Tofu
Aduki Bean
Chick-pea (Garbanzo)
Tempeh
Red Kidney Bean
Peanut Butter
Peanut (whole w/ shell)
Lentil
Lima Bean (fresh)
Lima Bean (dry)
Navy Bean (Great Northern)
Pinto Bean
Navy Bean Pod
Broad Bean
Pea w/ Pod

GRAINS

Amaranth
Triticale Flour
Rye Flour (dark)
Basmati Rice (long grain, parboiled)
Buckwheat Flour
Bulgur
Couscous
Barley Flour
Brown Rice (short grain)
Pearled Barley
Spaghetti (white flour)
Oatmeal
Whole Wheat Flour
Wheat Bran
Wheat Flakes
Hominy Grits
Gluten Flour (unsifted)
Whole Wheat Gluten Flour
Cornmeal
Corn Flour
Wheat Germ

VEGETABLES

Spirulina
Spinach (raw)
Collards (cooked)
Cauliflower (cooked)
Summer Squash
Brewer's Yeast
Broccoli (cooked)
Okra (cooked)
Bell Pepper
Dulse (Seaweed)
Eggplant (cooked)
Asparagus (cooked)
Cucumber (unpared)
Cabbage (common, raw)
Pumpkin
Brussels Sprouts (cooked)
Mustard Greens (cooked)
Wakame (Seaweed)
Corn (kernel off-cob)
Pea Sprouts
Crisphead Lettuce
Kale (cooked)
Mushroom (Agaricus C)

Onion (raw)
Hijiki (Seaweed)
Soybean Sprout
Swiss Chard (raw)
Watercress (chopped fine)
Chlorella (Seaweed)
Parsley (chopped)

NUTS AND SEEDS

Pine Nuts
Sunflower Flour
Coconut (fresh, shredded)
Sunflower (hulled)
Sunflower Butter
Pecan (shelled)
Pumpkin Squash Seed Kernel
Persian Walnut
Watermelon Seed
Cashew Nut
Almonds (shelled—whole)
Sesame Seed Meal
Sesame Butter
Sesame Seed (hulled)
Tahini

Filbert (shelled)
Brazil Nut (shelled)
Alfalfa Seeds

FRUITS

Plantain (raw)
Tomato (raw)
Pineapple (raw)
Date (whole, w/ pit)
Papaya (raw)

ROOTS

Sweetpotato (cooked)
Turnip Greens (raw)
Beet (cooked)
Potato (raw)
Carrot (raw)
Beet Greens (cooked)

FLUIDS

Coconut Milk
Soymilk

SINGLE FOODS

(IN ORDER OF "QUALITY" OF PROTEIN)

Pine Nuts
Amaranth
Triticale Flour
Spirulina
Sunflower Flour
Spinach (raw)
Rye Flour (dark)
Basmati (long-grain, parboiled)
Sunflower Seed
Buckwheat Flour
Collards (cooked)
Bulgur

Couscous
Brewer's Yeast
Barley Flour
Brown Rice (raw)
Broccoli (cooked)
Sunflower Butter
Pearled Barley
Coconut Milk
Pumpkin
Spaghetti
Soymilk
Whole Wheat Flour

Dulse (Seaweed)
Cowpeas (Black-eyed Pea)
Green Pea
Watermelon Seed
Mung Bean Sprouts
Soybean
Brussel Sprout
Black Bean
Cashew Nut
Red Miso (rice)
Wakame (Seaweed)
Hominy Grits
Almonds (shelled—whole)
Tofu

Corn (kernel off-cob)
Pea Sprouts
Aduki Bean
Chick-pea (Garbanzo)
Sesame Seed Meal
Tempeh
Red Kidney Bean
Peanut Butter
Peanut (whole w/ shell)
Sesame Butter
Sesame Seed (hulled)
Tahini
Gluten Flour (unsifted)
Wheat (Gluten Flour)

COMBINATIONS OF TWO FOODS

(IN ORDER OF "QUALITY" OF PROTEIN)

Hijiki Seaweed / Amaranth
Triticale Flour / Amaranth
Basmati (long-grain, parboiled) /
  Amaranth
Sunflower Flour / Amaranth
Pine Nuts / Swiss Chard (raw)
Sunflower Flour / Green Pea (dry)
Sunflower (hulled) / Amaranth
Whole Wheat Flour / Amaranth
Sesame Seed (meal) / Amaranth
Spinach (raw) / Pine Nuts
Buckwheat Flour (dark) / Basmati
  (long-grain parboiled)
Walnut, Persian / Amaranth
Pine Nuts / Amaranth
Bulgur / Amaranth
Brown Rice (raw, short-grain) /
  Amaranth
Sunflower (hulled) / Pine Nuts
Couscous / Amaranth
Watermelon Seed / Amaranth
Filbert (shelled) / Amaranth

Pine Nuts / Broccoli (cooked)
Sunflower Flour / Aduki Bean
Sunflower Flour / Alfalfa Seeds
Spaghetti / Amaranth
Pumpkin Squash Seeds Kernel /
  Amaranth
Broccoli (cooked) / Basmati (long-
  grain, parboiled)
Triticale Flour / Buckwheat Flour
  (dark)
Rye Flour (dark) / Pine Nuts
Barley Flour / Amaranth
Amaranth / Almonds (shelled—
  whole)
Rye Flour (dark) / Amaranth
Sunflower Flour / Lentil (whole, dry)
Pine Nuts / Cowpeas (Black-eye
  pea)
Pine Nuts / Basmati (long-grain,
  parboiled)
Pearled Barley / Amaranth
Triticale Flour / Green Pea (dry)

Sunflower Flour / Navy Bean pod

Oatmeal (cooked and oats) /
Amaranth

Triticale Flour / Pine Nuts

Sunflower Flour / Cowpeas (Black-
eye pea)

Pine Nuts / Green Pea (dry)

Spirulina / Amaranth

Sunflower Flour / Navy Bean (Great
Northern)

Sunflower Butter / Amaranth

Pine Nuts / Mung Bean Sprouts
(dry)

Pine Nuts / Collards (cooked)

Tempeh / Brazil Nut (shelled)

Cashew Nut / Amaranth

Sunflower Flour / Buckwheat Flour
(dark)

Triticale Flour / Coconut Milk

Corn Flour / Amaranth

Corn (kernel off-cob) / Amaranth

Triticale Flour / Broccoli (cooked)

Wheat Flakes / Amaranth

Sunflower Flour / Broccoli (cooked)

Pecan (shelled) / Amaranth

Sunflower Flour / Pine Nuts

Brussel Sprout (cooked) / Basmati
(long-grain, parboiled)

Sunflower Flour / Lima Bean (fresh)

Triticale Flour / Mustard Greens
(cooked)

Sunflower Flour / Soybean

Amaranth / Almonds (shelled—
whole)

Rye Flower (Dark) / Amaranth

Sunflower Flour / Lentil (whole, dry)

Pine Nuts / Cowpeas (Black-eye Pea)

Pine Nuts / Basmati (long-grain,
parboiled)

Pearled Barley / Amaranth

Triticale Flour / Green Pea (dry)

Sunflower Flour / Navy Bean pod

Oatmeal (cooked and oats) /
Amaranth

Triticale Flour / Pine Nuts

Sunflower Flour / Cowpeas (Black-
eye pea)

Pine Nuts / Green Pea (dry)

Spirulina / Amaranth

Sunflower Flour / Navy Bean (Great
Northern)

Sunflower Butter / Amaranth

Pine Nuts / Mung Bean Sprouts
(dry)

Pine Nuts / Collards (cooked)

Tempeh / Brazil Nut (shelled)

Cashew Nut / Amaranth

Sunflower Flour / Buckwheat Flour
(dark)

Triticale Flour / Coconut Milk

Corn Flour / Amaranth

Corn (kernel off-cob) / Amaranth

Triticale Flour / Broccoli (cooked)

Wheat Flakes / Amaranth

Sunflower Flour / Broccoli (cooked)

Pecan (shelled) / Amaranth

Sunflower Flour / Amaranth

Brussel Sprout (cooked) / Basmati
(long-grain, parboiled)

Sunflower Flour / Lima Bean (fresh)

Triticale Flour / Mustard Greens
(cooked)

Sunflower Flour / Soybean

Sweetpotato (cooked) / Amaranth

Sunflower Flour / Chick-pea
(Garbanzo)

Sunflower Flour / Lima Bean (dry)

Triticale Flour / Cowpeas

Spirulina / Brazil Nut (shelled)

Spinach (raw) / Basmati (long-
grain, parboiled)

Pine Nuts / Corn (kernel off-cob)

Brown Rice (raw, short-grain) /
Pine Nuts

Chard, Swiss (raw) / Amaranth
Sunflower Flour / Coconut Milk
Sunflower Flour / Brussel Sprout
  (cooked)
Green Pea (dry) / Basmati (long-
  grain, parboiled)
Sunflower Flour / Pea Sprouts
Pine Nuts / Kale (cooked)
Triticale Flour / Sunflower Flour
Cornmeal / Amaranth
Coconut (fresh, shredded)/
  Amaranth
Pine Nuts / Buckwheat Flour
  (dark)
Sunflower / Buckwheat Flour (dark)
Triticale Flour / Rye Flour (dark)
Sunflower Flour / Kale (cooked)
Pine Nuts / Brussel Sprout
  (cooked)
Sunflower Flour / Asparagus
  (cooked)
Sunflower Flour / Spirulina
Sunflower Flour / Red Kidney Bean
Sunflower Flour / Spinach (raw)
Pine Nuts / Almonds (shelled—
  whole)
Spinach (raw) / Amaranth
Wheat Bran / Amaranth
Triticale Flour / Spinach (raw)
Triticale Flour / Potato (raw)
Triticale Flour / Brussel Sprout
  (cooked)
Sunflower Flour / Mung Bean
  Sprouts (dry)
Brazil Nut (shelled) / Lima Bean
  (dry)
Common Cabbage (raw) /
  Amaranth
Turnip Greens / Triticale Flour
Mung Bean Sprouts (dry) / Basmati
  (long-grain, parboiled)
Eggplant (cooked) / Amaranth

Triticale Flour / Cauliflower
  (cooked)
Collards (cooked) / Amaranth
Collards (cooked) / Basmati (long-
  grain, parboiled)
Okra (cooked) / Amaranth
Triticale Flour / Asparagus
  (cooked)
Pumpkin (Squash Seed Kernel) /
  Pine Nuts
Turnip Greens / Amaranth
Crisphead Lettuce / Amaranth
Spirulina / Coconut Milk
Summer Squash / Amaranth
Triticale Flour / Sweetpotato
  (cooked)
Triticale Flour / Mung Bean
  Sprouts (dry)
Pineapple (raw) / Amaranth
Sunflower Flour / Soymilk
Beet (cooked) / Amaranth
Triticale Flour / Agaricus C,
  Mushroom
Sunflower Flour / Mustard Greens
  (cooked)
Spirulina / Aduki Bean
Triticale Flour / Collards (cooked)
Triticale Flour / Plantain (raw)
Sunflower Flour / Rye Flour (dark)
Watermelon Seed / Spirulina
Carrot / Amaranth
Cucumber (not pared) / Amaranth
Triticale Flour / Pumpkin Pulp
Sunflower Flour / Collards (cooked)
Triticale Flour / Onion (raw)
Triticale Flour / Tomato (raw)
Plantain (raw) / Amaranth
Pepper / Amaranth
Brazil Nut (shelled) / Amaranth
Sunflower Flour / Swiss Chard (raw)
Triticale Flour / Okra (cooked)
Whole Wheat Flour / Pine Nuts

Brewer's Yeast / Gluten Flour (unsifted)
Cauliflower (cooked) / Amaranth
Triticale Flour / Green Snap Bean (raw)
Potato (raw) / Amaranth
Brewer's Yeast / Watermelon Seed
Hijiki Seaweed / Pine Nuts
Tofu / Sunflower Flour
Spirulina / Pea Sprouts
Peanut (whole w/ shell) / Amaranth
Sunflower Flour / Pea (podded)
Tomato (raw) / Amaranth
Pine Nuts / Pearled Barley
Green Snap Bean (raw) / Amaranth
Sunflower Flour / Cauliflower (cooked)
Spirulina / Pine Nuts
Broccoli (cooked) / Amaranth
Triticale Flour / Crisphead Lettuce
Triticale Flour / Summer Squash
Asparagus (cooked) / Amaranth
Sunflower Butter / Pine Nuts
Mung Bean Sprouts (dry) / Amaranth
Sunflower Flour / Okra (cooked)
Tofu / Brazil Nut (shelled)
Triticale Flour / Pineapple (raw)
Triticale Flour / Cucumber (not pared)
Sunflower Flour / Crisphead Lettuce
Triticale Flour / Beet (cooked)
Triticale Flour / Common Cabbage (raw)
Spirulina / Whole Lentil (dry)
Sunflower Flour / Black Bean
Triticale Flour / Pepper
Pumpkin Pulp / Amaranth
Spirulina / Parsley (chopped)
Mustard Greens (cooked) / Amaranth
Sunflower Butter / Spirulina

Sunflower Flour / Green Snap Bean (raw)
Spirulina / Hijiki Seaweed
Sunflower Flour / Common Cabbage (raw)
Triticale Flour / Carrot
Spirulina / Buckwheat Flour (dark)
Spirulina / Chick-pea (Garbanzo)
Cowpeas (Black-eye Pea) / Basmati (long-grain, parboiled)
Spirulina / Green Pea (dry)
Spirulina / Sesame Seed Meal
Spirulina / Cowpeas (Black-eye Pea)
Triticale Flour / Kale (cooked)
Triticale Flour / Aduki Bean
Watercress (chopped fine) / Amaranth
Watercress (chopped fine) / Triticale Flour
Sesame Seed Meal / Pine Nuts
Triticale Flour / Eggplant (cooked)
Triticale Flour / Papaya (raw)
Sunflower Flour / Corn (kernel off-cob)
Cowpeas (Black-eye Pea) / Amaranth
Spirulina / Pumpkin, (Squash Seed Kernel)
Triticale Flour / Basmati (long-grain, parboiled)
Triticale Flour / Swiss Chard (raw)
Sunflower Flour / Potato (raw)
Triticale Flour / Spirulina
Spirulina / Alfalfa Seeds
Pine Nuts / Lima Bean (fresh)
Triticale Flour / Sunflower (hulled)
Sunflower Flour / Summer Squash
Spirulina / Basmati (long-grain, parboiled)
Triticale Flour / Pea Sprouts
Spirulina / Mung Bean Sprouts (dry)

Sunflower Flour / Agaricus C
Mushroom
Triticale Flour / Pecan (shelled)
Brewer's Yeast / Sunflower Flour
Turnip Greens / Sunflower Flour
Sunflower Flour / Cucumber (not
pared)
Triticale Flour / Sunflower Butter
Tomato (raw) / Sunflower Flour
Spirulina / Soymilk
Triticale Flour / Coconut (fresh,
shredded)
Sunflower Flour / Pumpkin Pulp
Spirulina / Black Bean
Brussel Sprout (cooked) /
Amaranth
Brewer's Yeast / Brazil Nut
(shelled)
Agaricus C Mushroom / Amaranth
Spirulina / Rye Flour (dark)
Tofu / Spirulina
Sunflower Flour / Onion (raw)
Triticale Flour / Lentil (whole, dry)
Buckwheat Flour (dark) /
Amaranth
Onion (raw) / Amaranth
Triticale Flour / Tofu
Wheat Bran / Triticale Flour
Kale (cooked) / Amaranth
Spirulina / Mustard Greens
(cooked)
Spirulina / Broccoli (cooked)
Soybean / Brazil Nut (shelled)
Triticale Flour / Alfalfa Seeds
Triticale Flour / Soybean
Papaya (raw) / Amaranth
Sunflower Flour / Plantain (raw)
Spirulina / Potato (raw)
Spirulina / Spinach (raw)
Spirulina / Soybean
Sunflower Flour / Eggplant (cooked)
Sunflower Flour / Brown Rice (raw,
short-grain)

Beet, Greens (cooked) / Amaranth
Soymilk / Amaranth
Pine Nuts/ Coconut Milk
Sweetpotato (cooked) / Sunflower
Flour
Triticale Flour / Soymilk
Brewer's Yeast / Spirulina
Soymilk / Pine Nuts
Spirulina / Barley Flour
Triticale Flour / Oatmeal (cooked
and oats)
Spirulina / Onion (raw)
Amaranth / Alfalfa Seeds
Sunflower Flour / Carrot
Spirulina / Agaricus C Mushroom
Spirulina / Plantain (raw)
Watercress (chopped fine) /
Sunflower Flour
Spirulina / Asparagus (cooked)
Spirulina / Cauliflower (cooked)
Sunflower Flour / Pepper
Summer Squash / Spirulina
Turnip Greens / Spirulina
Spirulina / Bulgur
Sweetpotato (cooked) / Spirulina
Spirulina / Collards (cooked)
Sunflower / Spirulina
Spirulina / Pumpkin Pulp
Spirulina / Couscous
Spirulina / Pineapple (raw)
Rye Flour (dark) / Buckwheat
Flour (dark)
Sunflower Flour / Pineapple (raw)
Sunflower Flour / Soybean Sprout
Tomato (raw) / Spirulina
Bean, Lima (fresh) / Amaranth
Whole Wheat Flour / Spirulina
Rye Flour (dark) / Basmati (long-
grain, parboiled)
Spirulina / Navy Bean, w/o Meat
Spirulina / Papaya (raw)
Spirulina / Cucumber (not pared)
Spirulina / Beet (cooked)

Spirulina / Crisphead Lettuce
Triticale Flour / Red Kidney Bean
Wheat Bran / Spirulina
Spirulina / Okra (cooked)
Spirulina / Navy Bean (Great Northern)
Spirulina / Common Cabbage (raw)
Sunflower Flour / Basmati (long-grain, parboiled)
Spirulina / Pecan (shelled)
Spirulina / Pearled Barley
Spirulina / Oatmeal (cooked and oats)
Spirulina / Coconut (fresh, shredded)
Persian Walnut / Triticale Flour
Spirulina / Pepper
Spirulina / Eggplant (cooked)
Sunflower Flour / Beet (cooked)
Spaghetti / Pine Nuts
Spirulina / Lima Bean (fresh)
Spirulina / Peanut (whole, w/ shell)
Spirulina / Swiss Chard (raw)
Spirulina / Red Kidney Bean (cooked)
Sunflower Flour / Hominy Grits
Spirulina / Kale (cooked)
Spirulina / Green Snap Bean (raw)
Triticale Flour / Lima Bean (fresh)
Triticale Flour / Pumpkin (Squash Seed Kernel)
Persian Walnut / Spirulina
Sunflower Flour / Papaya (raw)
Peanut Butter / Amaranth
Spirulina / Brown Rice (raw, short-grain)
Spirulina / Carrot
Spirulina / Corn (kernel off-cob)
Spirulina / Almonds (shelled—whole)
Spirulina / Lima Bean (dry)

Triticale Flour / Beet Greens (cooked)
Sunflower Flour / Pecan (shelled)
Sunflower Flour / Coconut (fresh, shredded)
Wheat Flakes / Spirulina
Watercress (chopped fine) / Spirulina
Spirulina / Peanut Butter
Wheat Flakes / Triticale Flour
Pine Nuts / Filbert (shelled)
Carrot / Basmati (long-grain, parboiled)
Spirulina / Beet Greens (cooked)
Soybean / Hijiki Seaweed
Triticale Flour / Soybean Sprout
Coconut Milk / Amaranth
Green Pea (dry) / Amaranth
Soymilk / Hijiki Seaweed
Triticale Flour / Brown Rice (raw, short-grain)
Spirulina / Cashew Nut
Triticale Flour / Pearled Barley
Wheat Flakes / Sunflower Flour
Kale (cooked) / Basmati (long-grain, parboiled)
Spirulina / Soybean Sprout
Wheat Bran / Sunflower Flour
Spirulina / Spaghetti
Sunflower (hulled) / Sunflower Flour
Sunflower Flour / Oatmeal (cooked and oats)
Triticale Flour / Sesame Seed Meal
Triticale Flour / Navy Bean pod
Hominy Grits / Amaranth
Whole Wheat Flour / Buckwheat Flour (dark)
Green Pea (dry) / Bulgur
Triticale Flour / Corn (kernel off-cob)
Tahini / Spirulina
Spirulina / Sesame Butter

Date (whole, w/ pit) / Amaranth
Persian Walnut / Sunflower Flour
Coconut Milk / Basmati (long-grain, parboiled)
Spirulina / Filbert (shelled)
Pine Nuts / Bulgur
Soybean Sprout / Basmati (long-grain, parboiled)
Spaghetti / Alfalfa Seeds
Whole Wheat Flour / Green Pea (dry)
Red Miso (rice) / Amaranth
Pine Nuts / Peanut (whole, w/ shell)
Spinach (raw) / Rye Flour (dark)
Soymilk / Basmati (long-grain, parboiled)
Lima Bean (dry) / Amaranth
Spirulina / Corn Flour
Pine Nuts / Barley Flour
Pine Nuts / Corn Flour
Green Pea (dry) / Couscous
Spirulina / Pea, Edible-Podded
Triticale Flour / Lima Bean (dry)
Bulgur / Buckwheat Flour (dark)
Soybean Sprout / Amaranth
Pine Nuts / Navy Bean
Brazil Nut (shelled) / Black Bean
Pine Nuts / Couscous
Triticale Flour / Almonds (shelled—whole)
Sunflower Flour / Corn Flour
Spirulina / Sesame Seed (hulled)
Spirulina / Cornmeal
Brazil Nut (shelled) / Red Kidney Bean (cooked)
Spirulina / Hominy Grits
Sunflower Flour / Pumpkin (Squash Seed Kernel)
Whole Wheat Flour / Triticale Flour
Pine Nuts / Red Kidney Bean (cooked)

Spirulina / Pinto Bean (red Mexican)
Wakame Seaweed / Amaranth
Green Pea (dry) / Barley Flour
Sunflower Butter / Buckwheat Flour (dark)
Pine Nuts / Lima Bean (dry)
Triticale Flour / Spaghetti
Rye Flour (dark) / Broccoli (cooked)
Triticale Flour / Peanut (whole, w/ shell)
Couscous / Buckwheat Flour (dark)
Soybean / Pine Nuts
Soymilk / Brazil Nut (shelled)
Sunflower Flour / Almonds (shelled—whole)
Soybean / Basmati (long-grain, parboiled)
Spirulina / Wakame Seaweed
Sunflower Flour / Pearled Barley
Triticale Flour / Navy Bean (Great Northern)
Lima Bean (fresh) / Basmati (long-grain, parboiled)
Sunflower (hulled) / Basmati (long-grain, parboiled)
Watermelon Seed / Lima Bean (dry)
Sunflower Flour / Peanut (whole, w/ shell)
Triticale Flour / Barley Flour
Triticale Flour / Bulgur
Sunflower Flour / Cornmeal
Sunflower (hulled) / Coconut Milk
Sunflower Flour / Beet Greens (cooked)
Sunflower Flour / Hijiki Seaweed
Triticale Flour / Hijiki Seaweed
Gluten Flour (unsifted) / Amaranth
Watermelon Seed / Triticale Flour

Watermelon Seed / Soybean
Triticale Flour / Date (whole, w/ pit)
Sunflower (hulled) / Rye Flour (dark)
Red Kidney Bean (cooked) / Amaranth
Tempeh / Spirulina
Spirulina / Dulse Seaweed
Sunflower Flour / Sunflower Butter
Brewer's Yeast / Couscous
Watermelon Seed / Pea (edible, podded)
Pine Nuts / Aduki Bean
Soybean Sprout / Pine Nuts
Brewer's Yeast / Gluten Flour Wheat
Triticale Flour / Couscous
Brewer's Yeast / Triticale Flour
Rye Flour (dark) / Collards (cooked)
Sunflower Flour / Spaghetti
Brewer's Yeast / Hijiki Seaweed
Navy Bean pod / Amaranth
Sunflower Flour / Filbert (shelled)
Soybean / Amaranth
Watermelon Seed / Pine Nuts
Barley Flour / Alfalfa Seeds
Bulghar / Broccoli (cooked)
Triticale Flour / Parsley (chopped)
Brewer's Yeast / Bulgur
Sunflower Flour / Red Miso (Rice)
Tofu / Hijiki Seaweed
Pumpkin, (Squash Seed Kernel) / Basmati (long-grain, parboiled)
Spirulina / Gluten Flour (unsifted)
Cowpeas (Black-eye Pea) / Bulgur
Sunflower Flour / Pinto Bean (Red Mexican)
Sunflower Flour / Wakame Seaweed
Sesame Seed Meal / Rye Flour (dark)
Bulgur / Brussel Sprout (cooked)

Pine Nuts / Cornmeal
Buckwheat Flour (dark) / Barley Flour
Sunflower Flour / Peanut Butter
Sesame Butter / Amaranth
Tahini / Amaranth
Whole Wheat Flour / Sunflower Flour
Buckwheat Flour (dark) / Pearled Barley
Cowpeas (Black-eye Pea) / Couscous
Brazil Nut (shelled) / Navy Bean (Great Northern)
Pine Nuts / Cashew Nut
Couscous / Broccoli (cooked)
Tofu / Pine Nuts
Sunflower Flour / Bulgur
Rye Flour (dark) / Green Pea (dry)
Triticale Flour / Cashew Nut
Sunflower Flour / Parsley (chopped)
Couscous / Brussel Sprout (cooked)
Rye Flour (dark) / Okra (cooked)
Dulse Seaweed / Amaranth
Triticale Flour / Peanut Butter
Triticale Flour / Filbert (shelled)
Spirulina / Red Miso (Rice)
Sunflower Flour / Couscous
Coconut Milk / Bulgur
Rye Flour (dark) / Pumpkin (Squash Seed Kernel)
Navy Bean (Great Northern) / Amaranth
Tempeh / Sunflower Flour
Pine Nuts / Navy Bean (Great Northern)
Brewer's Yeast / Dulse Seaweed
Watermelon Seed / Buckwheat Flour (dark)
Watermelon Seed / Green Pea (dry)
Tofu / Amaranth

Couscous / Coconut Milk

Tofu / Basmati (long-grain, parboiled)

Mustard Greens (cooked) / Bulgur

Sunflower Butter / Brussel Sprout (cooked)

Watermelon Seed / Lima Bean (fresh)

Watermelon Seed / Navy Bean (Great Northern)

Watermelon Seed / Soymilk

Sunflower Flour / Barley Flour

Spirulina / Broad Bean (mat-dry)

Watermelon Seed / Tofu

Spaghetti / Buckwheat Flour (dark)

Bulgur / Asparagus (cooked)

Bulgur / Mung Bean Sprouts (dry)

Triticale Flour / Wakame Seaweed

Bulgur / Alfalfa Seeds

Lima Bean (dry) / Basmati (long-grain, parboiled)

Aduki Bean / Amaranth

Watermelon Seed / Black Bean

Black Bean / Amaranth

Rye Flour (dark) / Mung Bean Sprouts (dry)

Brewer's Yeast / Basmati (long-grain, parboiled)

Rye Flour (dark) / Coconut Milk

Brazil Nut (shelled) / Pinto Bean

Pine Nuts / Peanut Butter

Watermelon Seed / Navy Bean pod

Mustard Greens (cooked) / Couscous

Red Kidney Bean (cooked) / Basmati (long-grain, parboiled)

Pine Nuts / Lentil (whole, dry)

Watermelon Seed / Lentil (whole, dry)

Sunflower Flour / Cashew Nut

Couscous / Alfalfa Seeds

Sunflower Flour / Sesame Seed Meal

Pine Nuts / Hominy Grits

Couscous / Mung Bean Sprouts (dry)

Rye Flour (dark) / Bulgur

Spinach (raw) / Bulgur

Couscous / Aduki Bean

Rye Flour (dark) / Corn (kernel off-cob)

Watermelon Seed / Cowpeas (Black-eye Pea)

Watermelon Seed / Sprouts Pea

Sprouts Pea / Basmati (long-grain, parboiled)

Sunflower Flour / Date (whole, w/ pit)

Couscous / Asparagus (cooked)

Watermelon Seed / Coconut Milk

Watermelon Seed / Chick-pea (Garbanzo)

Triticale Flour / Brazil Nut (shelled)

Brewer's Yeast / Barley Flour

Soybean / Couscous

Bulgur / Lima Bean (fresh)

Broccoli (cooked) / Barley Flour

Rye Flour (dark) / Couscous

Couscous / Lima Bean (fresh)

Green Pea (dry) / Pearled Barley

Dulse Seaweed / Chick-pea (Garbanzo)

Brewer's Yeast / Sesame Seed Meal

Brewer's Yeast / Sunflower Butter

Soybean / Bulgur

Bulgur / Aduki Bean

Spaghetti / Coconut Milk

Rye Flour (dark) / Brussel Sprout (cooked)

Collards (cooked) / Bulgur

Couscous / Lima Bean (dry)

Watermelon Seed / Red Kidney Bean (cooked)

Spinach (raw) / Couscous

Watermelon Seed / Brussel Sprout (cooked)
Lentil (whole, dry) / Couscous
Triticale Flour / Hominy Grits
Pine Nuts / Pea Sprouts
Chick-pea (Garbanzo) / Brazil Nut (shelled)
Triticale Flour / Chick-pea (Garbanzo)
Sunflower Butter / Spinach (raw)
Rye Flour (dark) / Brown Rice (raw, short-grain)
Basmati (long-grain, parboiled) / Pearled Barley
Triticale Flour / Corn Flour
Pea (edible-podded) / Amaranth
Brown Rice (raw, short-grain) / Basmati (long-grain, parboiled)
Bulgur / Lima Bean (dry)
Sunflower Butter / Rye Flour (dark)
Rye Flour (dark) / Brazil Nut (shelled)
Soymilk / Bulgur
Sunflower Butter / Green Pea (dry)
Aduki Bean / Basmati (long-grain, parboiled)
Soymilk / Couscous
Whole Wheat Flour / Coconut Milk
Navy Bean pod / Basmati (long-grain, parboiled)
Lentil (whole, dry) / Basmati (long-grain, parboiled)

COMBINATIONS OF THREE FOODS

(IN ORDER OF "QUALITY" OF PROTEIN)

Triticale Flour / Hijiki Seaweed / Amaranth
Hijiki Seaweed / Pumpkin (Squash Seed Kernel) / Amaranth
Rye Flour (dark) / Brazil Nut (shelled) / Lima Bean (dry)
Sunflower (hulled) / Hijiki Seaweed / Amaranth
Hijiki Seaweed / Pine Nuts / Amaranth
Spaghetti / Brazil Nut (shelled) / Amaranth
Brazil Nut (shelled) / Red Kidney Bean (cooked) / Lima Bean (dry)
Sunflower Flour / Chick-pea (Garbanzo) / Brazil Nut (shelled)
Tofu / Brazil Nut (shelled) / Lima Bean (dry)
Sesame Seed Meal / Hijiki Seaweed / Amaranth
Hijiki Seaweed / Date (whole, w/ pit) / Amaranth
Wheat Bran / Hijiki Seaweed / Amaranth
Hijiki Seaweed / Onion (raw) / Amaranth
Sunflower Flour / Hijiki Seaweed / Amaranth
Tofu / Brazil Nut (shelled) / Lima Bean (fresh)
Hijiki Seaweed / Beet, Greens (cooked) / Amaranth
Whole Wheat Flour / Hijiki Seaweed / Amaranth
Sunflower Flour / Green Pea (dry) / Alfalfa Seeds
Soybean / Brazil Nut (shelled) / Lima Bean (dry)
Hijiki Seaweed / Collards (cooked) / Amaranth
Brazil Nut (shelled) / Lima Bean (dry) / Amaranth
Hijiki Seaweed / Filbert (shelled) / Amaranth

Sunflower Flour / Amaranth / Alfalfa Seeds

Hijiki Seaweed / Pecan (shelled) / Amaranth

Hijiki Seaweed / Basmati (long-grain, parboiled) / Amaranth

Peanut Butter / Brazil Nut (shelled) / Amaranth

Hijiki Seaweed / Beet (cooked) / Amaranth

Hijiki Seaweed / Oatmeal (cooked and oats) / Amaranth

Filbert (shelled) / Brazil Nut (shelled) / Amaranth

Persian Walnut / Hijiki Seaweed / Amaranth

Soymilk / Brazil Nut (shelled) / Lima Bean (dry)

Hijiki Seaweed / Cashew Nut / Amaranth

Soybean / Brazil Nut (shelled) / Lima Bean (fresh)

Spinach (raw) / Hijiki Seaweed / Amaranth

Wheat Flakes / Hijiki Seaweed / Amaranth

Hijiki Seaweed / Papaya (raw) / Amaranth

Triticale Flour / Sesame Seed Meal / Amaranth

Hijiki Seaweed / Common Cabbage (raw) / Amaranth

Soybean Sprout / Hijiki Seaweed / Amaranth

Hijiki Seaweed / Pepper / Amaranth

Hijiki Seaweed / Mung Bean Sprouts (dry) / Amaranth

Brewer's Yeast / Gluten Flour (unsifted) / Brazil Nut (shelled)

Hijiki Seaweed / Plantain (raw) / Amaranth

Hijiki Seaweed / Cauliflower (cooked) / Amaranth

Sunflower Flour / Brazil Nut (shelled) / Pinto Bean (Red Mexican)

Hijiki Seaweed / Mustard Greens (cooked) / Amaranth

Hijiki Seaweed / Asparagus (cooked) / Amaranth

Hijiki Seaweed / Agaricus C Mushroom / Amaranth

Turnip Greens / Hijiki Seaweed / Amaranth

Hijiki Seaweed / Pumpkin Pulp / Amaranth

Hijiki Seaweed / Potato (raw) / Amaranth

Sunflower Flour / Navy Bean pod / Alfalfa Seeds

Hijiki Seaweed / Carrot / Amaranth

Triticale Flour / Sweetpotato (cooked) / Amaranth

Hijiki Seaweed / Pineapple (raw) / Amaranth

Persian Walnut / Triticale Flour / Amaranth

Hijiki Seaweed / Pearled Barley / Amaranth

Triticale Flour / Basmati (long-grain, parboiled) / Amaranth

Sunflower Flour / Cowpeas (Black-eye Pea) / Alfalfa Seeds

Red Miso (rice) / Brazil Nut (shelled) / Amaranth

Hijiki Seaweed / Coconut (fresh, shredded) / Amaranth

Triticale Flour / Sunflower (hulled) / Amaranth

Triticale Flour / Sunflower Flour / Amaranth

Hijiki Seaweed / Cucumber (not pared) / Amaranth

Tomato (raw) / Hijiki Seaweed / Amaranth

Sunflower (hulled) / Basmati (long-grain, parboiled) / Amaranth

Hijiki Seaweed / Barley Flour / Amaranth

Sweetpotato (cooked) / Hijiki Seaweed / Amaranth

Triticale Flour / Coconut (fresh, shredded) / Amaranth

Summer Squash / Hijiki Seaweed / Amaranth

Triticale Flour / Pineapple (raw) / Amaranth

Hijiki Seaweed / Rye Flour (dark) / Amaranth

Triticale Flour / Brazil Nut (shelled) / Amaranth

Hijiki Seaweed / Broccoli (cooked) / Amaranth

Hijiki Seaweed / Eggplant (cooked) / Amaranth

Hijiki Seaweed / Buckwheat Flour (dark) / Amaranth

Persian Walnut / Basmati (long-grain, parboiled) / Amaranth

Sunflower Flour / Navy Bean (Great Northern) / Amaranth

Triticale Flour / Oatmeal (cooked and oats) / Amaranth

Pine Nuts / Brazil Nut (shelled) / Lima Bean (dry)

Triticale Flour / Crisphead Lettuce / Amaranth

Hijiki Seaweed / Green Snap Bean (raw) / Amaranth

Watermelon Seed / Triticale Flour / Amaranth

Hijiki Seaweed / Crisphead Lettuce / Amaranth

Rye Flour (dark) / Brazil Nut (shelled) / Lima Bean (fresh)

Hijiki Seaweed / Bulgur / Amaranth

Sunflower Flour / Swiss Chard (raw) / Amaranth

Hijiki Seaweed / Okra (cooked) / Amaranth

Triticale Flour / Summer Squash / Amaranth

Triticale Flour / Pecan (shelled) / Amaranth

Sunflower Flour / Lima Bean (fresh) / Alfalfa Seeds

Peanut (whole, w/shell) / Brazil Nut (shelled) / Amaranth

Triticale Flour / Swiss Chard (raw) / Amaranth

Triticale Flour / Eggplant (cooked) / Amaranth

Hijiki Seaweed / Brussel Sprout (cooked) / Amaranth

Triticale Flour / Common Cabbage (raw) / Amaranth

Triticale Flour / Plantain (raw) / Amaranth

Triticale Flour / Beet (cooked) / Amaranth

Sunflower Flour / Lima Bean (dry) / Alfalfa Seeds

Turnip Greens / Triticale Flour / Amaranth

Watercress (chopped fine) / Hijiki Seaweed / Amaranth

Triticale Flour / Mustard Greens (cooked) / Amaranth

Triticale Flour / Cucumber (not pared) / Amaranth

Triticale Flour / Tomato (raw) / Amaranth

Triticale Flour / Carrot / Amaranth

Triticale Flour / Pine Nuts / Amaranth

Soymilk / Brazil Nut (shelled) / Lima Bean (fresh)

Brazil Nut (shelled) / Lima Bean (fresh) / Amaranth

Triticale Flour / Potato (raw, whole) / Amaranth

Sunflower Flour / Corn (kernel off-cob) / Amaranth

Sesame Seed Meal / Filbert (shelled) / Amaranth

Hijiki Seaweed / Swiss Chard (raw) / Amaranth

Wheat Flakes / Triticale Flour / Amaranth

Sunflower Flour / Crisphead Lettuce / Amaranth

Sunflower Flour / Green Pea (dry) / Amaranth

Soymilk / Hijiki Seaweed / Amaranth

Triticale Flour / Pumpkin Pulp / Amaranth

Brewer's Yeast / Watermelon Seed / Brazil Nut (shelled)

Triticale Flour / Okra (cooked) / Amaranth

Triticale Flour / Pepper / Amaranth

Tofu / Rye Flour (dark) / Brazil Nut (shelled)

Wheat Bran / Triticale Flour / Amaranth

Persian Walnut / Sunflower Flour / Amaranth

Triticale Flour / Spinach (raw) / Amaranth

Triticale Flour / Agaricus C Mushroom / Amaranth

Soybean / Rye Flour (dark) / Brazil Nut (shelled)

Oatmeal (cooked and oats) / Basmati (long-grain, parboiled) / Amaranth

Triticale Flour / Broccoli (cooked) / Amaranth

Sunflower Flour / Common Cabbage (raw) / Amaranth

Coconut (fresh, shredded) / Basmati (long-grain, parboiled) / Amaranth

Hijiki Seaweed / Couscous / Amaranth

Triticale Flour / Cauliflower (cooked) / Amaranth

Sweetpotato (cooked) / Basmati (long-grain, parboiled) / Amaranth

Swiss Chard (raw) / Basmati (long-grain, parboiled) / Amaranth

Sunflower Flour / Basmati (long-grain, parboiled) / Amaranth

Triticale Flour / Amaranth / Almonds (shelled-whole)

Sunflower Flour / Brown Rice (raw, short-grain) / Amaranth

Common Cabbage (raw) / Basmati (long-grain, parboiled) / Amaranth

Whole Wheat Flour / Triticale Flour / Amaranth

Filbert (shelled) / Basmati (long-grain, parboiled) / Amaranth

Sunflower Flour / Spinach (raw) / Amaranth

Sesame Seed Meal / Basmati (long-grain, parboiled) / Amaranth

Triticale Flour / Amaranth / Alfalfa Seeds

Rye Flour (dark) / Brazil Nut (shelled) / Amaranth

Triticale Flour / Green Snap Bean (raw) / Amaranth

Triticale Flour / Asparagus (cooked) / Amaranth

Sunflower Flour / Corn Flour / Amaranth

Triticale Flour / Sunflower Butter / Amaranth

Pineapple (raw) / Basmati (long-grain, parboiled) / Amaranth

Sunflower Flour / Coconut (fresh, shredded) / Amaranth

Crisphead Lettuce / Basmati (long-grain, parboiled) / Amaranth

Sunflower Flour / Summer Squash / Amaranth

Pecan (shelled) / Basmati (long-grain, parboiled) / Amaranth

Rye Flour (dark) / Pine Nuts / Alfalfa Seeds

Sweetpotato (cooked) / Sunflower Flour / Amaranth

Sunflower Flour / Asparagus (cooked) / Amaranth

Sunflower Flour / Broccoli (cooked) / Amaranth

Sunflower Flour / Okra (cooked) / Amaranth

Watercress (chopped fine) / Triticale Flour / Amaranth

Sunflower Flour / Broccoli (cooked) / Alfalfa Seeds

Sunflower Flour / Eggplant (cooked) / Amaranth

Pine Nuts / Basmati (long-grain, parboiled) / Amaranth

Basmati (long-grain, parboiled) / Amaranth / Alfalfa Seeds

Sunflower Flour / Pineapple (raw) / Amaranth

Triticale Flour / Rye Flour (dark) / Amaranth

Sunflower Flour / Kale (cooked) / Alfalfa Seeds

Triticale Flour / Papaya (raw) / Amaranth

Sunflower Flour / Brussel Sprout (cooked) / Alfalfa Seeds

Triticale Flour / Brown Rice (raw, short-grain) / Amaranth

Wheat Flakes / Basmati (long-grain, parboiled) / Amaranth

Triticale Flour / Onion (raw) / Amaranth

Hijiki Seaweed / Pine Nuts / Buckwheat Flour (dark)

Triticale Flour / Pumpkin (Squash Seed Kernel) / Amaranth

Sunflower Flour / Cucumber (not pared) / Amaranth

Wheat Flakes / Sunflower Flour / Amaranth

Sunflower Flour / Oatmeal (cooked and oats) / Amaranth

Triticale Flour / Collards (cooked) / Amaranth

Triticale Flour / Tofu / Brazil Nut (shelled)

Summer Squash / Basmati (long-grain, parboiled) / Amaranth

Sunflower Flour / Cornmeal / Amaranth

Sunflower Flour / Pecan (shelled) / Amaranth

Hijiki Seaweed / Kale (cooked) / Amaranth

Sunflower Flour / Brazil Nut (shelled) / Black Bean

Spaghetti / Soybean / Brazil Nut (shelled)

Sunflower Flour / Cowpeas (Black-eye Pea) / Amaranth

Eggplant (cooked) / Basmati (long-grain, parboiled) / Amaranth

Spaghetti / Amaranth / Alfalfa Seeds

Chick-pea (Garbanzo) / Cashew Nut / Brazil Nut (shelled)

Sunflower (hulled) / Sunflower Flour / Amaranth

Sunflower Flour / Pine Nuts / Amaranth

Beet (cooked) / Basmati (long-grain, parboiled) / Amaranth

Brazil Nut (shelled) / Lima Bean (dry) / Pearled Barley

Sunflower Flour / Pea (edible-podded) / Alfalfa Seeds

Persian Walnut / Sunflower (hulled) / Amaranth

Wheat Bran / Basmati (long-grain, parboiled) / Amaranth

Sunflower Flour / Carrot / Amaranth

Tomato (raw) / Sunflower Flour / Amaranth

Sunflower Flour / Lentil (whole, dry) / Alfalfa Seeds

Whole Wheat Flour / Amaranth / Alfalfa Seeds

Carrot / Basmati (long-grain, parboiled) / Amaranth

Sunflower Flour / Green Snap Bean (raw) / Amaranth

Sunflower Flour / Mustard Greens (cooked) / Amaranth

Cucumber (not pared) / Basmati (long-grain, parboiled) / Amaranth

Sunflower Flour / Green Pea (dry) / Broccoli (cooked)

Pumpkin (Squash Seed Kernel) / Basmati (long-grain, parboiled) / Amaranth

Sunflower Flour / Aduki Bean / Alfalfa Seeds

Triticale Flour / Corn (kernel off-cob) / Amaranth

Triticale Flour / Buckwheat Flour (dark) / Amaranth

Mustard Greens (cooked) / Basmati (long-grain, parboiled) / Amaranth

Hijiki Seaweed / Amaranth / Alfalfa Seeds

Spinach (raw) / Basmati (long-grain, parboiled) / Amaranth

Whole Wheat Flour / Basmati (long-grain, parboiled) / Amaranth

Sunflower Flour / Lima Bean (fresh) / Amaranth

Sunflower Flour / Pumpkin Pulp / Amaranth

Sunflower Flour / Cauliflower (cooked) / Amaranth

Sunflower Flour / Plantain (raw) / Amaranth

Triticale Flour / Mung Bean Sprouts (dry) / Amaranth

Sunflower Flour / Beet (cooked) / Amaranth

Tempeh / Sunflower Flour / Brazil Nut (shelled)

Triticale Flour / Filbert (shelled) / Amaranth

Sunflower Flour / Collards (cooked) / Amaranth

Sunflower Flour / Green Pea (dry) / Asparagus (cooked)

Plantain (raw) / Basmati (long-grain, parboiled) / Amaranth

Sunflower Flour / Kale (cooked) / Amaranth

Sunflower Flour / Pepper / Amaranth

Turnip Greens / Sunflower Flour / Amaranth

Basmati (long-grain, parboiled) / Asparagus (cooked) / Amaranth

Sunflower Flour / Mung Bean Sprouts (dry) / Amaranth

Tomato (raw) / Basmati (long-grain, parboiled) / Amaranth

Triticale Flour / Pearled Barley / Amaranth

Sesame Seed Meal / Brown Rice (raw, short-grain) / Amaranth

Sunflower Flour / Filbert (shelled) / Amaranth

Pepper / Basmati (long-grain, parboiled) / Amaranth

Hijiki Seaweed / Corn (kernel off-cob) / Amaranth

Okra (cooked) / Basmati (long-grain, parboiled) / Amaranth

Sunflower Flour / Brussel Sprout (cooked) / Amaranth

Sunflower Flour / Potato (raw) / Amaranth

Brazil Nut (shelled) / Pearled Barley / Amaranth

Triticale Flour / Cowpeas (Black-eye Pea) / Amaranth

Triticale Flour / Brussel Sprout (cooked) / Amaranth

Sunflower Flour / Green Pea (dry) / Crisphead Lettuce

Watercress (chopped fine) / Sunflower Flour / Amaranth

Pumpkin Pulp / Basmati (long-grain, parboiled) / Amaranth

Turnip Greens / Basmati (long-grain, parboiled) / Amaranth

Sunflower Flour / Agaricus C Mushroom / Amaranth

Sunflower Flour / Amaranth / Almonds (shelled-whole)

Hijiki Seaweed / Brown Rice (raw, short-grain) / Amaranth

Sunflower Flour / Rye Flour (dark) / Amaranth

Sunflower (hulled) / Sesame Seed Meal / Amaranth

Broccoli (cooked) / Basmati (long-grain, parboiled) / Amaranth

Sunflower (hulled) / Pine Nuts / Amaranth

Sunflower Flour / Spinach (raw) / Green Pea (dry)

Sunflower Flour / Asparagus (cooked) / Alfalfa Seeds

Wheat Bran / Sunflower Flour / Amaranth

Sunflower Flour / Buckwheat Flour (dark) / Alfalfa Seeds

Potato (raw) / Basmati (long-grain, parboiled) / Amaranth

Sunflower Flour / Red Kidney Bean (cooked) / Alfalfa Seeds

Whole Wheat Flour / Brazil Nut (shelled) / Amaranth

Triticale Flour / Beet Greens (cooked) / Amaranth

Collards (cooked) / Basmati (long-grain, parboiled) / Amaranth

Brewer's Yeast / Sunflower Flour / Brazil Nut (shelled)

Watermelon Seed / Filbert (shelled) / Amaranth

Onion (raw) / Basmati (long-grain, parboiled) / Amaranth

Sunflower Flour / Navy Bean pod / Amaranth

Hijiki Seaweed / Lima Bean (fresh) / Amaranth

Tempeh / Hijiki Seaweed / Brazil Nut (shelled)

Cauliflower (cooked) / Basmati (long-grain, parboiled) / Amaranth

Spaghetti / Pea Sprouts / Brazil Nut (shelled)

Sunflower Butter / Hijiki Seaweed / Amaranth

Soymilk / Brazil Nut (shelled) / Amaranth

Triticale Flour / Green Pea (dry) / Amaranth

Agaricus C Mushroom / Basmati (long-grain, parboiled) / Amaranth

Sunflower Flour / Mung Bean Sprouts (dry) / Alfalfa Seeds

Sunflower Flour / Green Pea (dry) / Common Cabbage (raw)

Sunflower Flour / Green Pea (dry) / Mustard Greens (cooked)

Soybean / Peanut (whole, w/ shell) / Brazil Nut (shelled)

Persian Walnut / Sesame Seed Meal / Amaranth

Triticale Flour / Spaghetti / Amaranth

Sunflower (hulled) / Brazil Nut (shelled) / Amaranth

Hijiki Seaweed / Amaranth / Almonds (shelled-whole)

Spaghetti / Lentil (whole, dry) / Brazil Nut (shelled)

Filbert (shelled) / Amaranth / Alfalfa Seeds

Whole Wheat Flour / Pine Nuts / Amaranth

Sunflower Flour / Papaya (raw) / Amaranth

Sunflower Flour / Onion (raw) / Amaranth

Brewer's Yeast / Hijiki Seaweed / Brazil Nut (shelled)

Sunflower Flour / Green Pea (dry) / Swiss Chard (raw)

Sunflower Flour / Swiss Chard (raw) / Alfalfa Seeds

Sunflower Flour / Lima Bean (dry) / Amaranth

Kale (cooked) / Brazil Nut (shelled) / Amaranth

Green Snap Bean (raw) / Basmati (long-grain, parboiled) / Amaranth

Tofu / Sunflower (hulled) / Brazil Nut (shelled)

Hijiki Seaweed / Cowpeas (Black-eye Pea) / Amaranth

Pine Nuts / Brazil Nut (shelled) / Navy Bean (Great Northern)

Sunflower Flour / Summer Squash / Green Pea (dry)

Brown Rice (raw, short-grain) / Basmati (long-grain, parboiled) / Amaranth

Tofu / Spaghetti / Brazil Nut (shelled)

Triticale Flour / Kale (cooked) / Amaranth

Sunflower Flour / Buckwheat Flour (dark) / Amaranth

Sunflower Flour / Mustard Greens (cooked) / Alfalfa Seeds

Whole Wheat Flour / Persian Walnut / Amaranth

Tofu / Brown Rice (raw, short-grain) / Brazil Nut (shelled)

Soybean / Hijiki Seaweed / Pine Nuts

Sunflower Flour / Spinach (raw) / Alfalfa Seeds

Papaya (raw) / Basmati (long-grain, parboiled) / Amaranth

Brazil Nut (shelled) / Black Bean / Amaranth

Brewer's Yeast / Watermelon Seed / Hijiki Seaweed

Sunflower Flour / Pine Nuts / Green Pea (dry)

Sunflower Flour / Pineapple (raw) / Green Pea (dry)

Sesame Seed Meal / Pine Nuts / Amaranth

Sunflower Flour / Green Pea (dry) / Okra (cooked)

Tofu / Pea (edible-podded) / Brazil Nut (shelled)

Sunflower Flour / Soybean / Alfalfa Seeds

Sunflower Flour / Green Pea (dry) / Buckwheat Flour (dark)

Mung Bean Sprouts (dry) / Basmati (long-grain, parboiled) / Amaranth

Pea (edible-podded) / Brazil Nut (shelled) / Amaranth

Triticale Flour / Cashew Nut / Amaranth

Brown Rice (raw, short-grain) / Brazil Nut (shelled) / Amaranth

Watermelon Seed / Pea (edible-podded) / Amaranth

Watercress (chopped fine) / Basmati (long-grain, parboiled) / Amaranth

Corn (kernel off-cob) / Basmati (long-grain, parboiled) / Amaranth

Sunflower Flour / Green Pea (dry) / Cucumber (not pared)

Soybean / Cowpeas (Black-eye Pea) / Brazil Nut (shelled)

Rye Flour (dark) / Basmati (long-grain, parboiled) / Amaranth

Tahini / Chick-pea (Garbanzo) / Brazil Nut (shelled)

Sesame Butter / Chick-pea (Garbanzo) / Brazil Nut (shelled)

Tofu / Cowpeas (Black-eye Pea) / Brazil Nut (shelled)

Sunflower Flour / Green Pea (dry) / Brussel Sprout (cooked)

Watermelon Seed / Pine Nuts / Amaranth

Rye Flour (dark) / Brazil Nut (shelled) / Navy Bean (Great Northern)

Hijiki Seaweed / Peanut (whole, w/ shell) / Amaranth

Persian Walnut / Pine Nuts / Amaranth

Soymilk / Brazil Nut (shelled) / Red Kidney Bean (cooked)

Basmati (long-grain, parboiled) / Amaranth / Almonds (shelled-whole)

Sunflower Flour / Green Pea (dry) / Cowpeas (Black-eye Pea)

Sunflower Flour / Green Pea (dry) / Cauliflower (cooked)

Sunflower (hulled) / Brown Rice (raw, short-grain) / Amaranth

Tomato (raw) / Sunflower Flour / Green Pea (dry)

Rye Flour (dark) / Brazil Nut (shelled) / Red Kidney Bean (cooked)

Spirulina / Brazil Nut (shelled) / Amaranth

Sunflower Flour / Navy Bean (Great Northern) / Amaranth

Spaghetti / Hijiki Seaweed / Amaranth

Sweetpotato (cooked) / Sunflower Flour / Green Pea (dry)

Sunflower Flour / Green Pea (dry) / Eggplant (cooked)

Cashew Nut / Basmati (long-grain, parboiled) / Amaranth

Sunflower Flour / Green Pea (dry) / Agaricus C Mushroom

Sunflower Flour / Green Pea (dry) / Coconut (fresh, shredded)

Sunflower (hulled) / Pine Nuts / Green Pea (dry)

Sunflower (hulled) / Amaranth / Alfalfa Seeds

Brazil Nut (shelled) / Red Kidney Bean (cooked) / Amaranth

Sunflower Flour / Pumpkin Pulp / Green Pea (dry)

Soymilk / Hijiki Seaweed / Pine Nuts

Sweetpotato (cooked) / Sunflower (hulled) / Amaranth

Sunflower Flour / Brazil Nut (shelled) / Amaranth

Peanut Butter/ Brazil Nut (shelled) / Lima Bean (dry)

Sunflower Flour / Green Pea (dry) / Green Snap Bean (raw)

Sunflower Flour / Green Pea (dry) /
Mung Bean Sprouts (dry)

Brazil Nut (shelled) / Navy Bean
(Great Northern) / Amaranth

Sunflower (hulled) / Oatmeal
(cooked and oats) / Amaranth

Soymilk / Rye Flour (dark) / Brazil
Nut (shelled)

Sunflower Flour / Coconut Milk /
Alfalfa Seeds

Triticale Flour / Bulgur /
Amaranth

Sunflower Flour / Green Pea (dry) /
Collards (cooked)

Cashew Nut / Brazil Nut (shelled) /
Amaranth

Triticale Flour / Barley Flour /
Amaranth

Whole Wheat Flour / Sunflower
Flour / Amaranth

Brussel Sprout (cooked) / Basmati
(long-grain, parboiled) /
Amaranth

Sesame Seed Meal / Swiss Chard
(raw) / Amaranth

Sunflower Flour / Pea (edible-
podded) / Amaranth

Sunflower Flour / Plantain (raw) /
Green Pea (dry)

Sunflower (hulled) / Corn (kernel
off-cob) / Amaranth

Sunflower Flour / Green Pea (dry) /
Carrot

Sunflower (hulled) / Coconut (fresh,
shredded) / Amaranth

Cashew Nut / Amaranth / Alfalfa
Seeds

Triticale Flour / Peanut (whole, w/
shell) / Amaranth

Triticale Flour / Date (whole, w/
pit) / Amaranth

Pine Nuts / Basmati (long-grain,
parboiled) / Alfalfa Seeds

Sunflower Flour / Potato (raw) /
Green Pea (dry)

Sunflower Flour / Pumpkin (Squash
Seed Kernel) / Amaranth

Spaghetti / Pine Nuts / Amaranth

Pine Nuts / Filbert (shelled) /
Amaranth

Tofu / Pine Nuts / Brazil Nut
(shelled)

Brown Rice (raw, short-grain) /
Pine Nuts / Amaranth

Pumpkin (Squash Seed Kernel) /
Brazil Nut (shelled) / Amaranth

Triticale Flour / Sunflower Flour /
Green Pea (dry)

Hijiki Seaweed / Corn Flour /
Amaranth

Pine Nuts / Amaranth / Almonds
(shelled-whole)

Spaghetti / Brazil Nut (shelled) /
Lima Bean (dry)

Watermelon Seed / Lima Bean
(fresh) / Amaranth

Soybean / Peanut Butter / Brazil
Nut (shelled)

Brazil Nut (shelled) / Amaranth /
Almonds (shelled-whole)

Sunflower Flour / Pepper / Green
Pea (dry)

Hijiki Seaweed / Pine Nuts / Mung
Bean Sprouts (dry)

Triticale Flour / Coconut Milk /
Amaranth

Whole Wheat Flour / Sunflower
(hulled) / Amaranth

Basmati (long-grain, parboiled) /
Pearled Barley / Amaranth

Sunflower Flour / Sesame Seed Meal
/ Amaranth

Sunflower Flour / Green Pea (dry) /
Beet (cooked)

Turnip Greens / Sunflower Flour /
Green Pea (dry)

Brazil Nut (shelled) / Navy Bean pod / Amaranth

Sunflower Flour / Collards (cooked) / Alfalfa Seeds

Sunflower Flour / Okra (cooked) / Alfalfa Seeds

Whole Wheat Flour / Sweetpotato (cooked) / Amaranth

Sesame Seed Meal / Oatmeal (cooked and oats) / Amaranth

Watermelon Seed / Brussel Sprout (cooked) / Amaranth

Hijiki Seaweed / Pine Nuts / Brussel Sprout (cooked)

Sunflower Flour / Hijiki Seaweed / Lentil (whole, dry)

Rye Flour (dark) / Brazil Nut (shelled) / Navy Bean (w/o meat)

Sunflower Flour / Crisphead Lettuce / Alfalfa Seeds

Wheat Flakes / Sunflower / Amaranth

Sunflower Flour / Green Pea (dry) / Corn (kernel off-cob)

Sunflower / Pineapple (raw) / Amaranth

Sunflower Flour / Pearled Barley / Amaranth

Sunflower Flour / Brazil Nut (shelled) / Navy Bean (Great Northern)

Cowpeas (Black-eye Pea) / Brazil Nut (shelled) / Amaranth

Whole Wheat Flour / Coconut (fresh, shredded) / Amaranth

Sunflower Flour / Green Pea (dry) / Onion (raw)

Watermelon Seed / Lima Bean (dry) / Amaranth

Triticale Flour / Lima Bean (fresh) / Amaranth

Brazil Nut (shelled) / Basmati (long-grain, parboiled) / Amaranth

Persian Walnut / Filbert (shelled) / Amaranth

Whole Wheat Flour / Pineapple (raw) / Amaranth

Tofu / Brazil Nut (shelled) / Red Kidney Bean

Spaghetti / Pine Nuts / Alfalfa Seeds

Sunflower Flour / Aduki Bean / Amaranth

Beet Greens (cooked) / Basmati (long-grain, parboiled) / Amaranth

Sunflower Flour / Cauliflower (cooked) / Alfalfa Seeds

Sunflower Flour / Spaghetti / Amaranth

Buckwheat Flour (dark) / Basmati (long-grain, parboiled) / Amaranth

Triticale Flour / Couscous / Amaranth

Sunflower Flour / Pine Nuts / Alfalfa Seeds

Pine Nuts / Brazil Nut (shelled) / Black Bean

Sunflower Flour / Rye Flour (dark) / Alfalfa Seeds

Watermelon Seed / Broccoli (cooked) / Amaranth

Soybean / Hijiki Seaweed / Amaranth

Triticale Flour / Corn Flour / Amaranth

Brewer's Yeast / Couscous / Brazil Nut (shelled)

Persian Walnut / Pumpkin (Squash Seed Kernel) / Amaranth

Persian Walnut / Oatmeal (cooked and oats) / Amaranth

Sunflower / Pecan (shelled) / Amaranth

Pine Nuts / Green Pea (dry) / Basmati (long-grain, parboiled)

Triticale Flour / Sunflower Flour /
Aduki Bean

Pine Nuts / Swiss Chard (raw) /
Amaranth

Sunflower Flour / Pecan (shelled) /
Green Pea (dry)

Sunflower Flour / Soymilk /
Amaranth

Tofu / Peanut (whole, w/ shell) /
Brazil Nut (shelled)

Watermelon Seed / Asparagus
(cooked) / Amaranth

Sunflower Flour / Coconut Milk /
Amaranth

Sunflower Flour / Green Pea (dry) /
Kale (cooked)

Sunflower Flour / Common Cabbage
(raw) / Alfalfa Seeds

Soybean / Brazil Nut (shelled) /
Red Kidney Bean (cooked)

Triticale Flour / Soybean / Brazil
Nut (shelled)

Brazil Nut (shelled) / Navy Bean
(Great Northern) / Lima Bean
(dry)

Sunflower Flour / Red Kidney Bean
(cooked) / Amaranth

Barley Flour / Amaranth / Alfalfa
Seeds

Watercress (chopped fine) /
Sunflower Flour / Green Pea
(dry)

Sunflower (hulled) / Summer
Squash / Amaranth

Sunflower Flour / Hominy Grits /
Amaranth

Bulgur / Amaranth / Alfalfa Seeds

Pumpkin (Squash Seed Kernel) /
Pine Nuts / Amaranth

Pine Nuts / Broccoli (cooked) /
Basmati (long-grain, parboiled)

Pine Nuts / Oatmeal (cooked and
oats) / Amaranth

Sesame Seed Meal / Rye Flour
(dark) / Amaranth

Persian Walnut / Brown Rice (raw,
short-grain) / Amaranth

Wheat Flakes / Sunflower Flour /
Green Pea (dry)

Kale (cooked) / Basmati (long-
grain, parboiled) / Amaranth

Pine Nuts / Mustard Greens
(cooked) / Basmati (long-grain,
parboiled)

Tofu / Sunflower Flour / Alfalfa
Seeds

Sunflower Flour / Hijiki Seaweed /
Pea Sprouts

Sunflower Flour / Green Pea (dry) /
Papaya (raw)

Sunflower Flour / Green Pea (dry) /
Lima Bean (fresh)

Hijiki Seaweed / Pine Nuts /
Broccoli (cooked)

Sunflower Flour / Beet Greens
(cooked) / Amaranth

Persian Walnut / Sunflower Flour /
Green Pea (dry)

Soymilk / Pea (edible-podded) /
Brazil Nut (shelled)

Spirulina / Chick-pea (Garbanzo) /
Brazil Nut (shelled)

Tofu / Brazil Nut (shelled) / Navy
Bean pod

Sunflower (hulled) / Crisphead
Lettuce / Amaranth

Sunflower Flour / Green Snap Bean
(raw) / Alfalfa Seeds

Whole Wheat Flour / Crisphead
Lettuce / Amaranth

Hijiki Seaweed / Lima Bean (dry) /
Amaranth

Cowpeas (Black-eye Pea) / Basmati
(long-grain, parboiled) / Amaranth

Sunflower (hulled) / Eggplant
(cooked) / Amaranth

Sunflower Flour / Pine Nuts / Aduki Bean

Whole Wheat Flour / Summer Squash / Amaranth

Triticale Flour / Soybean Sprout / Amaranth

Hijiki Seaweed / Coconut Milk / Amaranth

Whole Wheat Flour / Corn (kernel off-cob) / Amaranth

Couscous / Amaranth / Alfalfa Seeds

Brown Rice (raw, short-grain) / Brazil Nut (shelled) / Lima Bean (dry)

Spaghetti / Basmati (long-grain, parboiled) / Amaranth

Sunflower Flour / Soybean Sprout / Amaranth

Brewer's Yeast / Bulgur / Brazil Nut (shelled)

Pine Nuts / Oatmeal (cooked and oats) / Amaranth

Sesame Seed Meal / Rye Flour (dark) / Amaranth

Persian Walnut / Brown Rice (raw, short-grain) / Amaranth

Wheat Flakes / Sunflower Flour / Green Pea (dry)

Kale (cooked) / Basmati (long-grain, parboiled) / Amaranth

Pine Nuts / Mustard Greens (cooked) / Basmati (long-grain, parboiled)

Tofu / Sunflower Flour / Alfalfa Seeds

Sunflower Flour / Hijiki Seaweed / Pea Sprouts

Sunflower Flour / Green Pea (dry) / Papaya (raw)

Sunflower Flour / Green Pea (dry) / Lima Bean (fresh)

Hijiki Seaweed / Pine Nuts / Broccoli (cooked)

Sunflower Flour / Beet Greens (cooked) / Amaranth

Persian Walnut / Sunflower Flour / Green Pea (dry)

Soymilk / Pea (edible-podded) / Brazil Nut (shelled)

Spirulina / Chick-pea (Garbanzo) / Brazil Nut (shelled)

Tofu / Brazil Nut (shelled) / Navy Bean pod

Sunflower / Crisphead Lettuce / Amaranth

Sunflower Flour / Green Snap Bean (raw) / Alfalfa Seeds

Whole Wheat Flour / Crisphead Lettuce / Amaranth

Hijiki Seaweed / Lima Bean (dry) / Amaranth

Cowpeas (Black-eye Pea) / Basmati (long-grain, parboiled) / Amaranth

Sunflower / Eggplant (cooked) / Amaranth

Sunflower Flour / Pine Nuts / Aduki Bean

Whole Wheat Flour / Summer Squash / Amaranth

Triticale Flour / Soybean Sprout / Amaranth

Hijiki Seaweed / Coconut Milk / Amaranth

Whole Wheat Flour / Corn (kernel off-cob) / Amaranth

Couscous / Amaranth / Alfalfa Seeds

Brown Rice (raw, short-grain) / Brazil Nut (shelled) / Lima Bean (dry)

Spaghetti / Basmati (long-grain, parboiled) / Amaranth

Sunflower Flour / Soybean Sprout /
Amaranth

Brewer's Yeast / Bulgur / Brazil
Nut (shelled)

Brown Rice (raw, short-grain) /
Pumpkin (Squash Seed Kernel) /
Amaranth

Swiss Chard (raw) / Brazil Nut
(shelled) / Amaranth

Triticale Flour / Pine Nuts / Green
Pea (dry)

Triticale Flour / Sunflower Flour /
Lentil (whole, dry)

Whole Wheat Flour / Oatmeal
(cooked and oats) / Amaranth

Wheat Flakes / Sesame Seed Meal /
Amaranth

Sesame Seed Meal / Amaranth /
Almonds (shelled-whole)

Sunflower / Common Cabbage (raw)
/ Amaranth

Sunflower Flour / Sunflower Butter /
Amaranth

Sunflower Flour / Soymilk / Alfalfa
Seeds

Soymilk / Cowpeas (Black-eye Pea)
/ Brazil Nut (shelled)

Watermelon Seed / Collards
(cooked) / Amaranth

Soybean / Brown Rice (raw, short-
grain) / Brazil Nut (shelled)

Sunflower Flour / Peanut (whole, w/
shell) / Amaranth

Sunflower Flour / Green Pea (dry) /
Oatmeal (cooked and oats)

Sunflower Flour / Pea Sprouts /
Alfalfa Seeds

Whole Wheat Flour / Common
Cabbage (raw) / Amaranth

Rye Flour (dark) / Cowpeas (Black-
eye Pea) / Brazil Nut
(shelled)

Watermelon Seed / Swiss Chard
(raw) / Amaranth

Rye Flour (dark) / Pine Nuts /
Amaranth

Wheat Bran / Sunflower Flour /
Green Pea (dry)

Sesame Seed Meal / Common
Cabbage (raw) / Amaranth

Pumpkin (Squash Seed Kernel) /
Amaranth / Alfalfa Seeds

Watermelon Seed / Mustard
Greens (cooked) / Amaranth

Watermelon Seed / Mung Bean
Sprouts (dry) / Amaranth

Corn Flour / Basmati (long-grain,
parboiled) / Amaranth

Coconut Milk / Brazil Nut (shelled)
/ Lima Bean (dry)

Tofu / Hijiki Seaweed / Pine Nuts

Whole Wheat Flour / Brown Rice
(raw, short-grain) / Amaranth

Sunflower / Amaranth / Almonds
(shelled-whole)

Wheat Flakes / Whole Wheat Flour
/ Amaranth

Soymilk / Brazil Nut (shelled) /
Navy Bean (w/o meat)

Sunflower / Corn Flour / Amaranth

Watermelon Seed / Spinach (raw) /
Amaranth

Soybean / Brazil Nut (shelled) /
Amaranth

Pearled Barley / Amaranth / Alfalfa
Seeds

Whole Wheat Flour / Sesame Seed
Meal / Amaranth

Hominy Grits / Brazil Nut (shelled)
/ Amaranth

Soybean / Brazil Nut (shelled) /
Pearled Barley

Sunflower Flour / Potato (raw) /
Alfalfa Seeds

Whole Wheat Flour / Eggplant (cooked) / Amaranth

Sesame Seed Meal / Cashew Nut / Amaranth

Watermelon Seed / Basmati (long-grain, parboiled) / Amaranth

Sunflower / Beet (cooked) / Amaranth

Tofu / Brazil Nut (shelled) / Amaranth

Sunflower / Filbert (shelled) / Amaranth

Brewer's Yeast / Spaghetti / Brazil Nut (shelled)

Watermelon Seed / Sunflower / Amaranth

Sunflower / Spinach (raw) / Amaranth

Pine Nuts / Bulgur / Amaranth

Watermelon Seed / Cashew Nut / Amaranth

Sesame Seed Meal / Crisphead Lettuce / Amaranth

Sesame Seed Meal / Corn (kernel off-cob) / Amaranth

Sunflower Butter / Basmati (long-grain, parboiled) / Amaranth

Pine Nuts / Basmati (long-grain, parboiled) / Asparagus (cooked)

Spirulina / Brazil Nut (shelled) / Aduki Bean

Hijiki Seaweed / Green Pea (dry) / Amaranth

Watermelon Seed / Tempeh / Brazil Nut (shelled)

Watermelon Seed / Hijiki Seaweed / Amaranth

Sesame Seed Meal / Okra (cooked) / Amaranth

Sunflower Butter / Pine Nuts / Amaranth

Sunflower Flour / Pine Nuts / Chick-pea (Garbanzo)

Watermelon Seed / Brown Rice (raw, short-grain) / Amaranth

Triticale Flour / Brazil Nut (shelled) / Lima Bean (dry)

Hijiki Seaweed / Pine Nuts / Green Pea (dry)

Wheat Bran / Sunflower / Amaranth

Sunflower Flour / Summer Squash / Alfalfa Seeds

Spinach (raw) / Sesame Seed Meal / Amaranth

Sunflower Flour / Hijiki Seaweed / Aduki Bean

Sunflower / Pumpkin (Squash Seed Kernel) / Amaranth

Whole Wheat Flour / Pecan (shelled) / Amaranth

Sunflower / Cucumber (not pared) / Amaranth

Pine Nuts / Brazil Nut (shelled) / Red Kidney Bean

Whole Wheat Flour / Spinach (raw) / Amaranth

Pine Nuts / Chick-pea (Garbanzo) / Brazil Nut (shelled)

Sunflower Flour / Soybean / Amaranth

Sunflower / Okra (cooked) / Amaranth

Pine Nuts / Pearled Barley / Amaranth

Whole Wheat Flour / Beet (cooked) / Amaranth

Watermelon Seed / Common Cabbage (raw) / Amaranth

Spaghetti / Sesame Seed Meal / Amaranth

Sunflower Flour / Cucumber (not pared) / Alfalfa Seeds

Sunflower / Plantain (raw) / Amaranth

Sunflower Flour / Okra (cooked) / Amaranth

Watercress (chopped fine) /
Triticale Flour / Amaranth

Sunflower Flour / Eggplant (cooked)
/ Amaranth

Pine Nuts / Basmati (long-grain,
parboiled) / Amaranth

Basmati (long-grain, parboiled) /
Amaranth / Alfalfa Seeds

Sunflower Flour / Pineapple (raw) /
Amaranth

Triticale Flour / Rye Flour (dark) /
Amaranth

Triticale Flour / Papaya (raw) /
Amaranth

Triticale Flour / Brown Rice (raw,
short-grain) / Amaranth

Wheat Flakes / Basmati (long-
grain, parboiled) / Amaranth

Triticale Flour / Onion (raw) /
Amaranth

Hijiki Seaweed / Pine Nuts /
Buckwheat Flour (dark)

Triticale Flour / Pumpkin (Squash
Seed Kernel) / Amaranth

Sunflower Flour / Cucumber (not
pared) / Amaranth

Wheat Flakes / Sunflower Flour /
Amaranth

Sunflower Flour / Oatmeal (cooked
and oats) / Amaranth

Triticale Flour / Collards (cooked)
/ Amaranth

Triticale Flour / Tofu / Brazil Nut
(shelled)

Summer Squash / Basmati (long-
grain, parboiled) /
Amaranth

Sunflower Flour / Cornmeal /
Amaranth

Sunflower Flour / Pecan (shelled) /
Amaranth

Hijiki Seaweed / Kale (cooked) /
Amaranth

Spaghetti / Soybean / Brazil Nut
(shelled)

Sunflower Flour / Cowpeas (Black-
eye Pea) / Amaranth

Eggplant (cooked) / Basmati (long-
grain, parboiled) / Amaranth

Spaghetti / Amaranth / Alfalfa
Seeds

Sunflower / Sunflower Flour /
Amaranth

Sunflower Flour / Pine Nuts /
Amaranth

Beet (cooked) / Basmati (long-
grain, parboiled) / Amaranth

Brazil Nut (shelled) / Lima Bean
(dry) / Pearled Barley

Persian Walnut / Sunflower /
Amaranth

Wheat Bran / Basmati (long-grain,
parboiled) / Amaranth

Sunflower Flour / Carrot / Amaranth

Tomato (raw) / Sunflower Flour /
Amaranth

Whole Wheat Flour / Amaranth /
Alfalfa Seeds

Carrot / Basmati (long-grain,
parboiled) / Amaranth

Sunflower Flour / Green Snap Bean
(raw) / Amaranth

Sunflower Flour / Mustard Greens
(cooked) / Amaranth

Cucumber (not pared) / Basmati
(long-grain, parboiled) / Amaranth

Pumpkin (Squash Seed Kernel) /
Basmati (long-grain, parboiled) /
Amaranth

Triticale Flour / Corn (kernel off-
cob) / Amaranth

Triticale Flour / Buckwheat Flour
(dark) / Amaranth

Mustard Greens (cooked) /
Basmati (long-grain, parboiled) /
Alfalfa Seeds

Hijiki Seaweed / Amaranth / Alfalfa Seeds

Spinach (raw) / Basmati (long-grain, parboiled) / Amaranth

Whole Wheat Flour / Basmati (long-grain, parboiled) / Amaranth

Sunflower Flour / Lima Bean (fresh) / Amaranth

Sunflower Flour / Pumpkin Pulp / Amaranth

Sunflower Flour / Cauliflower (cooked) / Amaranth

Sunflower Flour / Plantain (raw) / Amaranth

Triticale Flour / Mung Bean Sprouts (dry) / Amaranth

Sunflower Flour / Beet (cooked) / Amaranth

Triticale Flour / Filbert (shelled) / Amaranth

Sunflower Flour / Collards (cooked) / Amaranth

Plantain (raw) / Basmati (long-grain, parboiled) / Amaranth

Sunflower Flour / Kale (cooked) / Amaranth

Sunflower Flour / Pepper / Amaranth

Turnip Greens / Sunflower Flour / Amaranth

Basmati (long-grain, parboiled) / Asparagus (cooked) / Amaranth

Sunflower Flour / Mung Bean Sprouts (dry) / Amaranth

Tomato (raw) / Basmati (long-grain, parboiled) / Amaranth

Triticale Flour / Pearled Barley / Amaranth

Sesame Seed Meal / Brown Rice (raw, short-grain) / Amaranth

Sunflower Flour / Filbert (shelled) / Amaranth

Pepper / Basmati (long-grain, parboiled) / Amaranth

Hijiki Seaweed / Corn (kernel off-cob) / Amaranth

Okra (cooked) / Basmati (long-grain, parboiled) / Amaranth

Sunflower Flour / Broccoli (cooked) / Amaranth

Sunflower Flour / Potato (raw) / Amaranth

Brazil Nut (shelled) / Pearled Barley / Amaranth

Triticale Flour / Cowpeas (Black-eye Pea) / Amaranth

Triticale Flour / Brussel Sprout (cooked) / Amaranth

Watercress (chopped fine) / Sunflower Flour / Amaranth

Pumpkin Pulp / Basmati (long-grain, parboiled) / Amaranth

Turnip Greens / Basmati (long-grain, parboiled) / Amaranth

Sunflower Flour / Agaricus C Mushroom / Amaranth

Sunflower Flour / Amaranth / Almonds (shelled, whole)

Hijiki Seaweed / Brown Rice (raw, short-grain) / Amaranth

Sunflower Flour / Rye Flour (dark) / Amaranth

Sunflower / Sesame Seed Meal / Amaranth

Broccoli (cooked) / Basmati (long-grain, parboiled) / Amaranth

Sunflower / Pine Nuts / Amaranth

Wheat Bran / Sunflower Flour / Amaranth

Sunflower Flour / Buckwheat Flour (dark) / Alfalfa Seeds

Potato (raw) / Basmati (long-grain, parboiled) / Amaranth

Whole Wheat Flour / Brazil Nut (shelled) / Amaranth

Triticale Flour / Beet Greens
(cooked) / Amaranth

Collards (cooked) / Basmati (long-
grain, parboiled) / Amaranth

Brewer's Yeast / Sunflower Flour /
Brazil Nut (shelled)

Watermelon Seed / Filbert
(shelled) / Amaranth

Onion (raw) / Basmati (long-grain,
parboiled) / Amaranth

Sunflower Flour / Navy Bean pod /
Amaranth

Whole Wheat Flour / Brown Rice
(raw, short-grain) / Amaranth

Sesame Seed Meal / Amaranth /
Almonds (shelled, whole)

Wheat Flakes / Whole Wheat Flour
/ Amaranth

Sunflower / Corn Flour / Amaranth

Watermelon Seed / Spinach (raw) /
Amaranth

Soybean / Brazil Nut (shelled) /
Amaranth

Pearled Barley / Amaranth / Alfalfa
Seeds

Whole Wheat Flour / Sesame Seed
Meal / Amaranth

Hominy Grits / Brazil Nut (shelled)
/ Amaranth

Soybean / Brazil Nut (shelled) /
Pearled Barley

Whole Wheat Flour / Eggplant
(cooked) / Amaranth

Sesame Seed Meal / Cashew Nut /
Amaranth

Watermelon Seed / Basmati (long-
grain, parboiled) / Amaranth

Sunflower / Beet (cooked) /
Amaranth

Tofu / Brazil Nut (shelled) /
Amaranth

Sunflower / Filbert (shelled) /
Amaranth

Brewer's Yeast / Spaghetti / Brazil
Nut (shelled)

Watermelon Seed / Sunflower /
Amaranth

Sunflower / Spinach (raw) /
Amaranth

Pine Nuts / Bulgur / Amaranth

Watermelon Seed / Cashew Nut /
Amaranth

Sesame Seed Meal / Crisphead
Lettuce / Amaranth

Sesame Seed Meal / Corn (kernel
off-cob) / Amaranth

Sunflower Butter / Basmati (long-
grain, parboiled) / Amaranth

Pine Nuts / Basmati (long-grain,
parboiled) / Asparagus (cooked)

Hijiki Seaweed / Green Pea (dry) /
Amaranth

Watermelon Seed / Hijiki Seaweed
/ Amaranth

Sesame Seed Meal / Okra (cooked)
/ Amaranth

Sunflower Butter / Pine Nuts /
Amaranth

Watermelon Seed / Brown Rice
(raw, short-grain) / Amaranth

Triticale Flour / Brazil Nut
(shelled) / Lima Bean (dry)

Wheat Bran / Sunflower /
Amaranth

Spinach (raw) / Sesame Seed Meal
/ Amaranth

Sunflower / Pumpkin (Squash Seed
Kernel) / Amaranth

Whole Wheat Flour / Pecan
(shelled) / Amaranth

Sunflower / Cucumber (not pared) /
Amaranth

Whole Wheat Flour / Spinach
(raw) / Amaranth

Sunflower Flour / Soybean /
Amaranth

Sunflower / Okra (cooked) / Amaranth

Pine Nuts / Pearled Barley / Amaranth

Whole Wheat Flour / Beet (cooked) / Amaranth

Watermelon Seed / Common Cabbage (raw) / Amaranth

Spaghetti / Sesame Seed Meal / Amaranth

Sunflower / Plantain (raw) / Amaranth

NOTES

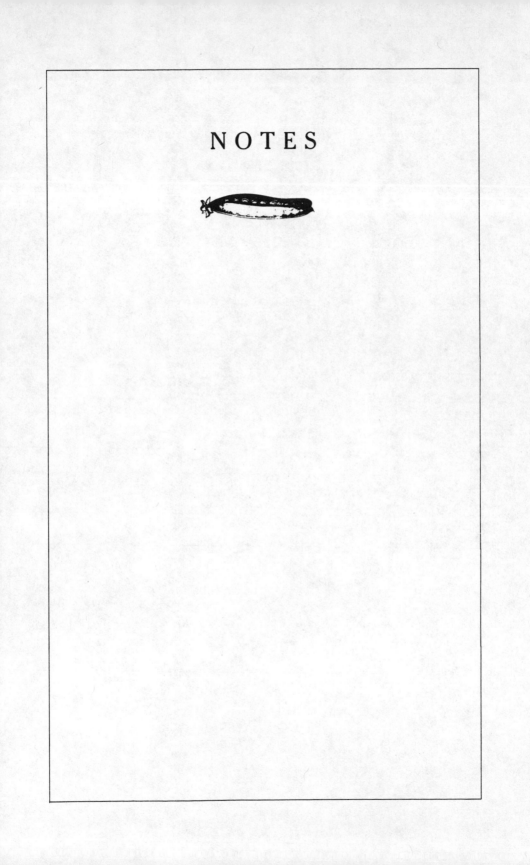

INTRODUCTION

1. Philip M. Boffey, "For First Time, Cut in Cholesterol Is Shown to Deter Artery Clogging," *New York Times*, 19 June 1987, p. 1.

2. *Cancer Facts and Figures: 1987*, American Cancer Society, at pp. 21–22.

3. *Guess What's Coming to Dinner—Contaminants in Our Food*, Americans for Safe Food, Center for Science in the Public Interest, March 1987, 14.

4. Ibid. 29.

5. Ibid. 17.

6. "U.S. Inspector Is Dubious About Quality of Meat," *New York Times*, 17 May 1987, p. 37.

7. Irvin Molotsky, "Chicken Inspection is Faulted," *New York Times*, 13 May 1987, p. C4.

1. WHAT IS VEGETARIANISM AND WHY CHOOSE IT AS A WAY OF LIFE?

1. Nancy Gustofson, M.S., R.D., "Vegetarian Nutrition: A Guide for Beginners," *Vegetarian Times* (April 1984): 31.

2. Irma B. Vyhmeister, Ph.D., "Vegetarian Diets, Issues and Concerns," *Nutrition and the M.D.* 10 (May 1984): 1.

3. "Diet Theory: Basic Arguments in Favor of Vegetarianism," *Vegetarian Times* (May/June 1979): 32.

4. Frances Moore Lappé, *Diet For a Small Planet* (New York: Ballantine, 1971).

5. Frances Moore Lappé and Joseph Collins, *Food First: Beyond the Myth of Scarcity* (New York: Ballantine, 1977).

2. FAMOUS VEGETARIANS

1. John Clark Smith, "Vegetarian As Art," *Vegetarian Times* (September/October 1979): 21.

2. Colman McCarthy, "Meatless Meals: A Change in America's Menu," *Washington Post*, 13 Jan. 1976, p. 19.

3. James F. Garrett, "George Bernard Shaw," *Vegetarian Times* (July/August 1977).

4. "Classics: The Vegetarian Diet According to Shaw," *Vegetarian Times* (March/April 1979): 50–51.

5. Barbara Sarkesian, "Thoreau," *Vegetarian Times* (December 1976/January 1977): 20.

6. Daniel Wesolowski, "Henry Thoreau," *Vegetarian Times* (November/December 1977): 39.

7. Sarkesian, "Thoreau."

8. Helen and Scott Nearing, "Living the Good Life at 95," *Vegetarian Times* (no. 23, 1978): 38–39.

9. Rynn Berry, Jr., "Cloris!," *Vegetarian Times* (May/June 1979): 15.

10. Judy Klemesrud, "Vegetarianism: Growing Way of Life, Especially Among the Young," *New York Times*, 10 March 1976, p. 47; Suzanne Sutton, "Superstars," *Vegetarian Times* (March/April 1977): 36–37.

11. Ann Johnson and Torney Smith, "Susan Smith Jones: More than Just a Pretty Face," *Vegetarian Times* (November/December 1979): 20–23.

12. Bob Lewanski, "Vegetarians Who Pump Iron," *Vegetarian Times* (March/April 1979): 19–22.

13. Robyn M. Grasing, "John Marino: A World Record Holder on Nutrition," *Vegetarian Times* (January/February 1979): 30–31.

14. "Still Skiing at Eighty Four," *Life and Health—National Health Journal* (vol. 1, 1973).

3 . A B R I E F H I S T O R Y O F V E G E T A R I A N I S M

1. Genesis 1:29.

2. Mervyn G. Hardinge, M.D., and Hulda Crooks, "Nonflesh Dietaries," *Journal of the American Dietetic Association* 43 (December 1963): 545.

3. George Parluski, "The History of the Vegetable Passion in the Orient," *Vegetarian Times* (March/April 1977): 17.

4. S. S. Altshuler, "The Historical and Biological Evolution of Human Diet," *American Journal of Digestive Disease* 1 (1934): 215.

5. "What's Wrong With Eating Meat?" *Amanda Marga Publications* (1977): 5.

6. "Vegetarianism: A New Concept?", *National Health Journal* 2nd ed., vol. 1 (Washington: Herald Pub. Assoc., 1973).

7. Colman McCarthy, "Meatless Meals: A Change in America's Menu," *Washington Post*, 13 Jan. 1976, p. 19.

8. Hardinge, "Nonflesh Dietaries."

9. Sarrat K. Majunder, "Vegetarianism: Fad, Faith, or Fact?", *American Scientist* 60 (March/April 1972).

10. S. Lepkovsky, "The Bread Problem in War and Peace," *Physiological Review* 24 (1944): 239; M. Hindhede, "The Effect of Food Restriction During War on Mortality in Copenhagen," *Journal of the American Medical Association* 74 (1920): 381.

11. A. Strom and R. A. Jensen, "Mortality From Circulatory Diseases in Norway, 1940–1945," *Lancet* 260 (1951): 126.

4 . P R O T E I N : U N R A V E L I N G T H E M Y T H S

1. Trish Hall, "Vegetarianism: More Popular if Less Pure," *New York Times*, 25 March 1987, p. C1.

2. Ibid.

3. Hara Marano, "The Problem with Protein," *New York* (5 March 1979): 51.

4. T. Osborne and L. B. Mendel, "Amino Acids in Nutrition and Growth," *Journal of Biological Chemistry* 17 (1914): 324.

5. John McDougall, M.D., radio interview with author on "Natural Living," WBAI, New York, 26 March 1987.

6. William Rose, Ph.D., "The Amino Acid Requirements of Adult Man, XVI, the Role of the Nitrogen Intake," *Journal of Biological Chemistry* 217 (1955): 997.

7. McDougall, radio interview.

5 . PROTEIN REQUIREMENTS

1. John McDougall, M.D., radio interview with author on "Natural Living," WBAI, New York, 26 March 1987.

2. Ibid.

3. Keith Akers, *A Vegetarian Sourcebook* (New York: Putnam, 1983).

4. Ibid.

5. William Rose, Ph.D., "The Amino Acid Requirements of Adult Man, XVI, the Role of the Nitrogen Intake," *Journal of Biological Chemistry* 217 (1955): 997.

6. John A. McDougall, M.D., and Mary A. McDougall, *The McDougall Plan for Super Health and Life-Long Weight Loss* (New Jersey: New Century Publishers, 1983).

7. McDougall, radio interview.

8. McDougall, *The McDougall Plan*, 99.

9. McDougall, radio interview.

6 . WHAT ARE OUR BEST SOURCES OF PROTEIN?

1. "Dangerous Chemicals in Meat," *Natural Living Newsletter*, no. 40.

2. Ibid.

3. Ibid.

4. *Journal of the American Dietetic Association* 25, no. 3 (March 1949): 202.

5. Ibid. 17, no. 6 (June/July 1941).

6. Ibid. (September 1948).

7. Ibid. 31 (1955).

8. Ibid. (September, 1964).

9. Ibid. 17, no. 1 (January 1941).

10. Robert Goodhart and Maurice Shils, *Modern Nutrition in Health and Disease* (Philadelphia: Lea and Febiger, 1980), 91.

7. EXCESS PROTEIN

1. John McDougall, M.D., radio interview with author on "Natural Living," WBAI, New York, 26 March 1987.

2. Ibid.

3. Hara Marano, "The Problem with Protein," *New York* (5 March 1979): 51.

4. Ibid.

5. Ibid.

6. McDougall, radio interview.

8 . ANIMAL PROTEIN AND ADDED CHEMICALS

1. Hara Marano, "The Problem with Protein," *New York* (5 March 1979): 52.

2. Osmo Turpeinen, M.D., "Effect of Cholesterol-Lowering Diet on Mortality from

Coronary Heart Disease and Other Causes," *Circulation* 59, no. 1 (January 1979): 1; Margaret A. Howell, "Diet as an Etiological Factor in the Development of Cancers of the Colon and Rectum," *Journal of Chronic Diseases* 28 (1975): 67–80.

3. Susan Lang, "Diet and Disease," *Food Monitor* (May/June 1983): 24.

4. Gary Null, *The New Vegetarian* (New York: Dell, 1978).

10. ECONOMICS: THE BIG-BUCKS BONUS

1. Nancy Gustafson, M.S., R.D., "Vegetarian Nutrition: A Guide for Beginners," *Vegetarian Times* (April 1984): 31–35.

2. Sam Zuckerman, "Food Ad Rogues' Gallery," *Nutrition Action* (September 1984): 5.

3. "Meat Quality: The Jungle Revisited," *The Farm Report* 1, no. 2 (1983).

4. Sarrat K. Majunder, "Vegetarianism: Fad, Faith, or Fact?", *American Scientist* 60 (March/April 1972): 179.

5. James B. Mason, *Vegetarian Times* (January/February 1980): 40.

6. William Stevens, "For Steaks, A Gilded Age is Fading," *New York Times*, 7 Jan. 1981, p. C1.

7. Ibid.

8. Gary Null, *The New Vegetarian* (New York: Dell, 1978).

9. James B. Mason, "Vegetarianism is a Human Rights Struggle," *Vegetarian Times* (June 1980): 47–49.

10. Glenn Lorang, "We Raise Wheat for Feed," *Western Field* (September 1972): 25.

11. Zuckerman, "Rogues' Gallery."

11. NATURAL RESOURCES: IN SEARCH OF ECOLOGICAL HARMONY

1. Frances Moore Lappé and Joseph Collins, *Food First: Beyond the Myth of Scarcity* (New York: Ballantine, 1977).

2. Ibid.

3. Alex Hershaft, Ph.D., *Solving the Population/Food Crisis by Eating for Life* (Washington, D.C.: Vegetarian Information Service, 1985).

4. Ibid.; Frances Moore Lappé, *Diet for a Small Planet* (New York: Ballantine, 1971).

5. Lester R. Brown and Edward C. Wolf, *Soil Erosion: Quiet Crisis in the World Economy*, World Watch Paper no. 60 (New York: 1984).

6. Lappé, *Food First.*

7. Lappé, *Diet for a Small Planet.*

8. Seth King, "Iowa Rain and Wind Deplete Farmlands," *New York Times*, 5 Dec. 1976, p. 61.

9. Curtis Harnack, "In Plymouth County, Iowa, the Rich Topsoil's Going Fast. Alas," *New York Times*, 11 July 1980.

10. Lappé, *Diet for a Small Planet.*

11. Ibid.

12. Ibid.

13. U.S. Department of Agriculture, *Soil and Water Resources Conservations Act —Summary of Appraisal*, Review Draft, 1980, 18.

14. Lappé, *Diet for a Small Planet.*

15. "Study Says Soil Erosion Could Cause Famine," *New York Times*, 30 Sept. 1984, p. 20.

16. Brown, *Soil Erosion.*

17. "Soil Erosion Could Cause Famine," *New York Times.*

18. Ibid.

19. Brown, *Soil Erosion.*

20. Lappé, *Diet for a Small Planet.*

21. *The Merriam-Webster Dictionary* (New York: Pocket Books, 1974).

22. George Bargstrom, paper presented at the annual meeting of the American Association for the Advancement of Science, 1981; radio interview with author 5 October 1979.

23. "The Browning of America," *Newsweek* (22 February 1981): 26.

24. Ibid.

25. Lappé, *Diet for a Small Planet.*

12 . FOOD RESOURCES

1. Alex Hershaft, Ph.D., *Solving the Population/Food Crisis by Eating for Life* (Washington, D.C.: Vegetarian Information Service, 1985).

2. "Meat, Cash-Crop Exports, Contribute to Starvation in Brazil," *Vegetarian Times* (August 1984): 8–10.

3. Sarrat K. Majunder, "Vegetarianism: Fad, Faith or Fact?", *American Scientist* 60 (March/April 1972): 177–179.

4. James Bonner, "The Population Dilemma," Bulletin no. 95 (January 21, 1965).

5. Frances Moore Lappé and Joseph Collins, *Food First: Beyond the Myth of Scarcity* (New York: Ballantine, 1977).

6. Frances Moore Lappé, *Diet for a Small Planet* (New York: Ballantine, 1971).

7. Ibid.

8. R. S. Harris, "Influence of Culture on Man's Diet," *Arch Environmental Health* 5 (1962): 144–152.

9. Ross Hume Hall, *Food for Naught* (New York: Vintage, 1974).

10. Lappé, *Diet for a Small Planet.*

11. Hershaft, *Solving the Population/Food Crisis.*

12. Lappé, *Diet for a Small Planet.*

13. Ibid.

14. Lappé, *Food First.*

15. Alan Benz, *The Nutrition Factor: Its Role in National Development* (Washington, D.C.: The Brookings Institution, 1973), 65.

16. Lappé, *Food First.*

17. Alan Riding, "Malnutrition Taking Bigger Toll Among Mexican Children," *New York Times*, 6 March 1978, p. 2.

18. Lappé, *Food First.*

19. Ibid.

20. Ibid.

21. Boyce Rensberger, "Can Eating Less Meat Here Relieve Starvation in the World?" *New York Times*, 28 Nov. 1974, p. 44.

22. *The Meat Sourcebook* (Chicago: The American Meat Institute, 1960), 43.

23. F. J. Schlink and M. C. Phillips, *Meat Three Times a Day* (New York: Richard Smith, 1946), 54.

24. Ibid.

25. Nathan Altman, "Revising the 'Basic Four'," *Vegetarian Times* (October 1977): 9–14.

26. Ibid.

27. Senate Select Committee on Nutrition and Human Needs, *Dietary Goals for the United States* (Washington, D.C., 1977).

28. Rudolph Ballentine, M.D., *Diet and Nutrition* (Honesdale, Pa.: The Himalayan International Institute of Yoga Science and Philosophy, 1978).

29. Altman, "Revising the 'Basic Four'."

30. Lappé, *Food First.*

31. Rensberger, "Starvation in the World."

13. PERSONAL TASTE

1. Frank J. Hurd and Rosalie Hurd, *Ten Talents* (Collegedale, Tenn.: The College Press, 1968), 5.

2. Ron Pikarski, "Bringing Vegetarianism into the Gourmet Limelight," *Vegetarian Times* (January/February 1980): 31–32.

3. Ibid.

4. Ibid.

5. Leslen Newman, "Natural Wonder," *Vegetarian Times* (March/April 1979): 80.

6. Ibid.

7. E. Neige Todhunter, "Food Habits, Food Fadism and Nutrition," *World Review of Nutrition and Dietetics* 16 (1973): 293.

8. Abhay Kumar Pati, "Ayurveda for Health," *International Journal of Holistic Health & Medicine* 1 (1982): 5.

9. Ibid.

10. Rudolph Ballentine, M.D., *Diet and Nutrition* (Honesdale, Pa.: Himalayan International Institute of Yoga Science and Philosophy, 1978), 317.

11. Pati, "Ayurveda."

14. RELIGIOUS BELIEFS

1. Mervyn G. Hardinge, M.D., and Hulda Cooks, "Nonflesh Dietaries," *Journal of the American Dietetic Association* 43 (1962): 545.

2. Suzanne Sutton, "Ellen White, Seventh-Day Adventists and Vegetarianism," *Vegetarian Times* (November/December 1977): 37.

3. J. C. McKenzie, "Social and Economic Implications of Minority Food Habits," *Proceedings of the Nutrition Society* 26 (1967): 198.

4. Louis A. Berman, "Why is Jewish Vegetarianism Different from All Others?", *Vegetarian Times* (April 1980): 44–45.

5. Hardinge, "Nonflesh Dietaries."

6. Nathaniel Altman, "The Spiritual Side of Vegetarianism," *Vegetarian Times* (November/December 1977): 36.

7. Hardinge, "Nonflesh Dietaries."

8. Darla Erhard, R.D., "The New Vegetarians," *Nutrition Today* (January/February 1974): 20.

9. Darla Erhard, "Nutrition Education for the Now Generation," *Journal of Nutrition Education* (1971): 135.

10. Erhard, "The New Vegetarians."

11. Erhard, "Nutrition Education."

12. Ibid.

13. Bhagwan Shree Rajneesh, "The Spiritual Side of Vegetarianism," *Vegetarian Times* (March 1980): 62.

14. Erhard, "Nutrition Education."

15. Ibid.

15. REVERENCE FOR LIFE

1. Nathaniel Altman, "The Spiritual Side of Vegetarianism," *Vegetarian Times* (November/December 1977): 36–38.

2. *Why Be A Vegetarian?*, Vegetarian Information Service Sheet.

3. Altman, "Spiritual Side of Vegetarianism."

4. James B. Mason, "Animals," *Vegetarian Times* (March 1980): 52.

5. Ibid., 53.

6. C. D. Van Houweling, Ph.D., "Drugs In Animal Feeds? A Question Without An Answer," *FDA Papers* (September 1967): 11–15.

7. Ross Hume Hall, *Food for Naught* (New York: Vintage, 1974), 91.

8. Mason, "Animals."

9. Hall, *Food for Naught*, 100.

10. Ibid.

11. W. Anderson, "Porcine Stress Syndrome Problem Updated by Vet," *Feedstuffs* (May 1972): 21.

12. Michael W. Fox, D. Sc., "Philosophy, Ecology, Animal Welfare, and the 'Rights Question'," *Ethics and Animals* (Clifton, N.J.: Humana Press, Inc., 1983), 308.

13. Michael W. Fox, D.Sc., "The Question of Animal Rights," *The Veterinary Record* (11 July 1981): 37–39.

14. Ibid.

15. "Cut Stress and You'll Control Dark Cutters," *Feedlot Management* 14 (1972): 50–51.

16. Hall, *Food for Naught*.

17. John Clark Smith, "Vegetarianism As Art," *Vegetarian Times* (September/October 1979): 20–21.

18. Dr. Michael W. Fox, D.Sc., "The Hidden Costs of Modern Farming," *A Special Awareness Report* (The Humane Society of the United States, 1981).

19. Richard Rhodes, "Watching the Animals," 91–92.

20. Louis A. Berman, "Why Is Jewish Vegetarianism Different From All Others?", *Vegetarian Times* (April 1980): 43.

21. DeDee Benrey, "The World According to Isaac Singer," *Vegetarian Times* (March 1983): 14.

22. Mark Braunstein, "On Being Radically Vegetarian," *Vegetarian Times* (March 1980): 72–73.

23. R. Brooks and J. R. Kemm, "Vegan Diet and Lifestyle: A Preliminary Study by Postal Questionnaire," *Proceedings of the Nutrition Society* 38 (1979): 15A.

24. Tamara Ross, "Animal, Vegetable, Mineral," *Nursing Mirror* (July 1980).

25. Ibid.

26. William K. Stevens, "For Steaks, A Gilded Age is Fading," *New York Times*, 7 Jan. 1981, p. C6.

27. Altman, "Spiritual Side of Vegetarianism."

28. James B. Mason, "Vegetarianism is a Human Rights Struggle," *Vegetarian Times* (June 1980): 48–49.

29. Ibid.

30. Ibid.

31. Fox, *Ethics and Animals.*

32. Ibid.

33. Ibid.

16. THE MACROBIOTIC WAY TO HEALTH

All this is original material from the author and from an interview with macrobiotic specialist Michio Kushi in February 1987.

17. DO WE NEED MEAT TO BE HEALTHY?

1. Mervyn G. Hardinge, M.D., "Do Human Beings Need Meat?" *Review and Herald* (27 February 1969).

2. Ibid.

3. Ibid.

4. Editorial, *Lancet* 2 (1959): 956.

5. Hardinge, "Do Human Beings Need Meat?"

6. Arturi I. Virtanen, *Federation Proceedings* 27, no. 6 (1968): 1374.

7. Hardinge, "Do Human Beings Need Meat?"

8. *Lancet* 285 (1963): 43.

9. William Adolph, "Vegetarian China," *Scientific American* (September 1938): 133.

10. Ibid.

11. Eleanor Williams, "Making Vegetarian Diets Nutritious," *American Journal of Nursing* (December 1975): 2168–2173; John W. T. Dickerson, Ph.D., and Ann M. Fehily, "Bizarre and Unusual Diets," *The Practitioner* 222 (May 1979): 643–647.

12. Williams, "Vegetarian Diets."

13. Catherine M. Stroble, R.D. and Lorelei Groll, "Professional Knowledge and Attitudes on Vegetarianism: Implications for Practice," *Journal of the American Dietetic Association.*

14. Ibid.

15. Ibid.

16. F. R. Ellis and Pamela Mumford, "The Nutritional Status of Vegans and Vegetarians," *Proceedings of the Nutrition Society* 26 (1967): 205–211.

17. Williams, "Vegetarian Diets."

18. Mervyn G. Hardinge, M.D., and F. J. Stare, "Do Human Beings Need Meat?", *Journal of Clinical Nutrition* 2 (1954): 73.

19. James G. Bergan, Ph.D., and Phyllis T. Brown, "Nutritional Status of 'New'

Vegetarians," *Journal of the American Dietetic Association* 76 (February 1980): 151–154.

20. D. S. Miller and P. Mumford, *Getting the Most Out of Food* (London: Van den Bergh, 1966), 9.

21. Johanna Dwyer, D.Sc., "Health Implications of Vegetarian Diets," *Comprehensive Therapy* 9, no. 4 (1983): 23–28.

22. J. A. Scharffenberg, M.D., "Vegetarian Diets," *American Journal of the Disabled Child* 133 (November 1979): 1204.

23. D. P. Burkitt, M.D., and N. S. Painter, M.S., "Dietary Fiber and Disease," *Journal of the American Medical Association* 229, no. 8 (19 August 1974): 1068–1074.

24. Ibid.

25. Ibid.

26. Ibid.

27. "Meat and Potatoes Still Number One," *USA Today*, 4 Dec. 1984.

28. Burkitt, "Dietary Fiber."

29. Ellis, "Nutritional Status of Vegans and Vegetarians."

30. W. S. Collens and G. B. Dobkin, "Phylogenetic Aspects of the Cause of Human Atherosclerotic Disease," *Circulation*, supp. II, 32 (October 1965): 7.

31. Davidson, Meiklejohn, and Passmore, *Human Nutrition and Dietetics* (1966), 287.

32. Philip L. White and Nancy Selvey, *Let's Talk About Foods* (Acton, Mass.: Publishing Sciences Group, 1974).

33. Alex Hershaft, Ph.D., and Lori Sonken, "Mark Hegsted: A Close-up of the Federal Government's Chief Nutritionist," *Vegetarian Times*, no. 41 (May 1983).

34. D. M. Hegsted et al., "Lysine and Methionine Supplementation of All-Vegetable Diets for Human Adults," *Journal of Nutrition* 56 (1955): 555.

35. "Meatless Diet Urged by Mexican Government," *Vegetarian Times* (June 1982): 7.

36. "AMA Attacks Vegetarian Diet," *Vegetarian Times* (May/June 1979): 8–10.

37. Ibid.

38. Ibid.

39. Ellis, "Nutritional Status of Vegans and Vegetarians."

18. CAN WE BE HEALTHY EATING MEAT?

1. "U.S. Eating Unfit Meat," *Science Newsletter* (28 August 1948): 133.

2. A. M. Liebstein, M.D., and Neil L. Ehmki, "The Case for Vegetarianism," *American Mercury* (April 1950): 27.

3. Ibid.

4. Nathaniel Altman, "The Meat Board Has Been Feeding You a Lot of Baloney About Nutrition," *Vegetarian Times* (October 1977): 13.

5. Neal Karlen and Jeff B. Copeland, "A 'Mystery Meat' Scandal," *Newsweek* (24 Sept. 1984): 31.

6. "School Meat Supplies Called Unsanitary," *USA Today*, 6 Sept. 1984, p. A4.

7. Karlen, "A 'Mystery Meat' Scandal."

8. Ibid.

9. Peter M. Schantz, "Trichinosis in the United States, 1975: Increase in Cases Attributed to Numerous Common-Source Outbreaks," *The Journal of Infectious Diseases* 136, no. 5 (November 1977): 712–715.

10. Ibid.

11. Edward P. J. Gibbs, "Persistent Viral Infections of Food Animals: Their Relevance to the International Movement of Livestock and Germ Plasm," *Advances in Veterinary Science and Comparative Medicine* 25 (1981): 71–95.

12. Harold E. Sours and Owan G. Smith, "Outbreaks of Foodborne Disease in the United States, 1972–1978," *The Journal of Infectious Diseases* 142, no. 1 (July 1980): 122–125.

13. "British Hospital Deaths: Spoiled Beef Is Cause," *New York Times*, 11 September 1984.

14. Life and Health Supplement.

15. Dr. Scott Holmberg, "Hidden Danger In Our Food," Channel 7 News (ABC), 7 November 1984.

16. Robert E. Fontaine et al., "Epidemic Salmonellosis From Cheddar Cheese: Surveillance and Prevention," *American Journal of Epidemiology* 3, no. 2 (1980): 247–251; "Officials Recall Cheeses after link to 28 Deaths," *New York Times*, 14 June 1985, p. A12.

17. "Fish Poisoning," *Lancet* (17 November 1979): 1059–1060.

18. Bill Keller, "Ties To Human Illness Revive Move to Ban Medicated Feed," *New York Times*, 9 Sept. 1984, p. 1.

19. *New England Journal of Medicine* (6 September 1984).

20. Holmberg, "Hidden Danger."

21. "Antibiotics Can Lead to Tainted Meat," *USA Today*, 6 Sept. 1984, p. D1.

22. Suzanne D. Caudry and Vilma A. Stanisick, "Incidence of Antibiotic-Resistant Escherichia Coli Associated with Frozen Chicken Carcasses and Characterization of Conjugative R Plasmids Derived from Such Strains," *Antimicrobial Agents and Chemotherapy* 16, no. 6 (December 1979): 701.

23. Liebstein, "The Case for Vegetarianism."

24. Bill Keller, "Ties to Human Illness Revive Move to Ban Medicated Feed," *New York Times*, 9 Sept. 1984, p. 1.

25. Holmberg, "Hidden Danger."

26. "Antibiotics Can Lead to Tainted Meat."

27. Bill Keller, "Raising All-Natural Beef: Hardy Few Deliver Goods," *New York Times*, 31 Oct. 1984, p. C1.

28. Ibid.

29. Ibid.

30. "Chloramphenicol Use by Cattlemen Said to Be Dangerous," *Vegetarian Times* (September 1984): 6.

31. Ibid.

32. Gary Null and Steve Null, *How to Get Rid of the Poisons in Your Body* (New York: Arco, 1977).

33. K. E. McMartin et al., "Diethylstilbestrol: A Review of its Toxicity and Use as a Growth Promotant in Food-Producing Animals," *Journal of Environmental Pathology and Toxicology* 1 (1978): 279–313.

34. "Hormonal Time Bomb?", *Time* (2 August 1971).

35. McMartin, "Diethylstilbestrol."

36. Ross Hume Hall, *Food for Naught* (New York: Vintage, 1974).

37. Harrison Wellford, "Behind the Meat Counter: The Fight Over DES."

38. Hall, *Food for Naught.*

39. "Evidence Mounts Against DES," *USA Today,* 7 Dec. 1984.

40. G. M. Fara et al., "Epidemic of Breast Enlargement in an Italian School," *Lancet* (11 August 1979): 295–297.

41. David Bauman and Timothy Kenny, "Cattle Drug May be Tied to Early Puberty," *USA Today,* 5 Dec. 1984.

42. "EPA Decides Carcinogen Is OK for Eggs and Chicken," *Vegetarian Times* (July 1984).

43. Fred Zahradnik, "EPA Suppresses Rural Water Study," *The New Farm* (January 1984).

44. Ibid.

45. Ibid.

46. Michael E. Fox, D.Sc., radio interview with author on "Natural Living," WBAI, New York, 5 June 1981.

19. VEGETARIANISM AND HEALTH

The articles referred to in this chapter represent just a small sampling of the literature substantiating vegetarianism's health benefits.

1. L. J. Beilin and B. M. Margetts, "Vegetarian Diet and Blood Pressure," *Biblthca cardiol.,* no. 41 (1987): 85–105.

2. L. J. Beilin et al., "Vegetarian Diet and Blood Pressure Levels: Incidental or Causal Association?" *The American Journal of Clinical Nutrition* 48 (1988): 806–10.

3. I. L. Rouse et al., "Vegetarian Diet, Blood Pressure and Cardiovascular Risk," *Australian & New Zealand Journal of Medicine* 14 (1984): 439–443.

4. B. Armstrong, A. J. Van Merwyk, and H. Coates, "Blood Pressure in Seventh-Day Adventist Vegetarians," *American Journal of Epidemiology,* vol. 105, no. 5 (1977): 444–449.

5. R. O. West and O. B. Hayes, "Diet and Serum Cholesterol Levels," *The American Journal of Clinical Nutrition,* vol. 21, no. 8 (August 1968): 853–862.

6. J. Ruys and J. G. Hickie, "Serum cholesterol and triglyceride levels in Australian adolescent vegetarians," *British Medical Journal* (July 10, 1996): 87.

7. L. A. Simons et al., "The Influence of a Wide Range of Absorbed Cholesterol on Plasma Cholesterol Levels in Man," *The American Journal of Clinical Nutrition* 31 (August 1978): 1334–1339.

8. R. L. Phillips et al., "Coronary Heart Disease Mortality Among Seventh-Day Adventists with Differing Dietary Habits: A Preliminary Report," *The American Journal of Clinical Nutrition* 31 (October 1978): S191–S198.

9. B. Armstrong and R. Doll, "Environmental Factors and Cancer Incidence and Mortality in Different Countries with Special Reference to Dietary Practices," *International Journal of Cancer* 15 (1975): 617–631.

10. R. L. Phillips, J. W. Kuzma, and T. M. Lotz, "Cancer Mortality among Comparable Members Versus Nonmembers of the Seventh-Day Adventist Church," *Banbury Report 4: Cancer Incidence in Defined Populations,* New York: (Cold Spring Harbor Laboratory, 1980), pp. 93–107.

11. R. L. Phillips, "Cancer Among Seventh-Day Adventists," *Journal of Environmental Pathology and Toxicology* 3 (1980): 157–169.

12. M. J. Goldberg, J. W. Smith, and R. L. Nichols, "Comparison of the Fecal Microflora of Seventh-Day Adventists with Individuals Consuming a General Diet: Implications Concerning Colonic Carcinoma," *Annals of Surgery* (July 1977): 97–100.

13. N. Turjman et al., "Faecal Bile-Acids and Neutral Sterols in Seventh-Day Adventists and the General Population in California," in Kasper and Golbel (eds.), *Colon and Cancer,* Falk Symposium 32, (Lancaster, England: MTP Press, Ltd., 1982), pp. 291–297.

14. B. M. Calkins et al., "Diet, Nutrition, Intake, and Metabolism in Populations at High and Low Risk for Colon Cancer," *The American Journal of Clinical Nutrition* 40, (October 1984): 887–895.

15. S. M. Finegold and V. L. Sutter, "Fecal Flora in Different Populations, with Special Reference to Diet," *The American Journal of Clinical Nutrition* 31 (October 1978): S116–S122.

16. P. P. Nair et al., "Diet, Nutrition Intake, and Metabolism in Populations at High and Low Risk for Colon Cancer," *The American Journal of Clinical Nutrition* 40 (October 1984): 931–936.

17. P. K. Mills et al., "Cohort Study of Diet, Lifestyle, and Prostate Cancer in Adventist Men," *Cancer,* vol. 64, no. 3, (August 1, 1989): 598–604.

18. B. J. Howie and T. D. Shultz, "Dietary and Hormonal Interrelationships Among Vegetarian Seventh-Day Adventists and Nonvegetarian Men," *The American Journal of Clinical Nutrition* 42 (July 1985): 127–134.

19. P. K. Mills et al., "Cancer incidence among California Seventh-Day Adventists, 1976–1982," *The American Journal of Clinical Nutrition* 59 (suppl., 1994): 1136S–1142S.

20. P. K. Mills et al., "Dietary Habits and Past Medical History as Related to Fatal Pancreas Cancer Risk Among Adventists," *Cancer,* vol. 61, no. 12 (June 15, 1988): 2578–2585.

21. P. K. Mills et al., "Risk Factors for Tumors of the Brain and Cranial Meninges in Seventh-Day Adventists," *Neuroepidemiology* 8 (1989): 266–275.

22. B. K. Armstrong et al., "Diet and Reproductive Hormones: A Study of Vegetarian and Nonvegetarian Postmenopausal Women," *JNCI,* vol. 67, no. 4 (October 1981): 761–767.

23. A. Sanchez, D. G. Kissinger, and R. L. Phillips, "A Hypothesis on the Etiological Role of Diet on Age of Menarche," *Medical Hypotheses* 7 (1981): 1339–1345.

24. J. Sabate, C. Llorca, and A. Sanchez, "Lower Height of Lacto-Ovovegetarian Girls at Preadolescence: An Indicator of Physical Maturation Delay" *Journal of the American Dietetic Association,* vol. 92, no. 10 (October 1992): 1263–1264.

25. F. A. Tylavsky and J. B. Anderson, "Dietary Factors in Bone Health of Elderly Lactoovovegetarian and Omnivorous Women," *The American Journal of Clinical Nutrition* 48 (1988): 842–849.

26. A. G. Marsh et al., "Cortical Bone Density of Adult Lacto-ovo-vegetarian and Omnivorous Women," *Journal of the American Dietetic Association,* vol. 76 (February 1980): 148–151.

27. E. Linkosalo, "Dietary Habits and Dental Health in Finnish Seventh-Day Adventists," *Proceedings of the Finnish Dental Society* 84, no. 2 (1988): 109–115.

28. D. C. Nieman et al., "Hematological, Anthropometic, and Metabolic Comparisons Between Vegetarian and Nonvegetarian Elderly Women," *International Journal of Sports Medicine* 10 (1989): 243–250.

29. J. Sabate et al., "Anthropometric Parameters of Schoolchildren With Different Life-styles," *American Journal of Diseases of Children,* vol. 144 (October 1990): 1159–1163.

30. D. A. Snowdon and R. L. Phillips, "Does a Vegetarian Diet Reduce the Occurrence of Diabetes?" *American Journal of Public Health* 75 (1985): 507–512.

31. H. A. Kahn et al., "Association Between Reported Diet and All-Cause Mortality: Twenty-One Year Follow-Up on 27,530 Adult Seventh-Day Adventists," *American Journal of Epidemiology,* vol. 119, no. 5 (1984): 775–787.

32. I. W. Webster and G. K. Rawson, "Health Status of Seventh-Day Adventists," *The Medical Journal of Australia* (May 19, 1979): 417–420.

33. N. Nnakwe, C. Kies, and L. McEndree, "Calcium and Phosphorus Nutritional Status of Lacto-ovo-vegetarian and Omnivore Students Consuming Meals in a Lacto-ovo-vegetarian Food Service," *Nutrition Reports International,* vol. 29, no. 2 (February 1984): 365–369.

34. D. C. Nieman et al., "Dietary Status of Seventh-Day Adventist Vegetarian and Non-Vegetarian Elderly Women," *Journal of the American Dietetic Association,* vol. 89, no. 12, (December 1989): 1763–1769.

35. I. F. Hunt, N. J. Murphy, and C. Henderson, "Food and Nutrient Intake of Seventh-Day Adventist Women," *The American Journal of Clinical Nutrition* 48 (1988), 850–851.

36. K. A. Lombard and D. M. Mock, "Biotin Nutritional Status of Vegans, Lactoovovegetarians, and Nonvegetarians," *The American Journal of Clinical Nutrition* 50, (1989): 486–490.

37. B. M. Calkins, "Consumption of Fiber in Vegetarians and Nonvegetarians," in G. A. Spiller and D. Chem, *CRC Handbook of Dietary Fiber in Human Nutrition,* (Boca Raton, Fl.: CRC Press, 1986), pp. 407–414.

38. T. D. Shultz and J. E. Leklem, "Vitamin B-6 Status and Bioavailability in Vegetarian Women," *The American Journal of Clinical Nutrition* 46 (1987): 647–651.

39. R. L. Phillips and D. A. Snowdon, "Mortality Among Seventh-Day Adventists in Relation to Dietary Habits and Lifestyle," in R. L. Ory (ed.), *Plant Proteins: Applications, Biological Effects, and Chemistry,* (Washington, D.C.: American Chemical Society, 1986).

40. U. D. Register, "The Seventh-Day Adventist Diet and Life-Style and the Risk of Major Degenerative Disease," in *Frontiers in Longevity Research:* 74–82.

41. S. F. Knutsen, "Lifestyle and the Use of Health Services," *The American Journal of Clinical Nutrition* 59 (suppl., 1994): 1171S–1175S.88.

INDEX

Additives, 47, 48, 163–65
Adolph, William H., 139
Aduki beans: Malayan Millet Salad, 213; Mykonos Bean Salad, 210; Vegetable Salad, 210
Advertising, 36–38, 68, 91–92
Agribusiness, 67–68, 69, 70, 75–76, 77–78, 85, 93, 95, 115–16, 158, 167
Alfalfa, 74; sprouts, 70–71
Almond: Cinnamon Millet, 197; Vegetable Almondine Bake, 231
Alslebens, Dr. Harry Rudolph, 31
Amaranth: Navy Bean Mushroom Sauté, 220, Peach Delight, 201; Squashed Potato Casserole, 222; Sweet Spice, 198
American Cancer Society, *xvii, xix*, 18, 33
American Cyanamid, 65
American Dietetic Association, 37, 38, 92, 181
American Dietetic Associations Journal, 91
American Egg Board, 68
American Health, 44
American Heart Association, *xv*, 18
American Journal of Clinical Nutrition, 170, 171, 173–74, 178, 184
American Journal of Nursing, 141
American Meat Institute, 36, 91
American Medical Association, 149
American National Cattlemen's Association, 69
American Vegetarian Society, 13
Americans for Sale Food, *xx*
Amino Acids, *xiv*, 23–24, 30–31, 36, 37, 38, 56; "limiting," 56, 57; and protein combinations, 39–40, 53–58
Ammonia, 44, 46
Androgen, 35
Angel Hair with Radicchio, 246
Animal Factories (Singer), 122–23
Animals: cost of, 61, 62–66, 67–68; and drugs and chemicals, *xx–xxii*, 47–52; and excess protein, 45–46; feeding, 84–88; inspection of, *xxiii, xxiv*, 153, 155; natural resources and, 73–80; popularity of, 35–38; protein, *xiv*, 19–20, 23–24, 30, 32–38; respect for life of, 6, 108–09, 114–23; treatment of, *xx*, 115–23
Annals of Surgery, 172–73
Antibiotics, *xxi–xxii*, 34–35, 47, 49, 64, 116, 153, 158–61
Aphthovirus, 156

Aplastic anemia, 160
Apple-Papaya Honey Pudding, 251
Arginine, 24
Armour Beef Company, 36
Arteriosclerosis, 34, 131
Arthritis, 41
Artichokes: Savory Stuffed, 243–44
Artificial flavorings, 164
Arugula-Orange-Pepper Salad, 204
Asparagus and Bulgur, 226
Atherosclerosis, 41, 48, 64, 131
Athletes, 10, 19, 44
Atkinson, Roy, 118
Australian & New Zealand Journal of Medicine, 170
Ayurvedic medicine, 102–04, 105

Babies, 27, 44
Bacon, Sir Francis, 12
Bacteria, resistant, 158–59
Baked Spaghetti Casserole, 233
Banana: Bulgur, 195; Carob Tofu Pudding, 252; Heavenly Delight, 254; Nutty Breakfast, 199; Tropical Paradise Rice Cereal, 196; Tropical Soy Milk, 203
Banana-Coconut Pecan Rice Cereal, 196
Bangladesh, 89–90
Barley, 193; Green Barley Split, 230; Pyramid Pea Casserole, 232
Bascom, Willard, 167
Basil, 194
Basmati rice, 193; Carmen Miranda Brazilian, 242; Macro Beans and, 223; Mellow Rice Salad, 208; Nice Rice Salad, 206; Raisin Salad, 206; Sweet-and-Sour Bean Stew, 221
B-complex vitamins, 72
Beans, 127, 133; Brazilian Broccoli, 237; Cashewy Soup, 88; Chopped Veggie Salad, 207; cooking, 192; Crunchy, with Turnips, 238; Favorite Vegetable Soup, 216; Hot Soup, 214; Italian Style Pinto Bean Soup, 215; Kidney Bean Bonanza, 225; Mexican Medley, 227; Navy Bean Mushroom Sauté, 233; Sassy Bulgur and, 224; Stuffed Potatoes with Kidney Beans and Soy Cheese, 241; Sweet-and-Sour Stew, 221; *see also* Lima Beans, Snap Beans
Beef, *xxiv*, 19, 33–34, 36, 66, 87, 88, 89, 90, 91–93
Benedictines, 12

Gentian violet, *xxi*
Gleason, Ron, 10
Grains, *xiv,* 40, 89, 94, 142; cooking,
    192–93; as livestock feed, 84–85, 86,
    95–96; and macrobiotic, 111, 127–28
Green Barley Split, 230
Green Revolution, 85–86

Hall, Ross Hume, 86
Halloween Spaghetti, 232
Hardinge, Dr. Mervyn G., 137–39
Harris, Dr. R. S., 86
Harrison, George, 9
Harvard Heart Letter, 186
Harvard University, 130–31
Haugen, Arden, 10
Health, *xvii–xxiv,* 4–5, 102–05, 137–67; and
    macrobiotics, 124–34; Health
    professionals, *xii*
Heart Association, 33
Heart disease, *xviii,* 34, 41, 46, 48, 64, 99,
    131, 146; diet and, 169–71
Hegsted, Dr. Mark, 149
Herbicide residues, 47
Herbivores, humans as, 147–48
Hershaft, Alex, 149–50
High-protein diet, 36, 43–45
Hijiki, 207
Hilligan, Roy, 10
Hinduism, 11–12, 109, 111–12
Hi-Protein Green and White and Bulgur,
    225
Histadine, 23, 24, 56
Histamine, 158
Holmberg, Dr. Scott, 157, 158–59
Honey, Apple-Papaya Pudding, 251
Hormones, *xxi, xxii,* 35, 47, 64, 116, 161–63
How to Get Rid of the Poisons in Your Body
    (Null and Null), 160
Human Nutrition and Dietetics (Davidson,
    Meiklejohn, and Passmore), 148
Hunza people, 139
Hyperactivity, 41

Indonesian Sprout Salad, 205
Inspection, *xxiii, xxiv,* 153, 155
International Journal of Vancer, 172
Intestines, 21–22
Iodine deficiencies, 133
Iron, 150, 151–52
Irrigation, 78
Island Lentil Dish, 237
Isoleucine, 22

Italian: Mushroom and Potato Salad, 211;
    Pinto Bean Soup, 215; Rice, 228

Jainism, 12, 109
Jamaican Squash Soup, 217
Japan, 109, 110
Jones, Jesse, 126
Jones, Susan Smith, 9–10
*Journal of Environmental Pathology and
    Toxicology,* 172
*Journal of the American Dietetic
    Association,* 36, 37, 175, 177, 181–83
*Journal of the American Medical
    Association,* 144, 162, 188
Judaism, 106, 108, 109, 119

Kefir, 50
Keys, 184–85
Kidney, 21, 42–45, 46, 148
Kidney Bean Bonanza, 225
Kingsford, Anna, 13
Kiwi Pudding, 251–52
Knight, Gladys, 9
Kombu: Stir-fry Garlic and, 249
Koran, 12
Kritchevsky, Dr. David, 48
Kushi, Michio, 125, 126, 130, 131, 133

Lacto-ovo-vegetarians, 4, 39, 50
Lacto-vegetarians, 4, 139, 152
Lancet, The, 138
Land use, 73–77, 88–91
Lappé, Frances Moore, 76, 83, 88, 89
Latin America, 89
Leachman, Cloris, 9
Lead, 166
Leadbeater, C. W., 109
Leafy vegetables, 45, 50, 132
Legumes, *xiv,* 40, 94, 142; *see also* Beans
Lentils, 192; Island Dish, 237
Leucine, 22
Life, respect for, 6, 108–9, 114–23
Lima Beans: and Chick-Pea Seaweed
    Salad, 212; Crunchy, with Turnips, 238;
    Snappy Bake, 239; *see also* Beans
Lindane, 116
Little Italy Spaghetti, 235
Liver, 43, 46
Livestock feed, 84–86
Livingston-Wheeler, Dr. Virginia, *xxiii–xxiv*
Locally grown foods, 125
Low, Gilman, 10
Lutalyse, 35
Lysine, 22